THE SUFI MESSAGE

VOLUME VII

Pir-o-Murshid
Hazrat Inayat Khan

HAZRAT INAYAT KHAN

In An Eastern Rose Garden

MOTILAL BANARSIDASS PUBLISHERS
PRIVATE LIMITED • DELHI

4th Reprint : Delhi, 2018
First Indian Edition: Delhi, 1989

Vol. VII ISBN : 978-81-208-0665-8 (Cloth)
ISBN : 978-81-208-0666-5 (Paper)
Set ISBN : 978-81-208-0494-4 (Cloth)
ISBN : 978-81-208-0495-1 (Paper)

Also available at :
MOTILAL BANARSIDASS
41 U.A. Bungalow Road, Jawahar Nagar, Delhi 110 007
1 B, Jyoti Studio Compound, Kennedy Bridge, Nana Chowk, Mumbai 400 007
203 Royapettah High Road, Mylapore, Chennai 600 004
236, 9th Main III Block, Jayanagar, Bengaluru 560 011
8 Camac Street, Kolkata 700 017
Ashok Rajpath, Patna 800 004
Chowk, Varanasi 221 001

Printed in India

by RP Jain at NAB Printing Unit,
A-44, Naraina Industrial Area, Phase I, New Delhi–110028
and published by JP Jain for Motilal Banarsidass Publishers (P) Ltd,
41 U.A. Bungalow Road, Jawahar Nagar, Delhi-110007

CONTENTS

Preface to the Series	7
Preface	9
Love, Harmony, and Beauty	11
Nature's Religion	21
The Personality of God	32
Silent Life	38
The Will, Human and Divine	46
Mind, Human and Divine	52
Will-power	57
Personal Magnetism	65
Love, Human and Divine	73
Intuition	82
Faith	87
The Effect of Prayer	98
The Mystery of Breath	102
Character and Fate	110
Gain and Loss	119
Stilling the Mind	124
Mental Creation	132
The Attainment of Power	139
What the Power of Breath can do	142
The Knowledge of Past, Present, and Future	145
Spirits and Spiritism	149
The Master Mind	153

The Desire of Nations	162
Democracy	170
Spiritual Democracy	176
The Freedom of the Soul (1)	180
The Freedom of the Soul (2)	188
The Freedom of the Soul (3)	193
The Ideal Life	198
The Journey to the Goal	204
The Presence of God	212
The Spiritual Hierarchy	221
Sublime Knowledge	229
Intellect and Wisdom	233
Simplicity and Complexity	239
Dependence	245
Friendship (1)	251
Friendship (2)	256
The Four Paths which lead to the Goal	262
Human Evolution	267

PREFACE TO THE SERIES

THE present volume is the first of a series including all the works intended for publication of Hazrat Inayat Khan (Baroda 1882-New Delhi 1927), the great Sufi mystic who came to the Western world in 1910 and lectured and taught there until his passing away in 1927.

A new edition of this series, which was published for the International Headquarters of the Sufi Movement in the West in the '60s, is now made available in the Indian subcontinent and the Middle East. In this way Hazrat Inayat Khan's inspired and universal vision of the Sufi Message returns to his own beloved country, where it originated and where interest in it is growing.

This book and other volumes of this series have not been written down by the author. They contain his lectures, discourses and other teachings as taken down in shorthand and other handwriting. When preparing for publication great care was taken, not only to avoid distortion of their intent and meaning, but also to leave intact, as far as possible, the flow of mystical inspiration and poetical expression which add so much to their spell, and without which a significant part of his message would be lost. Although speaking in a tongue foreign to him, he moulded it into a perfect vehicle for his thought, at times somewhat ungrammatical and unusual, but always as clear and precise as his often difficult and abstruse subjects would allow.

It goes without saying that neither in the present nor in the previous edition anything has been altered which would involve even the slightest deviation from the author's intention and no attempt has been made to transform his highly personal and colourful language into idiomatically unimpeachable English. Already so much is necessarily lost by the transfer of the spoken word to the printed page, that every effort has been made, as it should, to preserve the Master's melodious phrasing, the radiance of his personality, and the subtle sense of humour which never left him.

Hazrat Inayat Khan's teaching was nearly all given during the years 1918—1926. It covers a great many subjects, several of which were grouped in series of lectures and taken up again some years later. Certain subjects may cover nearly the same ground as others; stories and examples which abound in most of his works are met again elsewhere; and much of what he taught one finds repeated in several places. This was intentional, as repetition belonged to Hazrat Inayat Khan's method of teaching; it is for the student to become aware of the subtle differences in each context. For these and other reasons it would be difficult to follow a rigid system in publishing Hazrat Inayat Khan's works; a chronological grouping of his lectures would be very unsatisfactory, and a stringent classification according to subject-matter hardly feasible.

The complete series contains fourteen volumes. The last volume is the Index. This edition is the first one to present an index to the Sufi Message of Hazrat Inayat Khan.

Each volume is complete in itself, and therefore may be read without any necessity to study following or previous ones. However, one may get a spiritual and mental appetite to continue reading. One will find that a meditative way of reading will convey not only the words but also the spiritual power emanating from them, tuning mind, heart and soul to the pitch which is one's own.

W.v.L.

PREFACE

"In an Eastern Rose garden" is a collection of texts by Hazrat Sufi Inayat Khan on various subjects covering both inner life and life in the world. Many of these may serve as an informal guide book through one's life. It opens with a discussion on love, harmony and beauty, qualities which Inayat Khan considered to be the key notes of his practical religious and mystical philosophy.

Sometimes the religious aspect of man's development is stressed. For example in chapters on items like the personality of God, nature's religion, faith, the effect of prayer and the presence of God the need is stressed to create and realize the ideal in one's heart, reflecting the Divine Ideal. Other chapters cover practical aspects of life like magnetism, love, breath, character and fate, power, and friendship. Each time such a quality is treated in a way linking the outer characteristics with the spiritual perspective, thus opening up new avenues to the reader how to conduct one's life.

The mind, a concept containing both thinking and feeling, is essential in Hazrat Inayat Khan's mysticism and is highlighted in a couple of other chapters. The mind is considered as the other vehicle of the soul, besides the body, working through the body as an integrated mechanism. This dimension is discussed in terms of intellect and wisdom, simplicity and complexity, mental creation, the will, will-power, stilling the mind, the master mind. Very often this is done by highlighting the human versus the divine aspects, and then showing how to integrate these. A third group of themes may be presented as the inner aspects of the way to develop these qualities: silent life, intuition, dependance, sublime knowledge, the freedom of the soul, the ideal life, the journey to the goal, spiritual hierarchy, sublime knowledge, and the paths which lead to the Goal. These chapters at the same time may evoke in the reader the longing for treading this path, to discover the hidden qualities of one's being.

The Sufi way is not one of exclusion of the outer aspects of life. On the contrary, inner life can best be experienced in an active relationship with daily life in the world.

Although both spiritual and realistic, the philosophy of life presented in this book, has a yet wider scope. Life in the world is evolving in a process over a wide span of time. It is the wonderful opportunity for the human being to be in a position to actively contribute to this evolution. This book touches this subject as it discusses the knowledge of past, present and future, the desire of nations, democracy, the ideal life and human evolution. "In an Eastern Rose garden" presents the reader with inspiration and hope.

W.v.L.

LOVE, HARMONY, AND BEAUTY

HOW THE words 'love', 'harmony', and 'beauty' delight the heart of everyone who hears them! One may wonder what it can be in these words that is able to exert such a natural power upon the human soul.

The answer is that if there is anything in life which appeals to the human soul, it is love and beauty. If one asks, 'And what besides those?' then the answer is, 'There is nothing else'. Why is this? Because they are the very nature of life. Love is the nature of life, beauty is the outcome of life, harmony is the means by which life accomplishes its purpose, and the lack of it results in destruction.

When we reflect upon this whole creation we cannot but see that its purpose is to express an ideal of love, harmony, and beauty. Love could not have manifested itself if there were nothing to love, eyes could not have seen if there were nothing to see. What could love have done if there were no beauty? Love would have been silent. Love can only be said to exist after it has passed from silence into expression.

Now comes the question: what has made beauty? The answer is that it is love that has made beauty. When a Sufi calls you 'Beloved ones of God' he has this idea in his mind. Whatever God has created, He has created out of His love, He has created to be loved by Him, and therefore whatever He has created and all His creatures are His beloved ones.

We human beings have our prejudices; we like one, dislike another; we consider one worthy of high esteem, and another only worthy of low esteem, but to God they are all alike; they are His creation. It is just as it would be for a poet to have the little scrap of paper on which his song is written thrown away, or lost and not esteemed. How could he sing without his voice? So it is with the Creator; He cannot be pleased when His little scraps of paper are not appreciated.

God is love, and He has created man out of His love. How then can He be pleased if one has hatred or prejudice against a fellow-man, because one forgets that however unworthy he may seem to be, he is nevertheless the beloved one of God? He has created him in order to love him. Therefore God, the Father and Mother of all beings, is equally pleased with all His creatures.

But is not one thing more beautiful than another, one person more than another, in either external or internal being? What is the reason of this?

The reason is found when we consider the work of an artist, of a poet, of a composer of music, of a writer. We can see that one composition is much more beautiful than another. One picture may perhaps be the best the artist has painted in all his life. The poet may wonder, 'Have I written this verse? where can it have come from? It is so superior to all the others; it is marvellous how these words came to me.'

Just as we see this in the individual, so also do we see it in the work of the Creator. At the same time, love is the only power that has created, or that can create.

In this way God becomes the lover and the manifestation or object of love at the same time. In Sanskrit this is called by mystics *Shiva* and *Shakti*, or *Purusha* and *Prakriti*, or *Ishwara* and *Maya*, these three pairs of words. The one part is love, and the other part is beauty. Love has created beauty in order that it may be able to love. God is love; that is why He is called the Creator. The lover alone has the power to create, and that which he creates is for the purpose of receiving his love.

The Prophet has said, 'God is beautiful, and He loves beauty.' Now the word 'beautiful' does not refer to the form of God. God is formless. He has no personality until He manifests Himself to Himself. Therefore it is not His personality which is beautiful, for God is beyond that which in the ordinary sense of the word is called personality.

What then is the source of God's beauty? God is beautiful because He has created beauty. If there were no beauty in God, there could have been none in His manifestation. If there were no beauty in the thought of the poet, he could not write beautiful verse; if there were no beauty in the thought of the artist, he could never have painted the picture. One cannot see the beauty in the heart of the painter except in the beauty of the picture he has made. It is not only the picture which is beautiful, the heart of the painter was beautiful first. Consequently we become able to see the beauty not only in manifestation, but also before it was manifested; and before it was manifested it existed in love. In other words, we can see that the beauty was hidden in love; beauty is hidden in love, and the beauty that love has before it to love is its own beauty. Therefore, to whatever extent beauty is beautiful, so is love beautiful; even more so, for the Creator is more beautiful than the thing He has created.

All things that we make are the work of our hands. We are their creator, and we are greater than our hands. So it is with love. Love is greater than beauty, because love is the creator of the beauty that love loves in its life.

No doubt by loving, love becomes limited, limited as beauty; but then that is the purpose of love. If there were no beauty, His love could not have realized the latent joy of its own nature. The joy of its existence would die out.

As soon as we can think in this way, we come to see that the lover is vaster, incomparably vaster than the object he loves. The real love, the real beauty, is in the lover. The object that he loves is much smaller, although for the moment the lover is not aware of the difference. The lover thinks, 'You are the object before which I bow. You are the object of which I think day and night, before which I am helpless. You are the object that I admire, that I adore.' Yet he does not realize the vastness of his love, and indeed, strictly speaking, love is vaster than the lover.

When people begin to learn the lesson of love they are apt to be frightened at the pain and difficulties and troubles which they will have to face on behalf of love. When they compare their condition with that of the beloved, they think the beloved is much better off than they: 'The one who takes my thought, who gives me pain, who wounds my heart, is much happier. When I compare myself with the beloved I think he is much the happier.' And they go on thinking, 'If I were the beloved it would be much better'. Every soul experiences that thought, but once he has risen above it, then he begins to know love. The soul that has not escaped from this fails to realize the fullness of love.

There is another side to love, and that is selfishness, and the lover must escape from this. The true lover says, 'I will give everything, I will endure all things, all tortures, all torments that may have to be faced in life. I will bow in humility before whatever befalls me. I will give all that I have. I will bear all things, believe all things, hope for all things, and endure all things.' But the other side of love says, 'Are you crazy? Have you lost your senses? You are foolish. Why this complaining? See how happy the beloved is. Be happy like him, and be in his exalted position, instead of in this humility and degradation. Enter into this greatness and not into that destruction!' Then he proceeds to reason, and at length he understands. The one thing leads to destruction, the other promises safety. But in destruction there is the hand of God, while in safety there is the hand of Satan. All things that are selfish are taught by that power and by that knowledge which is the enemy of mankind. Satan is an enemy because he leads man away from the purpose of his life. He seeks to make the lover change places with the beloved and say, 'Your position is better than mine; now I would like to be like you'. And perhaps he will wait all his life to gain that coveted position, and it never comes because the beloved would not surrender the wealth when the chance was there.

The life of a person is quite changed after being melted in the fire of love. The fire of love will exalt him so that his power will even influence animals and birds; the wise and foolish will be attracted to him alike. Once he is purified, burned in the fire of love, he will become the attraction of every soul, of every being, invisible as well as visible. It is only the advice of Satan that keeps him from that. The master is he who suffers. We often reflect upon how Jesus Christ washed the feet of his disciples. What beauty there is in that service, in that humility! Should we find that beauty in a proud man? Could a proud man win the hearts of the world for centuries and centuries? The proud man is led by Satan; he becomes egoistic, selfish, cold; everyone in his presence will freeze, for his presence is like ice and cannot impart comfort.

But how forgiving is he who has been through all suffering! Was there anything else in Christ's life but forgiveness and tolerance? Always forgive, always tolerate, he said. It was because the love in the heart of the Master was so great that it appealed to everyone. Love was all the philosophy that his fishermen could understand, and if love were placed before philosophy and religion how devoted would the devotees become. The animals and the birds would be attracted by the power of man's heart aflame with love. As it is, man only frightens love away at the least suspicion of its appearance, and so love never wants to come nearer.

How often is the word 'love' used in everyday life for what is nothing but an amusement, a pleasure, a pastime, a degraded thing. Love is so much higher. It is not a thing that you can give to a person, or of which a person may say, 'I can develop it'. He cannot learn it, he cannot study it in a book; there is only this one thing to be done: to allow it to grow in the heart. A person cannot live without his heart, and the heart cannot exist without love. However loveless and cold a person seems to be, however wicked and cruel, he nevertheless has love, though it is hidden. There is a thick wall built round it. It has no means of coming out; it is continually kept within this shell, and it is uneasy and restless. That is why man becomes cold and unhappy, always wanting he knows not what, because he does not understand the only true inclination. The power of love has become captive in a thick shell, a shell of coldness, the frozen part of love, and this shell refuses outlet to the stream of love, the divine power which seeks to emerge through the heart. When a man does not give this love an outlet he becomes a burden to others; his presence becomes disagreeable to his surroundings, his influence becomes a burden to himself. For this reason some people even go mad. Not knowing what they want in life, they always blame others for not having loved them, and sympathized with them, or been kind to them. They do not realize that the key lies in themselves; in their heart lies the power to open and melt anyone's heart. It is our own power that can bring another to our feet.

Whoever learns this truth ceases to blame anyone for being cold to him, unkind to him, unsympathetic towards him. He finds that the cause lies in himself. By seeking the sympathy and good feeling of another person he covers up his own heart and stops it from expressing itself. The power of love is ever wishing to come out to impress itself upon its surroundings, and yet it is as if the doors were being ever closed to prevent God from coming out to fulfil the purpose of His own creation.

How beautiful are the words of the Prophet: 'The shrine of God is the heart of man'. How true that is! Is God to be found in a mosque, or temple, or church, or in any place where people sing hymns and offer their prayers? Can He be found where there is no love? He is not to be found in the houses that men have built for worship. These are only schools for children, and their playgrounds. Children like playing with toys, and yet they are preparing themselves for something else. When man has come to know the real beauty of God, he will find that it dwells only in one place: in the heart of man. God is love, and He is found in the heart of man.

He who understands this can worship God even in man, for when he abides by this philosophy he will always be aware that in every aspect and at every moment he may be injuring or hurting the feelings of God, that he is in danger of breaking the shrine of God in breaking the heart of his fellow-man.

It might be thought that the philosophers and mystics and sages, who are so near and close to God, might take too much liberty with the world. But they are, on the contrary, the most tender and sensitive towards mankind. They are ready to share anyone's trouble, to share anyone's sorrow, to share everyone's depression and despair. They are ready to console any and every person with their words, to help with their service, and to give their sympathy always to those who need it. They shrink at no sacrifice of time, money, pleasure, or comfort. As Christ teaches, 'Whosoever shall compel thee to go a mile, go with him twain'.

What does all this teach us? It is all a lesson in sympathy for one's fellow-man, to teach us to share in his troubles, in his despair. For whoever really experiences this joy of life, finds that it becomes so great that it fills his heart and his soul. It does not matter if he has fewer comforts or an inferior position than many in this world, because the light of his kindness, of his sympathy, of the love that is growing, the virtue that is springing up in his heart, all fill the soul with light. There is nothing now that he lacks in life, for he has become the king of it.

Such a person becomes a healer, a real healer. He heals a person with his glance, with a kind word, with his hand, by his comfort, by his nature. What a healing that is! Unpretentious, unassuming; the real healing is when a man is in sympathy with another's trouble and gives him a helping hand. He is the possessor of the true wine. He who can send from his eye the glance that proves the sympathy and help he is anxious to give, what a healing power he has! Is it not like a young bird being taken in beneath the brooding wings? There cannot be a more beautiful process of healing than this among all the different methods by which people have endeavoured to heal.

Some may ask what, then, should be the object which one should love in this life? Is there any particular object that a man can be recommended to love? Is it best to love one's parent or friends; to love one friend only or to love just one beloved of the opposite sex? Should one love something in the abstract, some spirit, some ideal, some name, or something which is beyond man's nature? Or should one love something idealized as the God whom one worships? There are many who say that there is no love which is useful but the love of God; all other forms are worthless. Another says that he or she can love no one who is of the opposite sex, having once been disappointed in this way. Another will say, 'I will love no human being; I can love my dog or my cat better. They do not disappoint me, whereas I was once disappointed in man.' Another says, 'I love my money, because if I am in need that is the only friend that comes to my rescue. The deposit I have in my bank does more for me than anyone can do. Why then should I not love my money?' And still another person says, 'If God is all, if He is to have all love, then why not love the chair, or the table, or a book, or the work that a person does—a work of art, a piece of music; is it not the same?' But all these questions are voiced by hearts which have once been disappointed, once broken. They broke and became closed, and once the doors of the heart are closed there is no light to guide its path. That is what is so beautiful in the little English song, 'The light of a whole life dies when love is done'. There is no light when love is done. When love is done, the heart is closed.

So often one meets with people who complain that the love on the part of the lover failed to satisfy and caused their despair and distress. What does the Sufi, what does the sage learn from this? He learns that it is those who love who gain. Those who have loved and not gone forward are those who have lost. The reason why they have gone back before reaching their destiny has been that they were dependent upon the object of love which disappointed them. The Sufi is aware of this great pit on the path. Whenever the lover, who was attracted by beauty, falls from his love, it is because he depended on the beauty. It was the beauty that he loved, and he could only stand as long as that beauty remained his ideal. The lover rises again when he consults with himself and says, 'I will make such an ideal as will allow my life to become self-sufficient. The ideal will be my excuse, but in reality I will raise my love. Whenever love was broken it was only because the ideal did not prove to be as the lover expected it to be. I will therefore avoid blinding my eyes with the external life, but will build the path on which to travel in my own heart. That ideal will suffice and provide everything that the beloved may lack.' This lover is the real lover, because love has a beauty too, and he produces from his own love the beauty which perhaps the beloved lacks, and he no longer notices the lack in his beloved. From this time on, the beloved becomes his love because he has made a beloved in his thought, in his imagination, and he can continually add to the beauty of the manifestation.

In this manner the song of love and beauty has been sung in all periods of history. Sa'di of Persia, Dante of Italy, and all the great ones who have loved and appealed to the heart of man, all of them have left words which still pierce through our hearts today because of the greatness of their ideal. They have themselves created their ideal in their own hearts. For all such there can no longer be any question of the beloved proving unworthy of love. The lover has become the creator of the love. Did not God create love? Have not we inherited this beauty of God? Can we not create love also? That which one can create can always be depended on.

There is another side to this question, and it is that the ideal of love which is created by man is according to his evolution. If he is material, he will appreciate material beauty in a person or object.

He cannot help this. It is not his fault. It is right for him to admire that which directly appeals to him. One person will prefer beauty of mind, of virtue, of personality, of some good manner, of some goodness which appeals to him; he values a beautiful personality, a sympathetic presence. Another person will perhaps like a soul because he finds in it his ideal of inspiration, intuition, peace of mind, and joy.

Therefore one cannot point to any particular object as the only object worthy of love, because beauty is only according to a person's evolution. He who is of lower evolution cannot love a higher object. But a person of higher evolution can love the lower as well as the higher. He who once loves cannot hate. The one who hates is he who cannot appreciate. Hatred is found in the lower grades of evolution, not in the higher; and the higher the evolution develops, the less the hatred and prejudice become. In the higher realm there is no poison, for the object is higher, the standard is higher, the sphere is greater. As high as one sets one's ideal, so high does one reach, and it is by raising the standard of beauty step by step that one rises up and up into the highest heaven.

It is by walking along and keeping ever on the path of love that even from the lowest depths the soul can reach the highest heaven. Man can even raise his ideal to that height in which he becomes able to love God the Formless, God the Nameless, who is above all goodness and virtue; not even He can be restricted to virtue, for He is beyond goodness.

There are sages who are moved to tears just by saying to themselves one word of essential truth, of abstract truth. What could have this effect? Is there some pain concealed in it? Is anything said to evoke sympathy? No, it is their ideal that is so high that they see the ideal beauty in the truth. The truth of being has become beautiful to them. Their beloved has become God, and when a word of truth is spoken in their hearing they are moved to tears. To these sages everything is a real manifestation of the beauty of God. If they hear music, in that music they feel God, in that music they see God. If they are standing before a picture, in the beauty of that picture they see their Beloved. If they are standing in a crowd, with all manner of faces, to them the whole picture is one harmony, one vision of the sublime, and they can see the whole beauty there. Whether it be desert, or sea, or sky, or land, whatever it is that is before their eyes has a vision of beauty to offer to them. And it is in this way that the whole of manifestation has become for them an immanence of the beauty of God.

NATURE'S RELIGION

ALTHOUGH it is no exaggeration to say that there are numberless religions in the world, and every religion has so many different sects and churches and chapels that this life is not long enough to study them—indeed it would be impossible even to count them in one lifetime—yet that which should really be studied proves to be something very different, for the thinker perceives that these many different religions have sprung out of one religion. Religion may begin in the East or the West, in the South or the North, yet it will always end in many religions. The more we ponder upon how all can have come from one, the plainer becomes the fact that all are expressions of one religion. And this religion is nature's religion.

The question as to what exactly this religion really is and how one may get to know it, can only be answered by those who have raised themselves beyond the limitations of ceremonial and dogma in which they are always first instructed. But rising above a religion does not mean giving up the religion. It means being fully benefited by the religion. Those who say they have given up their religion are not above it; those alone are above it who have arrived at a full understanding of the spirit of religion. As soon as the spirit of religion has become manifest, then indeed are the eyes blessed. The distinctions and differences of castes and creeds and religions all vanish away in one moment of time.

Once this is perceived, there ceases to be anything to criticize; it is all one what form of worship is to be used, what church is to be attended, what book is to be read. From now on it is seen that there is no such thing as a heretic, no such thing as a heathen, no difference between Kufr and Muslim. But until this truth is perceived there is always the thought, 'Whatever religion, or belief, or faith I have or hold, the scripture that I read, the church that I attend, is the only scripture, the only church, the only faith; this that I have understood and regarded as mine all through my life, this is the only path.'

It is like a person in pursuit of a bird. He looks at the branch of the tree which is still shaking after the bird has flown from it. He says, 'Oh, here is the bird', but he is only looking at the branch trembling hither and thither after the bird has sat there just for a moment. He calls the branch the bird. Another person may see a branch moving, but this time the branch is so strong that the bird could not possibly have moved it. Not understanding this, he thinks the bird sat on that branch. Thus it is with the truth.

Instead of understanding the spirit of the truth people have taught that religion lies in the name of the teacher. Importance is given to the name of the teacher, to the scripture, to the house in which worship is customary, to the priests or clergy who officiate. Prominence is given to being Brahmin or Buddhist, to belonging to certain communities formed in the name of a particular religion, to the castes set up, to the families formed, to those associations made in order to follow one particular creed, or ceremony, or law. Finally the loyalty to that particular religious system becomes its life, and this leads to the neglect—not only neglect, but actual hatred—of the religion followed by others. It is in this way that all wars and differences that have existed in all ages have arisen.

When one studies nature, one finds that nature cannot create itself without expressing its religion. The origin of all religion is love and beauty. If there were no love or beauty religion would never have existed, because beauty is the beginning of worship and prayer. The beginning of prayer and the first step of worship is admiration.

A child knows nothing about religion, and yet from the very first it is attracted to something that is beautiful, something that it can like. As it grows older it is only the form of its desires that changes; it still seeks to acquire the object of beauty. As it grows older still, it comes to recognize beauty in intellectual things. It is beauty that man bows down to. When a man gives honour and respect and reverence to another it is still because of the beauty which he perceives in some form or other in a person, and he has a natural inclination to bow before this beautiful living thing. Prayer and worship are acts of bowing to beauty, acts necessary to satisfy the predisposition with which every soul is born, the predisposition which is called love. And it is the innate desire of love to satisfy itself by admiring and bowing before someone, to respect someone, to have veneration for someone, to worship someone.

Man goes step by step from simple worship to the worship of the Most High, as he realizes a higher and higher ideal. We can see this when we study the history of religions. It is the desire to pay respect, the desire to idealize, that has made man worship idols or trees. Some people consider a certain tree sacred. And even in bowing before trees the desire of love is satisfied, its desire to humble itself, its desire to pay respect and reverence; and by this means the love of the heart has its outlet. Such people are not evolved enough to know where God is; He is not before their eyes as this idol is. How can He who is not seen be known? Therefore people bow before, beautiful flowers, beautiful herbs, beautiful trees in the forest. Others bow before rocks that have a certain form which attracts them and produces in them the desire to pay homage to this particular rock, thus bringing satisfaction to the soul's desire to bow and pay respect.

Then, as intelligence developed still more, people would perceive that sometimes they were higher than the rock before which they had previously bowed. They thought, 'That rock is low; we can touch it; we can reach the top of it; there are a thousand others like it'. Therefore they come to think, 'It is best to worship the sun, because there can be nothing higher than the sun. We cannot get near it. There is nothing as bright as the sun. When the sun appears, does it not take away all our gloom and worries and all the fears of the dark night also? It takes away all the conditions of death and destruction such as thieves, robbers, tigers, and lions in countrysides and villages; all clear away when the sun rises, and a new life begins; and with it come strength, vigour, energy and enthusiasm to go out into the world. This is the one thing that takes away fear, and when it goes away we are afraid again and hide in our little villages.'

And this worship of the sun lasted a long time. In places like Persia, and in places like eastern Russia where there is not always sun but always need of a fire, the people sought refuge from the cold weather by sitting near the fire. The light of the fire becomes company in loneliness, the heat of the fire brings comfort, the light takes away fear, the heat purifies everything that comes into it. So that is why in those countries which are cold they call fire sacred, and bow before it in obedience to the same innate yearning to bow and pay respect.

But man ascended still higher until he began to think, 'No, no; the sun which goes away and comes back, appears and disappears, is not constantly with us. So I will seek something that is constantly with us'. And what is that? Surely it is the imagination. Surely it is a spirit that is God. In Mongolia and China and in all those Eastern countries where numberless gods are worshipped, they say, 'The one thing that abides with us, day and night, in trouble and sorrow, in joy and sadness, is that spirit which is God'.

Then comes the time when the ruling power is seen in every object, in every being, in every plant, in every star, a controlling power ruling so many diverse objects. Thus it came about that the heroes were respected, kings were worshipped, and even every planet or star was thought to represent a separate god. This ideal of worship was developed among the Greeks and Hindus.

Then we come to the Semitic race, the race from which the beginning of the Bible is to be traced, the children of Israel. Abraham noticed people around him worshipping idols, people worshipping symbols, and people worshipping sacred cows, or beasts, or birds. He pondered on God, thinking, 'No, if Thou art anywhere, Thou must be somewhere within me, and I want to find Thee'. Once, lying awake, he repeated His name, and as he thus thought about Him he sought some sign of that One who is really worthy of worship. Again, in his visions he saw the star, and arose to ask, 'Art Thou the God?' And the answer came from within, 'It is not He. It comes and goes, for it is not stable nor steady. An object that is worthy of worship must be constantly before one'. Then, next day, he saw the moon and asked, 'Art Thou the God?' And the answer came, 'No, for the moon takes its light from the sun'. Then he saw the sun and asked the same question, and the answer came, 'No, that which appears or disappears, however perfect in its light and form, cannot be the eternal God'. And thus he perceived that God is a higher ideal than the sun, or moon, or anything that words can ever express; a God who is unseen and without form and without name, altogether beyond man's conception. That is how the ideal of one God began.

This great ideal came through different prophets, and was expressed in different ways. If Moses said, 'One God; no other gods but Me', Jesus Christ taught that there is not only one God, but also one Life; the whole of manifestation is one. The sun is not what we see; there is the sun, there is the manifestation which we see, and there is that which proceeds from the sun—all three aspects of the one. 'I and my Father are one', 'That which proceeds from the Father and the Son is one': these sayings contain the three aspects, and they create a puzzle in man's mind; he can remain in this puzzle all his life. There is the thing itself, there is its manifestation, and there is that which proceeds from it, always this trinity in one. In all ages the message was given with truth and wisdom as each messenger came, but how could all understand the truth when not everyone has even been able to understand another? Language can hardly express it, and it is hard to understand.

The same difficulty arose at the time of Mohammad. He said to his people, who were the worshippers of so many gods, 'There is no god but the one God'. They asked, 'Where is He? Is He in our temples? Is He in the Ka'ba?' He said, 'No, His temple is in man's heart'.—'How far away is He?'—'He is nearer to you than yourself.'—'In what can we find Him?'—'In all things and all beings.' —'What is His sign?'—'He is beyond all signs and yet all are His signs. He cannot be restricted to one centre or one form or one name, because all names are His names, all forms are His form, all in heaven or earth are His beings, and there is only One!'

If you want to find Him you will find Him in the higher intelligence. When intelligence manifests itself on the surface, that is God. In manifesting Himself, He has assumed various forms; through each of these He seeks gradually to attain to the same state of absolute being. Every form: rock, animal, bird, man, everything, is always striving to climb to the surface. The Bible tells us to raise our light on high; it is covered under a bushel. The bushel is the manifested part of our life; all these forms that cover the inner intelligence, which in its original aspect is the root of being, are the bushel. The inner intelligence, the light, has become veiled under the manifestation, and it is the desire of nature to unfold it again, so as to allow it to behold its original being, which it does through all changes that take the form of death and destruction.

This great truth, so difficult to express, must needs be uttered by every prophet, every teacher, every saint who has brought the message, in that language which their hearers could best understand. If the teacher perceived that the method used by the hearers was good, he would advise them to continue in the same mode of worship, to continue to go to such a temple or such a church, until they were able to perceive what is the real truth hidden behind all these things.

Having grasped the idea of God, there comes the question of the mode of worshipping Him. Religion offers many ways of worship; but various religions offer many modes of worship which have become the law of each religion, and how can that law be obeyed by the whole world? Let us ask the ministers of any religion, of Islam, of Christianity, of Buddhism, of Hinduism, whether their own law can become the law for the religion of the whole world. Though each one of them will say yes, yet surely it is not meant to be so. All men are not alike; the tendencies of every people differ; their habits are not the same. For instance the law of the Hindu is to go to the Ganges in the morning and bathe in it. How would that do in London? How could one bathe in the Thames in December before offering one's prayers? Everybody will agree that no one could do such a thing. Again, a Muslim obeys the law of leaving his shoes outside the mosque, and then goes to wash his hands and feet, and make his ablutions in running water; then he stands on the marble floor of the mosque, and offers up his prayers. If the same mode of worship were to be the law for Russia, where there is so much cold and snow underfoot, to prostrate oneself on the marble would mean to be frozen to death in one day; and then one would never live to take the name of any religion again.

In this way we see that one faith and religion and law cannot be promoted and advocated in the same way in all different lands and places. The different faiths are bound gradually to become unrecognized and forgotten, and those who wish to promote their own customs would cease even to imagine such a thing, could they realize that every person has a different temperament, that every form of religion is a form of worship of the same God. Nature teaches every soul to worship God in some way or other, and often provides that which is suitable for each. Those who want one law to govern all have lost sight of the spirit of their own religion. And it is in people who have not yet learnt their own religion that such ideas are commonly found. Did they but know their own religion, how tolerant they would become, and how free from any grudge against the religion of others!

So it is too with the manner of worship. It does not matter in what way a person offers his respect and his reverence to the deity he worships. It only matters how sincere he is in his offering. In one house of God we find that people do not wear hats; in Hindustan, Persia, and Arabia they put on turbans to go to the mosque. That is their custom. It makes no difference whether one person prays standing, another sitting, another kneeling, another prostrating himself, another in company with other people, and another alone. All that matters is that the heart of the worshipper is pure, that the mind is connected with God, that there is sincerity and earnestness.

There is a story that a farmer's boy, who was taking care of his father's cattle in the jungle, had heard a teacher of religion in his village. This teacher was teaching about God and glorifying the name of God. The young boy was so impressed that when he went to the jungle next time he experienced that innate tendency to worship someone, and so in the jungle he began to say aloud, 'Oh, God, I have heard so much about You; You are so good and kind that I feel that if You were here by me I would take such good care of You, more than of all my sheep, more than of all my fowls. In the rain I would keep You under the roof of my grass-shed; when it was cold, I would wrap You in my blanket, and in the heat of the sun I would give You a bath. I would put You to sleep with Your head on my lap, and I would fan You with my hat, and I would always watch You and guard You from wolves. I would give You bread of manna, and butter-milk to drink; and to entertain You I would sing and dance and play my flute. O God, come and see how I would tend You.' Then Moses, the Messenger of God, came up and heard all that the boy said, and answered, 'Oh boy, how foolish is this conversation! God, the unknown and unseen, who is in the heavens, the one before whom there is no might, no strength that can stand, He is almighty; the power is all His. He is beyond form and name and colour; He is beyond the perception and comprehension of man.'

The boy was disheartened, and afraid of what he had done. But the next message from God to Moses was, 'We are very displeased indeed with you that you have alienated a devotee who did not know us. If he did not know us as you do, at least he knew us as far as his mind could grasp. All our devotees picture us in different forms and according to different qualities of love, and we receive their love through whatever form or garb it is directed to us. They are all our creatures and we receive it even if they worship the sun. We have sent you to unite our children to us, and not to separate them from us.'

How we would hesitate to air our wisdom did we but realize that the first step of approach to God is sincerity and earnest love for Him! We should never call anyone heathen or pagan. We should never consider anybody in this world as unworthy. We do not know in what form a person is worshipping God. We do not know the earnestness in a man's heart; yet that is what is really important.

It is not only the learned, or so-called educated and enlightened persons, who perceive the meaning of the law of right and wrong. Even among savages there is some sense of it, because it is an instinct; it is the law by which the savage lives. We may think many people are doing wrong, yet we do not know what is wrong for them and what is not wrong; we do not know what is right for them and what is not right. We ourselves may be doing many things that we think right, but really are wrong to others; and others do things that appear to us to be wrong, and yet are acting rightly in their case. It is just a matter of looking at it from the other person's point of view.

How few there are in this world who stop to think whether the actions of another are right for him! We are so ready to accuse another, and we are so ready to hide our own faults. Did we but look at right and wrong from his standpoint, we should find that the meaning of right and wrong would change. It is wrong for a little child to go out without asking its parents, because perhaps it will meet a motor-car from which it cannot protect itself. But would the same thing be wrong for a grown-up? It is only during the age of childhood that the act is wrong, later it is right.

Did we but study the object of life, we should come to understand the nature of right and wrong; and once we knew the nature of right and wrong we would not need to consult the law of the scripture, for that law itself would then begin to reveal to us its own truth. Nature herself can tell us what is right and wrong for us and for another person.

The secret of it all is found in the answer to the question: why is man here? The answer is, that he is here to attain the satisfaction of his innermost desire. And what is that innermost desire? It is first joy, then peace. But the attainment of each is contrary, because joy comes from activity of life, and peace comes from rest.

All this activity that a person experiences and enjoys by his senses, is a glimpse of joy. The greater joy comes when he can experience through his inner self also, through his mind. For there is another joy, that of the mind when it is delighted with a thing of truth or delicacy, or a beautiful thought. Beautiful music, beautiful verse, beautiful imagination, all bring delight. It is perhaps a greater joy than the joy of a delicious dish, for some persons would give anything for a verse which they would never give for a delicious dish.

But there is a still greater joy, that of the heart, the innermost being of a person; the joy when this heart can express itself and experience love. There are many in this world who only live in the body; their heart is dead, their mind is dead; they seek their highest joy only in the body. But there are others who live in mind as well as in body. It is like the difference between a thoughtful man and an ordinary man. When a man is thoughtful he has become a different man. This idea is expressed by the word 'gentleman'. There are very few who could be truly called gentlemen, though many pass for such. The gentleman is he who is beginning to live in his mind, whose mind is becoming alive, who enjoys life too, yet is not delighted merely with the experience of the senses.

But he whose heart is awakened is higher than a gentleman. Such a one can sympathize with another; his sympathies are awake to consider another, to think for another, to serve another, to sacrifice for another. He is not merely a gentleman, he is a saint. The power of sympathy and love takes away the gross self which used to demand all for itself. Once that is taken away, man thinks in a far higher way. 'Whatever I can do for another, that will I do; I will sacrifice all I have; the loss is no matter; it is a satisfaction'. To satisfy the heart, what a thing it is! This also is a part of joy, but it is not peace.

Joy is experienced by worldly attainment; peace is the attainment of heaven. In the ordinary sense we call it peace to be at rest in an armchair, on cushions, or in bed. But when the body is on a comfortable couch, does that mean that the mind is resting on cushions also? Cannot the mind go through torture at the same time? If that be the case, of what benefit is the peace and comfort of the body? The whole being must have peace. The mind must have peace from anxieties, worry, and from the greed that gives us ambitious desires and that we call 'wrong' and 'sin'. When all this has gone, the mind is at rest. Then, when the heart is at peace and has done its work of love, the heart has enough; it ceases to be interested in any particular object in life, but is equal towards all. When there is no demand there is peace, and this peace helps towards peace of the soul.

These are the two desires which we hold. It is when we do not know the manner in which to attain these two desires that sometimes the joy of one part of our being takes away the peace of the other; or the peace of one part of our life takes away the joy of the other part of our being. It is when man once knows this that he is able really to master himself, to manage his life's affairs as he wishes, to have a better idea of what is right and what is wrong, and of what is sin and what is virtue.

This knowledge is gained through a study of life rather than of books. If we only knew how much the study of life can tell us! One could go into the British Museum and read every book in the building, and yet not obtain satisfaction. It is not study, it is not research, it is not enquiry which gives this knowledge; it is actually going through the experiences of life, witnessing life in its different aspects and in its different phases or spheres; that is what reveals the ideal of life.

A man may know about the whole world's doings, saying to himself, 'In the morning I will go from my home to the office, and will find out all about the world from my paper before I go'. But all he has learnt is what the newspapers feed him with; for how often next day is the news of today contradicted! Still he is satisfied, thinking he has learned so much about the world in the morning. And in the evening he is ready to discuss these topics at the dinner-table, and next day there is again something fresh; but is that knowledge?

How wonderful is the sight that is given to us, how marvellous is the mind, how great a treasure is the light of the soul! Can these be intended only for things like that? If we only knew the value of our life, the value of our soul, we would give the precious time that is ours to keen observation with calm perception, combining the attitude of a student with the care of a scientist.

Look not on life as a person would watch a play on the stage; rather look upon it as a student who is learning at college. It is not a passing show; it is not a place of amusement in which to fool our life away. It is a place for study, in which every sorrow, every heartbreak brings a precious lesson; it is a place in which to learn by one's own suffering, by the study of the suffering of others; to learn from the people who have been kind to us as well as from the people who have been unkind. It is a place in which all experiences, be they disappointments, struggles, and pains, or joys, pleasures, and comforts, contribute to the understanding of what life is, and the realization what it is.

Then do we awake to the religion of nature, which is the only religion. And the more we understand it, the greater our life becomes, and the more of a blessing will our life be for others.

THE PERSONALITY OF GOD

THAT ETHICAL view of God which conceives of Him as a personality is really a conception of the self; the divine love, power, and inspiration are really within oneself. But when someone who has not truly studied and understood the subject of God's personality begins to talk about it, he is apt to destroy the religious beliefs of many besides his own. Not only is he apt to go astray himself, through failing to assimilate the knowledge from the ethical point of view, but he will also confuse others in their faiths and beliefs.

After reading a few ethical books and after considering the Christ-idea and the idea of God from the ethical point of view, a person may go and talk to a friend who has simple faith in Jesus Christ and has never considered ethics or science or philosophy but has always held a picture of the Lord before him, fearing to displease the Lord, devoted to him. He may say 'There is no such person as Jesus Christ. He never came to earth; it is a myth; it is only an ethical ideal.' What happens? The plant of devotion, the ideal in the heart, the plant that grows and develops more and more is broken by him, and his friend is driven either to shut the doors of his heart, which should be protected, or to give up his faith. To yield is to go astray, and yet not to yield may be to go astray also.

There is a danger, then, of an ethical point of view destroying one's own religion and understanding; but there is an even greater danger of its doing so to the religion of others.

The Sufi always tries to keep the ideal of God, not only as a philosophy, but as a religious philosophy. It has always been clothed with religion so that the ideal of a Master, a Saviour, of God might be presented not only as a bare truth. For of all those who have the ethical point of view there may perhaps not be one in a thousand who has experienced trouble, distress, sorrow, and the pains of life in such a way as to be able to use this ethical knowledge in his life. The majority of people with an aptitude for study obtain the ethical knowledge, but proceed to criticize their own religion or that of others, and endeavour to destroy the faith which others have; such is human nature.

It is human nature to take others and lead them astray from their path. It is rare for anyone to ask himself, 'Have I gone astray? I will at least not mislead another.' The true parent would think like that. He would say, 'My children shall be happier; they shall not make the mistakes which we have made'. So once the love of human kind has developed in the heart of man, he begins to understand other people as the parent does his children, and to say to himself, 'If others lead you astray, at least I will not do so'.

In reality the ideal of God is a bridge connecting the limited life with the unlimited. Whoever goes over this bridge passes safely from the limited to the unlimited life. The bridge may be taken away, it is true, and one may yet swim across the chasm; but one may be drowned too. The ideal of God is a safe bridge which takes you safely to the goal.

There are four paths or stages that lead a person to spiritual knowledge, from the limited to the unlimited.

The first stage is *Shariat*. This is where the God-ideal is impressed upon mankind as authority, as fear of God. This really means conscientiousness, not fear as is usually thought. If we love, we do not wish to displease; love does not force us to act, but it asks us to be conscientious and take care not to cause the least disharmony with the one whose happiness we want. The first lesson is to idealize someone who is above the personalities of the earth, more than mortal, a protector more than a father; a guardian, a king, mightier than the nations; richer than all the super-millionaires in this world. Wonderful though the goodness is that we see in a mother, causing us to realize how kind and merciful she is, it is nothing compared with the perfection of the kindness and mercy of God. That which attracts us in the mother is limited; unlimited mercy and kindness are only to be seen in God. We perceive that all things that give protection, peace, fear, or love are only found in their perfection in the one ideal, and that is in God.

The one who realizes this offers his prayers to God, worships Him, thinks of Him, and holds the God-ideal in his mind; and a kind of connection comes to be established between him and the ideal, so that in times of depression, of despair, of sorrow and helplessness he has the ideal within immediate reach. He can say, 'I know someone greater, a greater friend than anyone in the world, to whom all respect and worship and humility are due'.

This stage of Shariat is that in which a person asks himself what will please Him, or displease Him. He learns his religion from his parents, from his friends. A good action pleases, a bad action displeases, and pride displeases most; he learns everything very easily by seeing what displeases another. How easy it is; and yet they still go to a clergyman or to a priest, to ask what pleases God. And all the time it is just what pleases man that pleases God, and therefore if we please all around us, we please God; if we displease them, we displease God. A man who has attained to this stage realizes what reward comes to him when he pleases the world, and what happens when he does not. Just think of the peaceful state of the one who has done some good to another, what condition is his when he retires to bed at night; what joy, what peace, what sense of safety! Whereas the person who has harmed another, stolen something, caused trouble or pain, his punishment is with him also. The reward and the punishment can be seen in our own day; there is no need to wait for heaven or hell; every day is heaven or hell once we realize what reaction our own works bring upon ourselves.

The next stage is called *Tariqat*. In this stage one finds what it is that really matters; what it is that is really wrong, and what it is that is really right; how some wrong is hidden under what people call right, and right is hidden under what we call wrong. It is now that a man begins to understand the nature of things. What the whole world calls wrong may be right. Although he pleases the world, at the same time he thinks of the pleasure of God first. He goes on until instead of finding the pleasure of God in the world, he also finds it in his own being, by his own conscience, by his own intelligence. He also begins to be able to say, 'Yes, it is true there is a Creator, it is true I am a creature; but what has God created me from? whence has He created the whole world? is it from Himself or from substance, and if substance has existed, where did that come from?

Having begun to think in this way he begins to find that if there is any substance, it is something that He made out of Himself. One can see that by considering one's own thoughts. When a person notices that a thought has come to him to do a certain thing, where was it before? How did it arise? Surely, his mind has in that case created something out of nothing, or out of himself. Mind is one thing, thought is one thing, but at the same time the thought is of the mind, the mind has created the thought, and yet the thought is not another substance, it is the substance of mind itself. But the mind as the knower of the thought and the creator of the thought stands at the back of the thought, and when the thought has disappeared the mind is there just the same. When the thought has gone the mind is still there. So it is with God. He has created all things; they are sustained a certain time and then lost from the sight of man, but at the same time they have come from Him, they are lost from Him, and He remains the same.

This then is the second stage, when a man begins to understand the Creator.

The third stage is that of *Haqiqat*. It is in this stage that man begins to realize the truth of the whole being and he will think, 'The one whom I have called God, whose personality I have recognized, and whose pleasure or displeasure I have sought, has been seeing His life through my eyes, has been hearing through my ears; it was His breath that came through my breathing, His impulse which I felt, and therefore I know that this body which I had thought to be my own is really the true temple of God. I did not realize that this body was the shrine of God.' Not knowing that God experiences this life through man, one is seeking for Him somewhere else, in some person aloof and apart from the world, whereas all the time He is in oneself.

It is not meant that such a person should set to work to break people's beliefs, and say that God is both in heaven and in his body. Someone would answer, 'If God is in my body, I will no longer worship that God; I thought God was pure and in the heavens, but if He dwells in my body, I cannot bear that idea for one moment.' That person will be frightened and go astray. That is why in India it is considered a great sin to awaken anyone who is asleep. If a man is asleep, do not wake him; let him sleep; it is the time for him to sleep; it will not do to wake him before his time.

Thus a mystic understands also that a person who is taking his time to wake up must not be awakened to give him the mystic's idea; it would be a sin, because he is not prepared to understand it, and his beliefs would be shaken. Let him go on thinking God is in Benares; let him think He is in the temple of Buddha; let him think He is in heaven; let him think He is in the seventh heaven above the sky. It is the beginning; he will evolve in time and arrive at the same stage. The rest he is having just now is good for him. The awakening comes, all in its good time.

This explains what is meant by saying that Sufism is a religious philosophy; the philosophy is clothed with religion, that it may not break the ideals and faiths and beliefs of those who are beginning their journey towards the goal. Externally the religion, inwardly the philosophy. The one who wants to understand will understand. 'He who hath ears to hear, let him hear.'

It also explains why people in the past have pictured their philosophy in myths, as did the Hindus and the Greeks in their stories of gods and goddesses. Even in the carvings in wood and stone, as at Elephanta and so many other places, truths are represented in pictures, which convey to the seer and the reader the truths underlying all religions.

The fourth stage is *Marefat.* This is the knowledge which enables a person who has arrived at it to call God 'Truth'. He applies no other name to God but only truth; in the end of his journey he has found the divine light which is truth, the light illuminating his whole being, the whole universe; and even if a thousand universes were there, they would be illuminated by it.

In the Bible it is said that first there was the Word, and there was Light. That means, that the first or highest knowledge is the truth. Light gives knowledge, words give knowledge; in fact, they are knowledge. The Qur'an says that Allah is the light of the heaven and the earth. That means the illumination to which one attains.

The story of Aladdin, who went in search of the lamp, teaches the same lesson. In the end man arrives at the stage where in the shrine of God he finds the light, the light of truth which illuminates all his life, the light that suffices the whole being. When this light comes, all the fear of God, the confusion, the puzzle are gone, because all such things are due to lack of light. Whatever difficulty might be before us would not dismay us if there were a light for us to see through it. That which breaks the heart or brings despair is a difficulty or a trouble through which we cannot see; this means that our trouble in life is always lack of light and nothing else; that every difficulty can be solved, and if we understand the nature of our difficulty, we can see our way through. It is the lack of light which prevents our seeing into our trouble, as well as the way out of it, and it is the light which gives us the power to see into our difficulty as well as showing the way out of it.

Therefore what we need in our life is the lamp of Aladdin. That is what is gained at the fourth stage of development, which is called Marefat.

SILENT LIFE

WHEN WE look at the universe we find there are two aspects of existence: firstly, life; secondly, the condition which compared with what we call life seems to be lifeless. The one aspect of existence we call life, the other aspect we overlook. We divide it into periods and call it time, or we compare it with objects and call it space.

We say that an object is alive, when it shows some activity and consciousness, meaning that it can move and see and think. An object that cannot see and is not active, we call dead. Whatever seems to be devoid of activity and consciousness is called a thing; when it has consciousness and activity, it is called living.

What is the source of this consciousness and activity? The circulation of the blood, the energy of the movements of the body, the activity of the nerves and muscles, if we could only know what it is that keeps them in action! A person may say that it all goes on mechanically like a clock, but the clock is not the source of the movement. The mind is the source of the clock; the mind has made the clock, has thought about it, has wound it; it continues to depend upon man to keep it going. Therefore behind 'clock' is 'man'. Even if it only wants winding once a year, still there is man behind it, whom we do not see.

It is the same with the whole mechanism of nature: all is mechanical and runs according to certain laws, and yet there is a source or origin of things hidden behind it all. As the artist is hidden behind his art, as the scientist is hidden behind his invention, as the mind is hidden behind the body, as the cause is hidden behind the action, so there is always one aspect of life which is hidden behind that other aspect which alone is recognized as life.

Both science and religion show that consciousness has evolved through different stages, from mineral to vegetable, from vegetable to animal, and from animal to humanity. It is regarded as the achievement of modern science that this thought has been reached, but its source lies in the traditions of the past. Rumi's Masnavi tells us the experience of consciousness from the mineral up to the plant:

> I died as a mineral, and rose a plant,
> I died as a plant, and rose again an animal,
> I died as an animal, and rose a man.
> Why then should I fear to become less by dying?
>
> I shall die once again as a man,
> To rise an angel, perfect from head to foot.
> Again, when I suffer dissolution as an angel,
> I shall become what passes the conception of man.

Science today stops at man, but the poem says that from man I shall rise to be an angel, and from angel I shall ascend to that stage of being which passes man's comprehension. This poem was written in the thirteenth century.

This proves Solomon's saying, 'There is nothing new under the sun'. When man discovers something today, he in reality only brings to light something which existed in the past, either as history or as tradition. Even before Rumi one finds this idea in the Qur'an.

What can we learn from this? Every activity which we call 'life' has sprung from a source that is silent, and will always be silent; and every activity, however different in aspect, peculiar to itself, and unlike others in its effect, is still the activity of a tiny part of that life which is as wide as the ocean. Call it world, universe, nation, country, race, community, one individual, or only a particle, an atom—its activity, its energy springs in each case from one inseparable and eternal silent aspect of life. And it has not only sprung from it, but it also resolves itself into it. One throws a pebble into the water, water that is still and calm; there comes an activity, it comes for one moment, and then it vanishes. Into what does it vanish? It vanishes into the same silence in which the water was before. Water is a substance that is active by nature, and the silence, the stillness, the calmness that it shows is just the original state, the effect of its original source. This means that the natural inclination of every thing and every being is silence, because it has come from silence, and yet it is active, because it is activity that produces activity; and its end is silence.

Therefore sages, mystics, and philosophers who have probed into the depths of life have seen that what we call life is death, and that what we call no life is the real life.

A Hindustani poet says, 'Raise your eyes, friend, from what you call life to that which perhaps you do not recognize as life, and then you will find that what you had once called life is nothing but death, and what you thought was nothing, is really life'.

When one comes to the essence of the teachings of Christ one will see that from beginning to end the whole attitude of the Master is to tell mankind that there is a life beyond, which is higher than this which one calls life and which yet is not life; that is to say, higher in quality, not beyond in time.

The life one recognizes is only the mortal aspect of life. Very few have ever seen or been conscious of the immortal aspect at all. Once one has realized life, that which one has hitherto called life is found to be only a glimpse or shadow of the real life that is beyond comprehension. To understand it one will have to raise one's light high from under the cover that is hiding it like a bushel. This cover is man's mind and body; it is a cover that keeps the light active on the world of things and beings. 'Do not keep your light under a bushel' means that we are not to keep the consciousness absorbed in the study of the external world, and in its pleasures and enjoyments. Man is always apt to say that the religious thinker is a dreamer, lost in vague ideals, having no proof of what he believes, and far from what he himself would call the reality. He never thinks that what he calls real has in its turn become unreal to the one to whom the silent life has become reality. Can you call this life real which is subject to such changes every moment? Every activity and the object of everyone's life—riches, power, love, friendship, childhood, youth, health, pleasure, displeasure, happiness, and poverty—all change sooner or later. Can anybody think that such things are reality? What can one call all this that is subject to change, whose source is unseen and whose end is unseen, and which is subject to death and destruction, after which it is seen no more? Is that reality? Or are not the realities perhaps really behind the scene, from whence everything came and to which everything goes?

Perhaps many of us have experienced at some time or other, in our own home, or in a church, a temple, or other religious place, how there is a kind of silence as we sit there. Compared with a bazaar, a market, or a factory there is no activity. If under such circumstances we noticed the condition of our own self, of our mind, of our thoughts, of our body, and have felt any comfort, have we then asked ourselves why we felt comfort and rest? Then, take another experience: we may be a few moments or a few hours in the woods, away and apart from everybody. It may seem as if even the trees and the leaves are keeping silence. The feelings that we have at such a time cannot be expressed in words. These feelings cannot be called pleasure, because what we are accustomed to in pleasure or in joy is not the same. We can only say, 'That peculiar pleasure, that peculiar joy'. There is no name for it, and yet it is a true experience of the soul.

Then there is a still greater and deeper experience: when a person is in a wilderness, near rocks in the desert, where there is no sound even of birds or beasts, when there is absolute silence. In the East, did not all the prophets from the time of Abraham, Moses, David, and in the time of Christ and Mohammad, all the prophets of the Old Testament and the New, and of the Qur'an, receive their inspiration from the same source? The history of Moses on Mount Sinai, the Prophet of Nazareth in the wilderness, the Prophet Mohammad on Ghar-e Hirá, did they not all drink from the silent life? Though God is in all activities and forms and names, it is His other aspect, solid, firm, eternal, all-sufficient and powerful, all-intelligent, undivided and inseparable, from which the inspiration came as a perfect inspiration, so that the world could take it as the sacred Word, in all ages and in all times.

Then, coming to the cause of idol-worship, a person might wonder about the old custom of Brahmins and Buddhists, who went into the temple of Buddha or Krishna, and sat before an idol which neither spoke to them nor took notice of them. He might think, 'What could they gain? It has a mouth and speaks not, it has hands yet cannot move'. And so people mocked at them, scoffed at them, and called them heathen and pagan. But they did not know of this silence that was impressed upon the worshipper. This human form sitting before them, silent and quiet and not speaking, or hearing, or thinking, absolutely quiet; just think what it means.

When a man is among friends he may get tired; sometimes he enjoys their society, but when he does not enjoy it, he thinks, 'I am drained of all vitality'. Why is this? It is the impression of their minds that has been produced in his mind. Perhaps someone has insulted him, or snubbed him, or told him this or that, and he goes among his friends bringing all his troubles with him; and then he leaves still saying, 'I am tired'. If he is working in a factory, it is reasonable to be tired in body; but why should he be tired in society where people are laughing and chatting? It is because their condition of mind is not like his.

But before the idol there is perfect harmony. See, here is someone sitting quiet. A quiet human form which does not speak; what rest! It may not help, but it does not disturb. It keeps the worshipper silent; that was the idea.

What do we learn from this? Every effort was made by the teachers of religion to waken men to that aspect of life that is overlooked in ordinary life which they call 'life'. The purpose of concentration, contemplation, meditation, all that is the essence of religion or mysticism or philosophy, is nothing but this one thing: to attain to that depth which is the root of our life.

A Marathi poet has said, 'O mind, my restless mind, my mind with its thoughts of a thousand things which it supposes will make it happy, saying, "If I had that, I should be happy; if I had this, I should feel life was not wasted". O, my mind, will you tell me who in this world is happy?' The mind says, 'If I had the wealth which I see others have, I should be happy'. But are these others happy? They in their turn say they would be, if they had something still higher!

The secret of happiness is hidden under the veil of spiritual knowledge. And spiritual knowledge is nothing but this: that there is a constant longing in the heart of man to have something of its origin, to experience something of its original state, the state of peace and joy which has been disturbed, and yet is sought after throughout its whole life, and never can cease to be sought after until the real source has at length been realized. What was it in the wilderness that gave peace and joy? What was it that came to us in the forest, the solitude? In either case it was nothing else but the depth of our own life, which is silent like the depths of the great sea, so silent and still. It is the surface of the sea that makes waves and roaring breakers; the depth is silent. So the depth of our own being is silent also.

And this all-pervading, unbroken, inseparable, unlimited, ever-present, omnipotent silence unites with our silence like the meeting of flames. Something goes out from the depths of our being to receive something from there, which comes to meet us; our eyes cannot see and our ears cannot hear and our mind cannot perceive because it is beyond mind, thought, and comprehension. It is the meeting of the soul and the Spirit.

Therefore the idea of understanding the spiritual ideal is to attain to that state of being, of calm and peace and joy and everlasting happiness, which neither changes nor ceases to exist. It is to realize what is said in the Bible, 'Be ye perfect even as your Father in heaven'. Those words do not tell us to remain imperfect as everybody on earth. No, they mean the idea of all perfection, all unity, no separation. It is the opposite of the idea that religion should keep part of humanity separate, saying, 'You do not belong to our church, our mosque, our temple!' It is the opposite of loyalty to this particular sect or community, or to that particular sacred book, to this particular teaching, or to that particular truth. Is not the source of all truth hidden in every man's heart, be he Christian, Muslim, Buddhist or Jew? Is not each part of that life which we call spiritual or divine? To be just this or that is the same as not going further than this or that. The bliss found in solitude is hidden within every human being; he has inherited it from his heavenly Father. In mystical words it is called the all-pervading light. Light is the source and origin of every human soul, of every mind.

The Sufi looks upon life as one life, upon all religions as his religion: call him a Christian and he is that, call him a Muslim or a Hindu and he is that; call him whatever you like, he does not mind. A Sufi does not think about what people call him. Who calls him Sufi? It is not he. But if he does not call himself something, someone else is sure to find a name for him. Cats and dogs do not declare their names; it is man that gives them a name. If you call yourself 'New Thought', it will be made into the name of a new sect some day; if you call yourself 'Higher Thought', that will be a sect one day; call yourself what you will: philosophy, theosophy, religion, mysticism, it is only the one thing, it is nothing but the constant longing of the soul of the human being. After experiencing all the different aspects of the life of activity, the longing to attain to that state of peace or calm seems in the end to be the only object that the soul wishes to achieve.

A person may keep thinking that perhaps he will be happy when he is a king, or rich, or an officer; then he will gain his desire, and as long as he has not got it, the sweetness of the thought lies only in the hope. As long as there is hope there is sweetness; after fulfilling the desire, the hope has gone. Then he hopes for something else. It is hope that is sweet, not the object. The object is never sweet; it is the sweetness of the hope that makes the object seem sweet.

'If I could reach that height!' a man says. So long as he has not reached that height, the dream of reaching the height, of one day experiencing that position, experience, or imagination, the dream of being comforted by it, so long he has the sweetness of the hope. But when it has come, the sweetness is finished. Then begins a new hope, always hoping, hoping. And still behind it all is that one inclination, common to all, the inclination of which he does not know the nature. No person would live did he not have the hope of something for which he was waiting.

Hope is the only food of life. Then reason says, 'Yes, I am looking forward to my change from this place to the next; to get my inheritance some day; then I shall be all right; I shall be all right when I get that position, that house, that comfort'. Man has always something before him, imagining, building, preparing and holding it in the mind all the time, and yet when he does get it, there is always another hope.

It is only those who are blessed by perceiving the origin and source of all things who awaken to the fact that the real inclination of every life is to attain to something which can not be touched or comprehended or understood. The hidden blessing of this knowledge is the first step to perfection. Once awake to this fact, man sees there is something in life that will make him really happy and give him his heart's desire. He can say, 'Though there are many things in life which I need for the moment and for which I shall certainly work, yet there is only that one thing, around which life centres, that will satisfy me: the spiritual attainment, the religious attainment, or, as one may even call it, the attainment of God'. Such a one has found the key to all happiness, and has found that all the things he needs will be reached because he has the key to all. 'Seek, and ye shall find: knock, and it shall be opened unto you . . . Seek first the kingdom of God, and all these things shall be added unto you.' This kingdom of God is the silent life; the life inseparable, eternal, self-sufficient, and all-powerful. This is the life of the wise, whatever be the name given to it; this is the life which the wise contemplate. It is the face of this life that they long to see; it is the ocean of this life that they long to swim in; as it is written, 'In Him we live and have our being'.

These are the ones who are really happy, who are above all unhappiness, above death and the destruction of life.

THE WILL, HUMAN AND DIVINE

THE WILL is the same, whether it be human or divine. The only difference is that in one aspect it is the whole, in the other aspect it is a part; in one aspect it is almighty, in the other it has only a certain might, or a certain power; in one aspect it is unlimited, in the other it is limited.

The difference between the divine and the human will is like the difference between the trunk of a tree and its branches; and as from the boughs other branches and twigs spring, so the will of one powerful individual has branches going through the will of other individuals. In a tree there is a trunk, and there are some prominent or large branches; from these there spring many smaller branches. So there are the powerful beings, the masters of humanity. Their will is God's, their word is God's word, and yet they are branches, because the trunk is the will of the Almighty. As the branches grow, so we too grow; as the branches develop, we develop; as the branches flourish, we flourish; as the branches bear fruit, we bear fruit; as the branches are capable of rising, we too rise. Whether the branch be large or small, every branch has the same origin and the same root as the stem. Therefore, whether a person be holy or wicked, wise or foolish, he has in his innermost spirit the same essence and the same power that the wise have.

There is no reason for anyone to feel discouraged by his weaknesses or deficiencies, or by his actions that have dissatisfied him, or by anything in life that has failed. He should forget the past that has failed him, and begin to construct and mould his future as he would wish it to be, considering that as a branch is not separate from the bough, and the bough is not separate from the stem, so with all our limitations we are not separate from the will of the Unlimited One.

In Sufi terms these two aspects of will are called *Kaza* and *Kadr*. Sometimes we think, 'If I could see that friend it would be so pleasant', and at the same time there comes a desire, 'If I could have some nice flowers', and then a friend comes bringing a bunch of our favourite ones. Or we may desire to have fish to eat, and the cook brings a savoury dish of fish. Sometimes this is due to the strength of one's own will, and sometimes it is the soul working in harmony with the divine will. One only knows when it is in harmony with the divine will and when not by noting the results, and the one who knows beforehand is the seer.

Sometimes things are accomplished without the least effort. When it is the divine will it is like something floating on water; it advances without effort. Problems and actions may be achieved in a moment then, whilst at other times the smallest problem cannot be solved without great difficulty. One finds that some persons are very clever and experienced in industrial work or in politics; and they have striven very hard to attain their goal, and yet have accomplished nothing; they are always a failure. And there are others who take up a thing, and without much effort, without much worry on their part, they complete it and attain their goal.

All this is accounted for by harmony with the divine will. Everyone experiences such a thing at some time or other. When things are in harmony with the divine will, everything is there; we just cast a glance towards a thing and it is found, as in the saying, 'Word spoken, action done'. When we strive with all the material in our hands and yet cannot achieve our desire, that is when the matter is contrary to the divine will. Our success or failure all depends upon the harmony or disharmony of our individual will with the divine will.

But if our individual will is a branch of the divine will, if its source is the same, how can it ever be out of harmony? Sometimes the hand sympathizes with the foot, at other times it does not. We hurt ourselves many times just because of disharmony; we may cut ourselves, our fingers for instance. If then, I, who am one person, can cause harm to myself, and suffer thereby, why should it not be possible that the human will should be out of harmony with the divine, so that the divine suffers thereby? It is possible to act in a way contrary to the divine will, even though one is only a branch of it. In a fountain there is a big stream which flows up and then breaks into many drops. The stream is like the divine will, and the different drops like the wills in us. One drop goes higher, another lower, one falls to the left, another to the right, one goes north, another south. But the source of all this activity is one; it is one thing that turns into so many, scattering in all directions. Thus from unity there has come variety.

The sages have therefore taught the part played by contentment. It is said, 'Resist not evil,' and yet how many give in to evil instead! The real meaning of the scripture is: suppose a person is angry with us, if we partake of his anger we resist him; the fire that he sets alight in our minds we allow to become alight in ourselves, and we have resisted. Do not resist evil in that way. Do not partake of the evil of another. If you are quiet and calm, your calmness and quietness will have a greater effect on the other than his anger, so that true resistance is practice of contentment. Patience is the best quality that man can cultivate. We are always apt to become excited or annoyed when another person does not understand us. Why get excited if he cannot understand us? If a person is foolish or cannot do things right, by becoming excited we make him still more foolish, still more stupid. We cannot help him in that way, and we partake of his quality by allowing ourselves to oppose him. If we kept our mind tranquil, if we had patience, we should keep in harmony. Harmony is the greatest thing to learn in life. All the disagreement between couples, friends, people in business and politics, comes from lack of patience. If we just had patience and contentment, we could teach ourselves much better.

Contentment teaches resignation. But this resignation is not exactly what people mean by fate. The true recognition of fate is like the drop realizing that it is foolish to fight against the ocean. The drop is part of the ocean. Why want to fight it? If the drop does not resign itself, of what profit will it be? Why believe that what we think is right, and no one can be right who thinks otherwise? We should remember that another person does not see as we see, because each one sees only a reflection of the highest Ego that works in man though he is unconscious of it. To him it is right, but to the other it need not appear right. It is only right for that one person, for that one moment; later it may not appear so. The limited being cannot claim the perception of the Unlimited; thus we cannot regard our own will as being the universal Will unless our will is in harmony with the will of God. We should therefore practise harmonizing our will with that of our fellow-men, by tolerance, patience, endurance; because in this world every ego is working for itself, however near or dear another may be. Everyone thinks, 'What can I make another person do for me?' He wants everybody to be in harmony with his way of life. That is why there is a world full of rebellion, like the thorns in the rose-bush.

It may seem a great sacrifice and torment to practise patience, but it is the only way to get out of the whirlpool; it is the only way that one can conquer life's difficulties. If anybody has ever conquered, he has only done so by this means; never by the means of resistance, but always by the way of resignation. All teachers have taught this way, saying, 'Prostrate thyself on the ground; prostrate thyself before God; kneel down'. Some of us fail to appreciate this, but the messengers do not leave anything unspoken; it is we who do not understand what they say. People fight for their religions; if we were just to learn the one instead! The question should always be: have we learned our own religion? To have learned it means to practise it and see its benefit. However fast we may try to run away from it, we will still find this lesson to learn. We have to make ourselves strong and prepared to withstand all that befalls us. Therefore we must develop our will-power first by such morals, and be able to harmonize our will with the others.

One thinks one can develop will-power by fighting, but that is not so, because by fighting we make very little progress; by fighting with ourselves we progress a hundred times more. Our greatest enemy is ourself. All weakness, all ignorance keeps us from the truth of our being, from all the virtues hidden in us and all perfection hidden in our souls. The first self we realize is the false self. Unless the soul is born again it will not see the kingdom of heaven. The soul is first born into the false self; it is blind. In the true self the soul opens its eyes. Unless the false self is fought with, the true self cannot be realized. Therefore endurance is necessary, patience is necessary.

If only we could fight with ourselves so that we became able to give pleasure to others! Sages are as harmonious with a pious person as with a wicked one, as harmonious with a wise man as with a foolish, with a rich as with a poor man. We feel friendly towards some, not towards others; we get on well with some, but with others there is always disharmony while with others again everyone feels peaceful and happy.

The lions could not harm Daniel because of the harmony of his will with the universal Will. The lions represent the destructive elements in the human mind. They represent wars, disappointments, rivalries, jealousies, envy, passions, and so forth, in different horrible guises. Our ego is the lion of lions, and if this is conquered, then these external lions—the different egos around us—are conquered also, and wherever we go, with anyone, whether foolish or wise, good or bad, we now have peace.

To learn the lesson of how to live is more important than any psychic or occult learning. Every day we think we have learnt the lesson, but if we had the world would have become a heaven for us by now. We may seek the higher knowledge or the higher things, but the very smallest thing, the control of all the creatures of the mind, which seems as nothing compared with the higher knowledge, once learnt and acted upon is greater than all. This is a great step; yet how difficult to gain this, how reasonless it seems! But when we pause to think of the difference between ourselves and animals, we see the greatness in this simple thing of yielding the will. If there is one animal in a place and another one comes to it, the first one wants to bite or bark, or even drive him out of his sight. A dog will do that even though he has finished his dinner and does not want to eat the food that has attracted the hungry dog to the place.

There is an Eastern parable of a dog going to a certain town. His journey was a very long one, taking two or three days as a rule, and yet he arrived before sunset of the same day. The dogs of that town were all very surprised to see him so soon. 'Yes, it was a very long journey', the dog said, 'but I attribute my speed to the kindness and help of my fellow-dogs. Since I left home, whenever I felt tired and tried to stop a moment to rest, four or five would run up and bark at me and want to bite me. So I had to run on without staying to rest in that place, or to search for food. And so it went on at every place I came to, until in the end I have arrived here at my destination.'

This illustrates the animal nature. Man's selfishness shows itself in wanting to get the better of his fellow-man. If we developed humanity we should do differently. We should be satisfied with a slice of bread if there were another in need, but as it is, it happens that even when we are fed ourselves, we do not wish anyone else to share the food. The human heart can only be really satisfied by knowing that the other person is happy. True pleasure lies in the sharing of joy with another. From the day that we realize this we begin to act as human beings; hitherto we have not done so even though we have human forms.

Sages have always repented of all things that make them animal. It is human beings that repent; the animals are pleased with everything that they do. The Bible says, 'Repent, for the kingdom of God is at hand'. This has to be done all day long. Once one has realized it, the kingdom of God is at hand. The sinner can become righteous at any moment if he makes up his mind; the difficulty is to make it up. The next thing is to carry it out. Revolutions and harmony, war and peace, are all parts of a whole being. But contentment and perfect resignation open up a harmonious feeling and bring the divine will into harmony with our own. Our blessing now becomes a divine blessing, our words divine words, our atmosphere a divine atmosphere, although we seem to be limited beings; for our will becomes absorbed into the whole, and so our will becomes the will of God.

MIND, HUMAN AND DIVINE

THE MIND is not the brain, but that faculty, that intangible and imperceptible activity of which the brain is merely a vehicle. Man limits things that are unlimited and beyond his power of measurement, and therefore he has pictured God in human form or given sacredness to the forms of animals. A person of larger mind has a larger view, and perhaps sees good in everybody, whereas one with a mind always wanting to find some evil will be able to find a trace of evil even in a good person. That means that man is accustomed from childhood to measure and understand things according to his way of understanding, and to examine them in the limited way peculiar to himself.

The Vedantas, which represent the ancient philosophy of the Hindus, using Sanskrit, the mother of languages, employ the word *Manu* or *Manushi* for 'man'. *Mana* is mind, and the English word 'man' has the same origin. This shows that the origin of man's being is his mind; and his external form is so much before his eyes that it hides the other aspect of his being, which seems, in comparison to this, to be invisible. His body is here, but his mind may be in China; the real *he* is not here.

In the story of the Prophet's life his journey to heaven is related. It is said that a heavenly animal came down to earth and took the Prophet to heaven. This means that the Prophet visited heaven in his mind. It is the state of mind which is heaven; it is the state of mind which is hell; it is the state of mind that makes one great, or feeble, or insignificant, strong or weak. In the Hindu writings it is said, 'Your success or failure depends entirely on your mind. If your mind has failed, no one can bring success; but even if everything has gone wrong, and your mind is set on success, the success is there!'

The more we think of the mind, the more we understand the nature of the human being. The tendency to sin or virtue, the temperament, the attitude towards right and wrong, failure and success, in fact all changes in life, are entirely dependent on the condition of the mind. The dream tells the state of the mind at the time; the mind is in full play when a person is asleep. It is not free during the waking hours because of the occupations of the day. The dream will show the state of a patient's mind. It is a disturbance of the mind that produces coma.

Whatever a man desires, that desire informs us of the state of mind he is in, and those who understand the mind well, know the mind of another simply by studying the desires and tendencies of his life. Love of a rose, a lily, a jasmine, of sweet, sour, salt, or savoury things expresses the particular tendency of a person's mind, the mood he is in. Modern education omits the study of the truth which teaches us that unity comes from nature's variety, whereas the sole aim of the mystic is to keep near to the idea of unity and to find out where we unite.

There is an Arabic saying, 'If you wish to know God, you must know yourself'. How little man knows while he is in the intoxication of individualism! He thinks, 'I am a separate being; you are another; there is no connection between you and me, and we all have our own joys and free will'. Did man but know it, his life is dependent not only on the objects and things that keep the body alive, but also on the activity of a thousand minds in a day. Every time a man laughs it is the reflection of his mind, controlled by the power of another person's mind. Why does he feel sometimes sad, sometimes glad, sometimes cheerful, sometimes enthusiastic, sometimes tired without reason, sometimes depressed and exhausted? We meet so many minds throughout the day and night which are reflected in our own mind; and so the thoughts are changed, seemingly without reason, yet the whole activity of life depends on these thoughts and is changed according to them.

Who then can say, 'I am an individual, independent and free, I can think as I wish, and I can do what I wish'? We are not doing what we wish; we are not thinking what we wish. There are various thoughts around us in the form of men and animals and entities which influence our mind and feeling and thought; we cannot escape them. No one can escape being affected by another person's mind. There is always some person stronger than us, and always someone weaker than ourselves. We are connected with one another. Our lives are tied together, and there is a link in which we can see one current running through all. There are many globes and lamps, and yet one current is running through all.

The mystic seeks to realize this constantly and to impress it on his mind in whatever he may see. What, for him, are the waves of the sea? Are they not the sea itself? Their individuality exists only in so far as one wave rises and falls. It rises and falls, but it merges into the sea. The new wave is a different wave altogether. What, for him, is the tree? There is one stem; the leaves spring from it, change their colour, and drop off. But at the same time the life of the whole tree depends on the root and stem, and any damage done to either of these affects every branch and bough, every part of the tree. What, for him, is the body? Eyes, nose, head, which of them is his self? The hand has a separate name, the fingers have separate names; every part has a different name. Myriads of thoughts, myriads of imaginations, myriads of feelings! Can we ever number their variety? The different emotions, the different kinds of sorrows, the different grades of joy, can we ever distinguish them or classify them? Our being has so many aspects, but what is it after all that calls itself 'I', 'me'? It is one, not many. It is simply that if we had no body or mind, we could not realize that we exist. Through all this variety one realizes, 'I am one'.

The same ideas work further in the mind, until man finds that oneness which exists behind all these numerous names and forms, and in which he will unite with his Lord. This shows that the experience of individuals, the thoughts, feelings, and knowledge of individuals, and the experience of nations, of races, throughout all ages and periods of history, have not belonged only to individuals, not even to the multitude, to the nations, the races, but have always gone back till they came to that depth where they were assimilated with what is called the divine mind.

All the different minds are the different leaves of one tree. Some minds are branches, some are boughs of the tree, and there is only the one source to which all are attached. No object or life can exist without one central point in which everything meets and joins together; and that meeting-ground is the divine mind. The Brahmins therefore taught people to bathe at the place where rivers meet; the purification of life was symbolized by bathing at Sangam. Those who really understood knew that this pictured the divine mind, that in life purification lies in touching that depth of life's sea in which the myriads of forms and names all join. The activity of all beings is directed from that centre. The Qur'an says that no single atom moves independently of the hand of God. That is, no activity of any kind takes place, either here or in the starry space, without the impulse from within, from that depth of life where all minds and the effects of all activity unite.

Coming now to the moral side of the subject, we may ask in what way we should carry on our life. Should we be satisfied by depending on one power working? That would be just like paralysis of a part of the body. The hand would not move. Just think, where have our thoughts and impulses come from?

Should we then act upon every impulse that comes? Should we not take action in every case, seeing they all come from God? No, for it is the realization of the mind that makes things right or wrong, good or bad, spiritual or material. It is your own thought; not the action. It is as you make it. Although the impulse is from within, if it is wrong, you have made it wrong; if it is right, it is because you make it so. The law justifies you. There is no other law. It is your law.

Every mind whether stupid or wise, wicked or virtuous, loves goodness and beauty. What is good? Good is that which is beautiful, what you admire, what you cannot help admiring. You admire the beauty of a person's kindness, beauty of action, feeling, and thought. Nobody tries to see ugliness or to follow the path of evil. Is there anyone who will say, 'Please do not be kind to me; please deceive me?' No one likes to be fooled. Wickedness is to seek to gain and not to give; but even the wicked person is still awake to beauty.

The mystic is guided by his own mind. That which we seek in life we must give to another; if it is kindness, give it; if goodness, give it; if service, give it. The whole secret of happiness in life lies in this. When we seek happiness in the kindness of another, it means that we depend on the kindness of another person to make us happy; and as long as we look to another to make us happy, we keep expecting that which we ought ourselves to have given. Not till then do we know what justice is.

The world is a dome, where every action is the echo of another.

Do good: it will come back; if not from one person, it will come from another. That is the echo. You do not know from which side it will come. It will come a hundredfold more than you give.

If we give love, will we get coldness? If we do good, can we get evil? We cannot be a judge of the action of another until we ourselves are selfless. Only then will justice come to us; only then will we understand the nature of justice. Self is the wall between us and justice. There is only one thing that is truly just, and that is to say, 'I must not do this'. But when we say this to another we may be wrong.

The mystic develops his mind in this manner, purifying it by pure thought, feeling, and action, only following this one line of thought. Pure means free from sense of separateness. Whatever difference in principles of right and wrong religious faith may show, no two individuals will ever differ in this one natural principle. Every soul seeks after beauty; and every virtue, righteousness, good action, is nothing but a glimpse of beauty.

Once having this moral, the Sufi does not need to follow a particular belief or faith, to restrict himself to a particular path. He can follow the Hindu way, the Muslim way, the way of any Church or faith, provided he treads this royal road: that the whole universe is but an immanence of beauty. We are born with the tendency to admire it in every form, and we may not blind ourselves by being dependent on one particular line of beauty. We will not get it from another. Give it. Let us make our action, our thought beautiful, and let others profit by it.

How is the perfection of mind reached that we have to touch? It is reached through contemplation, through realization and understanding of the one current running through the whole of life. We begin to contemplate on that. The mind which we call in religious language the Almighty, and in mystical terms the divine mind, is the depth of life, the depth of activity, with which all activity and every activity is connected.

Therein lies the whole of religion. The mystic's prayer is to that beauty, and his work is to forget the self, to lose himself like a bubble in the water. The wave realizes, 'I am the sea', and by falling into the sea prostrates itself before its God. As it is said, 'Be ye perfect, even as your Father which is in heaven is perfect'.

WILL-POWER

WHEN THE mind enquires into the nature of will-power, it becomes a question whether it is a power of the mind, a power of thought, or a power of the brain. Those who cannot see beyond the power of the brain, call it brain-power; those who cannot see beyond the mind, call it a power of the mind. Those who cannot conceive of the existence in man of anything above the feelings, consider will-power to be a power of feeling. A Sufi understands it to be the divine power.

It is the divine will that is manifested throughout the whole universe, which has created the whole universe; and it is part of the divine will that manifests itself through us. Everything we do in life is governed and directed by that power. Were it not that there is but one power to govern and direct, how would it have been if one foot determined to go to the North, and the other to the South? Our two eyes might have turned in opposite directions, one to the West, the other to the East, had there not been one will-power behind them to direct their gaze towards one object. When lifting a certain thing, one hand might have gone up and the other down, had there not been one will-power to govern both, and cause them to join in the one movement. This shows that each individual has one will-power which governs several organs of our physical existence as well as our thoughts and imaginations; all are directed consciously or unconsciously by the one power. We could not have accomplished one single thing in life had will-power not been at work.

But there are two ways in which the will-power works: firstly, when it is lighted with the light of intelligence; secondly, when it is not so lighted, but works by itself. When it works by itself, we call it accidental. We do things accidentally which we have not intended to do. But when will-power makes our mind and body work consciously, then the light of intelligence is followed and the will-power is acting consciously. This is the difference between various happenings. In the one we are conscious of what we are thinking, we are conscious of what we are speaking and of what we are doing in proportion to our will-power and to the light that is thrown upon it from the light of our intelligence. But we have acted without will-power when we have to say, 'I have done something I should not have done; I have said something I should not have said; I have thought something which I should not have thought.' When a person says, 'What I did is terrible; I said something I should not have said', it means that during the time he said or did it the will-power was there, but the strength and light of intelligence had not fallen upon it to the extent to which they should.

There are two aspects of our being: the will-power or governing power, and the vehicles, the mind and the body. Both are governed and controlled by that one governing power. In one aspect of our being we are king, in the other aspect we are minister, and in a third aspect we are servant. We are minister when our mind works, and we are servant when the body works. We are king when the will-power works.

When this power loses its control over the mind, then our thoughts become disordered; they dwell in any regions and wander on any lines, even those which our moral standard has perhaps not drawn for them. And our body also works in a disorderly way when the power of the will is lost. Therefore all illnesses, all failures, all disappointments and faults in life are caused by just one thing: weakness of will-power.

Man, not knowing this, sometimes considers the will-power to be a power of thought and mind. He does not know that behind mind there is something else. When the will is behind it, the body is powerful too. There was a well-known Indian faqir who was able to lift an elephant. How can a man lift an elephant? However strong he may be, what comparison can there be between the two? What power is at work? It was his will-power that was greater than the elephant's.

The great and wonderful things that man has done in this world that we see around us, are all the outcome of man's will. Animals, with all their strength, have not that will. Therefore puny man stands before the elephant and says, 'Sit down', and the elephant sits down; 'Stand up', and the elephant stands up. With all the strength in its body, still the elephant listens to him. That is how the faqir lifted the elephant. Man makes tigers, lions, horses work; he even makes his thought and will act through inanimate things; even through objects his will-power can be manifested. But when man does not realize its effect upon living creatures, how can he experience his power over objects?

Jelal-ud-Din Rumi, in his Masnavi, speaks of fire, air, water, earth, and ether as beings, while man calls them things. To man they are things, to God they are beings, obedient servants. Whatever He wishes, they do. As the servant acts according to his master's desires, so these elements act as God desires. Further, not only does the will of God work through elements, but the will of man also, in proportion to the power of his will. A loaf of bread given with will-power can cure a man's disease more successfully than a medicine, if there is enough will-power with it. The lesson of Christ, that if one has faith even as a grain of mustard one can remove mountains, can be understood after one has realized that it is the will-power which does the work.

In the East there are superstitions which have a mystical meaning. When a person goes into a new business, or goes on a journey, his relatives give him flour or rice in his hand, or some betel nuts, with the wish that he may meet with success. The token itself is nothing; but behind it there is will-power, and the person who received it has believed; therefore he has responded to the will-power attached to the gift. There is a harmony. The one who wishes to have good luck receives it.

Nevertheless, it is not to be inferred from this that a man should be prepared to believe in superstitions or become superstitious. It is to show that he must know the value of will-power, and use it in his profession, his business, his home, in all things. Is it not a desirable thing to have will-power; is it not desirable to have physical strength? If we are satisfied with feebleness of body, it may be that we are also satisfied to be without will-power.

All light is for us, inspiration is for us; why not use it as long as we know how to use it to make the best of life? If one wishes to abuse power, one may abuse bodily power, fighting everybody, boxing and wrestling. But that is another part of life. Power is necessary and should be developed; but when man is anxious to develop power, either of body or of mind, he ought to remember that the will-power is behind it all; that if the will is developed, the physical and mental power can easily be obtained. The will-power governs the body and the mind.

Now coming to the question of the will of man as opposed to the will of God: which is which? We understand the difference when we perceive that the nature of will-power differs only according to whether it exists in its fullness, or whether it is limited. The will-power in its fullness is divine power; the will-power in its limited state is the individual will. And if there is anything that can be called the source of the whole creation, it is the divine will, it is the will of the absolute Being. If we do not desire to call it will, we may call it force, strength, or might. But force, strength, might, energy, are all dead words. Force can be without intelligence, energy without intelligence, mind without intelligence; but will means force, energy, might, with intelligence. Therefore it is called divine will instead of divine energy. A person with a materialistic mind would call it energy. But why energy? Is our intelligence energy? It is beyond energy. Is our will only energy? It is energy with intelligence. Therefore divine will is energy, but with divine intelligence. In all there is intelligence.

If we observe nature keenly, we see how divine wisdom is working. The animals and birds of tropical countries have fur and feathers which differ from those one finds in the Himalayas and other cold regions. They have suitable bodies, suitable skins; their life, their whole existence is adjusted to the place where they live.

Man's desire, the desire of his senses, is matched by the possession of every sense, every organ of sense, each suited to gratify the desire of his being. The eye meets the requirement of the sense of sight. With all our intelligence and great research no one can make a new eye so adaptable and fitted for the purpose. This wisdom makes us understand and believe that behind all this there is an intelligent God and Creator, not only a life or energy or force; it makes us ask why anyone should want to call Him force or energy, and not God.

The light which we see of the stars and planets is not their own. It is the light of the sun which illuminates the planets and is reflected from them; it is the same light that they receive which they reflect. So it is with man: it is the will of God that is reflected in man. Although every star is not necessarily a sun, yet its light ultimately comes from a sun.

If man has divine light in him, why should he commit sin or do evil, and why should there be anything that we call wrong or a sin? If it is God's will, how can it be sin? We understand this when we consider the difference between wrong and right, sin and virtue, good and evil. These differ with different people. It depends upon the standards of each one's evolution; it depends on the goal or ideal which each one has placed before him. That is why the Prophet said, 'The religion of each person is peculiar to himself'. It is a great fault on our part when we accuse another person of an untrue or false belief, an untrue or false religion. We do not know that perhaps he has a religion which is suited to himself. His evolution or attainment in life, his temperament, his standard of morals are different; therefore we ought, if only we could, to keep to our own religion. The standard that we believe in for our own good is quite enough.

Our intelligence and experience of this life on earth create within us a world of experiences; and these experiences teach us, by comparing one with the other, that this one is for our happiness; that one is not. That which is for our happiness we call virtue, and that which does not contribute to our happiness we call vice. In this way the world which we make into our own is a world of personal experiences, either in our own lives or seen through the lives of others. Therefore it is quite natural that a person in Tibet should have a different religion from a person in France; and a man in Persia a different one from a man in Colombo. Although mankind is the same everywhere, a man's religion is his experience in life, and therefore his own evolution, his own experience, added to the temperament of the people with whom he lives. He can see what is good for him, and what is not; what is right and what is not right; what gives him happiness, and what keeps him from it. The world itself becomes a scripture or book to the soul. If he does not consult it, he is thoughtless. But the one who consults with the world that he has created within himself, is wise. Sometimes in his world he has decided a certain thing is a sin or evil, and yet when it comes to an action, or thought, or speech, he cannot follow the moral he has already made for himself, either because of the weakness of his mind or body, or because of the weakness of his will. He fails to fulfil the law of his own world, of his own scripture that he has written. Thus he falls, and that is considered by him to be sin. It is the same with virtue. We have our own sins, our own virtues, which we have made from our own experiences.

If a child throws a knife at somebody, it has not committed a crime, because it has not yet set that action down as a crime in its world of experiences; it has not gathered it into that world. It only becomes a crime when the child knows it to be criminal. After that it becomes responsible for its deed. 'Judge not, that ye be not judged; for with what judgment ye judge, ye shall be judged.' We judge others according to our world of good and bad; the same world, the same scripture that is our religion judges us also, when we do wrong. And no one would do wrong if his will-power helped him to do right, for how could he do something which the scripture of his own heart tells him to be wrong, had not his will-power failed him? Therefore those who repent after their crimes, faults, and failures show thereby that it is not that they wanted to do or have these things, but that their will-power failed them. The will-power was not strong enough to help them to carry out their own standard of good, as it should help all men through the journey of life.

How can will-power be developed? Are there any exercises by which it can be developed? Are there any rules to follow? Is there any knowledge to acquire? All these three are required.

The first exercise to help the will-power to develop would be to check every act, word, and thought which we do not wish to occur; to avoid unintentional actions, speech, and thoughts. The other exercise that is necessary for the development of the will-power is that of seeing that neither our mind nor our body rules us, but that we rule our body and our mind. Desires such as appetite, thirst, sleep, even the desire of moving or standing or walking, all these desires should be under control. There should be a time in every day when every desire of the body is checked. See if you can do it; and then as long as you can let the body go without listening to it, do so. It takes a great deal of trouble to rule the body, for it is not willing to be ruled.

Yogis, faqirs, Sufis may be seen sitting, standing in one posture for hours together. All the postures adopted are to control and govern every atom of the body, so that it may be under the control of the will. I do not mean that one should devote all one's time to these things, or even that one should have certain exercises for this. When one understands the matter, and carries it out in one's everyday life, then one's life becomes a continual progress.

Next, there is the control of the mind. The mind sometimes does not listen. We want to think of our business, and perhaps the mind thinks of the state of our health, or about a neighbour. It insists on thinking of something else. It may be as unruly as a wild horse which cannot be controlled. So the next step to gain control of it is by concentration, by absorption, by meditation. Concentration should be practised in everyday life. It is necessary that our bodies and minds should act according to our will in our profession, in our office, in our ordinary life.

There is a tradition of the Brahmins that Rama had two sons, Kusha and Lahu. They went with their mother to a city, where they dwelt with a great hermit of the time. Lahu, a young lad, went out to wander through the town and look at its beauty. To his great surprise he found a beautiful horse running without a rider. And when he enquired whose horse it was, people said, 'This horse is let loose with the intention that anyone who can catch it shall be crowned as king of this country'.

The lad, with the enthusiasm of growing strength and hope in life, thought, 'What a good thing it would be if I could catch this horse'. So he ran after it and tried to catch it; but every time he approached the horse, it slipped away. Again he ran after it. And again when the horse was only a little distance away, he was just able to touch it but again it slipped away. This went on for a long, long time. He was away so long that his mother became uneasy about him, not knowing where he had gone. So she told Kusha that his young brother had gone out and not returned. Kusha went out and discovered that Lahu was after this horse. He was very glad to note his brother's ambition. He knew, however, that he would never catch the horse unless he were instructed what to do. Finally, Lahu, knowing now how to catch the animal, succeeded and was able to bring it before the authorities, who declared him to be their king.

This story tells us about will-power. The mind is just like a wild horse, and the will is the only thing which can catch it. The thoughts and imaginations are all so unruly that we cannot think or feel what we wish. If we were able to do so, then neither could sorrow touch us again, nor could unhappiness come near, because it is the thoughts and imaginations which bring sorrow. If we could think what we wished to think, if we could feel what we wished to feel, life would be a heaven for us. When we do not feel what we wish to feel, when we do not think what we wish to think, it is just because of lack of will-power. That which is the governing power cannot hold it.

The elder brother of the story is the teacher who shows the path to his younger brothers who are groping in darkness. He is sent with a message from God, the Father and Mother of His children on earth, to guide his younger brethren. Those who are seeking after the power to control this vehicle, and have the ambition or desire to obtain the crown of life, to them will be granted the inheritance of the kingdom of their country.

PERSONAL MAGNETISM

EVERYONE sees how great is the influence of personal magnetism upon success in everyday life, profession, business, family, and daily occupations.

Sometimes we notice that we go to a shop to buy a certain thing, and there is something about the manner of the salesman that impels us to decide to visit the same shop the next time we need that kind of article. Even if it is a long way to the shop, we prefer not to go to one which is nearer. Similarly it sometimes happens that a person goes to a hotel or boarding-house or restaurant, and someone treats him in such a way that he decides to return to that place rather than visit another.

So with doctors, solicitors, barristers, scientists, professors, and teachers of all kinds. A doctor may be well-versed in his knowledge, he may have a great many degrees, but if he lacks this personal magnetism, instead of curing patients he may make them worse. Sometimes a doctor cures the patient before giving him the prescription. Just by a word of kindness, by a manner, a tenderness, a sympathy he makes the patient feel so much better that the disease which before was too much to bear, appears to be curable after all. Half the pain has gone with just seeing the doctor, such a difference does personality make. It is a great healer.

Then there may be a solicitor or barrister who antagonizes his client as soon as he sees him, and so the latter does not wish to go to him next time. Another person will impart courage and hope; his personality, his speech, everything, will show that he is the man to follow, to go to for help.

In family life disagreement or agreement often arises for the same reason. The father, mother, husband, or wife may have personal magnetism which can hold the family together. When this magnetism is lacking, a person finds it better to be among friends than to be with a relative; he would rather go out than stay at home. The home becomes a strange place, because there is not that magnetism for which he lives. It is as if in mid-winter a person comes to his room and finds it cold because there is no fire there; he wishes that he were somewhere else where there is a fire. Personal magnetism can create beauty around one, can attract one, can make a person attractive to his fellow-men, serviceable to them. It is soothing; it is healing.

What is this personal magnetism? Is it a development of psychic power or occult power? Is it an education, or is it refinement? The answer is that education helps personal magnetism, because knowledge is light, and light is beautiful, and it always helps. But this is not personal magnetism. People may be very well educated and at the same time very disagreeable. Sa'di says that an educated man who does not put what he has learnt into practice, is like a donkey loaded with books: he is carrying them on his back, but he does not know it or act accordingly. He has a load of knowledge which serves no purpose. If his education has not made a man human, what is the use of education? It is just learning for the purpose of earning money.

One may think, if magnetism is not education, is it then psychic power? Not necessarily, though it is the natural psychic or occult power that we call personal magnetism. It is not necessary to attain this kind of power by a certain practice or study; one should already have it; and when it is used in the right way it is personal magnetism.

Is magnetism then politeness? Is it polish? As polish is the fashion today, every person learns it when he mixes with people; but this is not necessarily personal magnetism, though he may think he has a winning manner. If there can be any real explanation of personal magnetism, it is the making of one's own personality into that which one expects from others. A man usually makes the mistake of expecting things from others and not doing them himself. For instance a man is very pleased if he is well received in a friend's house, if he is spoken kindly of, and treated well, if his vanity is satisfied by the action of others. He is very glad if others have a good opinion of him and overlook his defects. But seldom does he pause to do the same himself.

If we only tried to give to others all the things we demand from them; if we overlooked their bad points instead of expecting them to overlook ours; if we only thought, 'How inconsiderate I was that time when I spoke so rudely to so and so'; if we only gave others all that we would like them to give us, that would create a personal magnetism; if we did to them all the things that we expect from them!

The word 'gentleman' in the English language is a very good one in this respect. It has come to refer merely to dressing well; but the ideal behind it is good. It is the ideal of gentleness, and gentleness is the essence of personal magnetism. There cannot be a better lesson than that given in the Bible where it is said, 'Blessed are the meek, blessed are the poor in spirit'. But the difficulty is that man pays little attention to all these things; he thinks they are too simple. And at the same time if you ask him the meaning of 'poor in spirit', he will find it very difficult to answer. Not many will know what that means. It may be understood by comparing the spirit of man with the spirit of an animal. If a tiger is lying in a certain place, and you want the tiger to get up, he will roar. If a man is lying there, and you say, 'Will you please let me sit there', he will say, 'Certainly', because his spirit is poorer than the spirit of the tiger. And that is also the difference between a man and a gentleman. The gentleman is he who shows that poorness of spirit in himself, a spirit of accommodating another, letting another sit in his place if he wants to. He feels that it does not matter if another person sits in his place; it is really better. There is a person who, if we talk roughly to him, returns our words four times more rudely and coarsely. There is another person who, if we talk roughly to him, bears it and perhaps does not give an answer at all or perhaps he understands and consequently avoids a fight or quarrel in his search for peace. It is written, 'Blessed are the peace-makers'. This is not merely the kind of peace which prevents fighting and bloodshed and strife; we may make this kind of peace many times a day from morning to night. There are a thousand matters about which we can quarrel and get annoyed with one another. So throughout our daily life, at all times, there are opportunities of making peace.

We always admire a person who shows gentleness in his movements, in sitting, walking, in his voice or words, in his thought; we admire it consciously or unconsciously. There is always a charm in gentleness, and yet man neglects it when the time comes to practise it. That which should come first comes last. If only man realized how much he likes gentleness on the part of others! If a person has gentleness of voice or expression or word, it is so charming, so winning; we know this so well and yet we always forget it at the critical moment.

Poorness of spirit comes from meekness. Meekness is mildness, which is contrary to what we call roughness. Roughness of action or roughness of speech is contrary to mildness or meekness. Our eyes naturally always enjoy softness of colour rather than striking tones, because of the aggressive power in the latter which our eyes cannot bear. We experience the same thing with the sun and moon. We do not like to look at the sun, and in India we enjoy the moonlight nights so much, we wish the moon shone every night. Why? Because it is mild; it shows meekness. Our power is the power of light; our strength of speech, thought, and action is of the same kind and the same nature as the light of the sun and moon respectively. If the light is too strong, it irritates; if it is mild, it soothes. So if we treat everyone with gentleness, our personality is always welcome wherever we are. The same gentleness in our speech will always give us success, and we will always have friends. If only we had control over our words; if only our words were always of that meek nature!

Among the musicians and poets of the East special attention is given to education in meekness and mildness. There is a Sanskrit saying, 'Art becomes twice as graceful when art and mildness go together'. How true it is. When we admire the art of the artist and say how beautiful it is, and he answers, 'O, it is nothing, it is your kindness that causes you to admire it', his magnetism becomes great.

From a king down to the most ordinary person, it is mildness that wins the whole world. People of all positions in life and all grades of evolution can do such a great work with this one little possession. Sa'di says, 'If your word is sweet, you conquer the world; wherever you go you win men's hearts'. Is it not what Christ means when he says to the fishermen, 'Follow me, and I will make you fishers of men'; that is, 'I will teach you those manners of humanity by which you will win everyone you may come in contact with'? Do you think a person can become a fisher of men by his cleverness, by his artificial polish? False is false, gold is gold. The true gold will last; the false gold will lose its brilliance.

Polish is just like false gold. A person may wish to win wife, husband, father, brother, all by his cleverness, by his polish, but he will prove to be false even on a very unimportant occasion. Polish may please the eyes, but it cannot please the heart. One can polish one's actions, but one cannot polish one's heart; the polish of the heart comes from the feeling. When the action of the heart is not in harmony with the roughness of the feeling, the feeling will come out all the same. All that is real will come out; the polish is only beautiful for a moment. It may show a person to be very gentle and clever for a moment, but it does not last. His friends will leave him in a short time. The relatives will all know in time that it is just external, all cleverness, not that which will last for ever. It is the truth that lasts for always. All the beautiful qualities should be true qualities, not false, because the value lies in the true and not in the false.

In ancient times people of great descent, royal princes, people of educated and religious families, used to go out into the world, and were not recognized as such because there was no international communication in those days; no nation knew its neighbour. Yet it happened that these persons were always recognized by their manner, recognized as belonging to such a family.

Evolution has made all humanity a family; and now is the time when every individual should consider that as a member of the family of the whole of humanity he ought to show himself as being human in nature, and show how superior he can be to the animals and the lower creatures. If we only did what animals do, if we only ate, drank, slept, bit each other, got the better of one another, we should not accomplish anything great. Their whole life is spent in pursuit of their food. In the night animals join together and make a noise in the jungle. If we also enjoy ourselves in that way, then our amusements and joys and comforts are no greater than those of animals, unless we show some quality in our personality which animals do not possess.

A Hindustani poet, Amir, says, 'It is much more precious than any wealth to collect the wealth of a good manner'. Because by a good manner we can make another person as kind as our own father and mother; as kind and sympathetic as our own brother and sister, as respectful as our own son and daughter, if we only have that manner. If we know how to be motherly, how to be fatherly to the young, if we know how to behave respectfully towards our elders, if we know how sympathetic and polite and good we ought to be to those who are poor or are servants, or who depend on us, if our manner is beautiful, there is no heart we can fail to win. The children of the wealthiest people may, owing to the ill manner of the parents, want to sacrifice all their fortune, their father and mother, in order to get away from them; they would even sacrifice life itself. As with children, so with less near relatives. They cannot attract as long as they have no good manner; all the physical magnetism passes away. During youth, a man may be very magnetic, but when his youth passes away his attraction may be lost. But the attraction of personal magnetism grows with years and can be used at all times. Even an old man is attractive, so that people will say, 'What a nice person. By going to him we can feel so filled with joy and comfort'. Although even the nearest and dearest will not always desire to spend time with an old person, they find themselves attracted to an aged one who has personal magnetism.

The Prophet said, 'God is beautiful, and He loves beauty'. What is beautiful in life? It is not only trees and plants and flowers and the external physical world; the higher beauty is the beauty of personality. By the beauty of personality our heart is filled with joy; by the beauty of nature only the eyes are satisfied, the heart is not satisfied. It is the beauty of personality that fills our heart with joy; there is something imparted to us which we cannot explain. Animal magnetism passes away with the strength of the animal. Animal beauty all goes when the person is ill and his physical energy is lost; there is no longer any attraction.

Personal magnetism helps in all conditions. If a person is poor, it makes him rich, because his personality is such that he receives the attentions, the service, and all his life's demands with less trouble, even in spite of his humble position in life. Do we not see around us how a person of beautiful personality, however helpless, will always attract the good, the bad and all around him? If a person lacks it, however rich, however educated, however great in position, he will only attract those who are forced into his society, or such as are looking to get some of his wealth. His relatives, forced to be with him, only long for the time when he is no more, and his wealth will be theirs.

Let us think about the Prophets. There are so many followers of Christ in the world today, and perhaps it is true that not everyone understands his teachings or follows him because of his teaching. But if there is anything of him which is known to the world, if there is any of his fragrance left in the world, it is his personality. He was ready to forget and overlook the faults of others; he was ready to attend to the service of the poor, ready to play and be equal with little children. He never said, 'I am a teacher from God, and people must come and bow before me.'

That, then, is the attitude: the poorness of spirit, the harmony in life, the harmonious temperament.

From the highest to the lowest we always find people in a state of disharmony. In clubs, associations, meetings, institutions, parliaments, all will dispute and fight. This teaches us that however evolved a person may be in his education, his position, or his power and wealth, he has not mastered the law of harmony by these.

Whoever has mastered the law of harmony has developed humanity within himself. He will harmonize equally with the wise and with the foolish. It is not because he is wise that he harmonizes with the wise, nor because he is foolish that he harmonizes with the foolish. Foolish men gave their lives for Christ; wise men worshipped him for his wisdom. 'They left their nets' and the fishing where they had spent all their lives because Christ harmonized with them. He answered their questions; he was tolerant.

So with the story of Krishna. He is looked on as the incarnation of God, one of the greatest teachers the Hindus ever had. He was a child with little children, a cowherd with every cowherd, he was harmonious with everybody; he was wise among the learned, and was merry among the happy. He was not a king; he was not poor; he was one among all. The young and the old, everybody loved him. When he played the flute the cows and the deer and all the animals of the jungle would come to listen. It was not the mere skill of his music, for music is not attractive if the personality is not attractive; it was his personality that attracted them.

There were two friends speaking together, and one said, 'That funeral which is passing is of a person who is going to heaven'. Another funeral, passing later, caused this friend to remark, 'For this person, the place is hell'. The younger of the two friends asked, 'What do you know about it?' 'O', said the other, 'it is so simple: behind the first one were people walking with tears in their eyes, and they all looked so sad. So he must have won their hearts by his personality. His magnetism must have made such an impression that all the people appeared sad and sorrowing. But with the other funeral there were few people, and they were laughing in their sleeves and winking, and everybody had a smile, which shows that they were very pleased to get rid of him.'

Whatever possession, whatever power, whatever honour, whatever wealth, whatever property we have, is of no use in the end, for all is passing. But if there is any one thing which is worth gaining in life because it lasts for ever, it is humanity.

LOVE, HUMAN AND DIVINE

LOVE, whether it is human or divine is considered to be sacred, in the view of the mystics, philosophers, and thinkers. That it is possible to regard it thus is shown by the fact that in its root it is beyond both the human and the divine. As it is written in the Bible, 'God is love', three words which open up an unending realm for the thinker who desires to probe the depths of the secret of love.

In ordinary life we make this word mean affection for our surroundings, for our relatives or our beloved, but when we think deeply about it we see that from start to finish it represents the power underlying the power of all activities and all intelligences.

When we study life from the material standpoint we see there are four different stages: the mineral kingdom, the vegetable kingdom, the animal, and the human. And of these four domains it is said by a dervish, 'God slept in the mineral kingdom; He dreamed in the vegetable kingdom, He woke in the animal, and He realized Himself in the human.' And this gradual progression shows us that underlying it there is a sense of life which has expressed itself in every step towards the completed development of love.

In the mineral kingdom we find no tendency towards love. But as the intelligence develops in the vegetable kingdom, we feel that sympathy is reflected from us into the flowers. The plants perceive and feel that which comes from us. A loving person may attend to plants and rear them and water them with love and sympathy, and they flourish; but in the hands of another it may not be so. If we only watched plants closely we should see how much they feel our presence and our love. They flourish according to our love; the more love we give, the more fragrance, the more sweetness. Man is always working on farms and in gardens, thinking of them as material things, looking to see how plants can be improved by material means; if he could only believe it, there is a still higher means of helping them to grow, a spiritual means: the use of love and sympathy.

There is a story in the East of Puran Bhagat, who was once living in exile in the forest; and after a long time, during which he had developed the true love in his thought and feeling and spirit, he returned to his country. The first thing he wished to do was to sit in his garden, which had gone to ruin during his absence. He went down to it in the guise of a sage, and began to water it with his little water bowl. The garden at once began to flourish, and in a short time it became such a miracle of beauty that everyone in the city began to talk about it and say, 'This must be some spiritual man, since the garden begins to grow and flourish'. The touch of the saints and sages and prophets makes things grow.

Every kind of power lies in this one thing which we call by the simple name: love. Charity, generosity, kindness, affection, endurance, tolerance, and patience—all these words are different aspects of one; they are different names of only one thing: love. Whether it is said, 'God is love', or whatever name is given to it, all the names are the names of God; and yet every form of love, every name for love, has its own peculiar scope, has a peculiarity of its own. Love as kindness is one thing, love as tolerance is another, love as generosity is another, love as patience is another; and yet from beginning to end it is just love. It is love's different manifestations in different directions which distinguish themselves differently and have different purposes.

According to Sufi metaphysics love has two different aspects, Jelal and Jemal; and each aspect of love has its peculiar sphere. The Jelal of love is the power of love. You may call it psychic power, will-power, or power of mind; yet it is one power working through different channels. And this is the power of love; its power manifests and acts according to its force. Its force is greater when it is unlimited, and less when it is limited. That which is called imagination, thought, perception, conception, inspiration, and intuition, comes from the Jemal aspect of love.

In the third stage of evolution, which is called the animal kingdom, love is still more manifest. The animal is more capable of perceiving and feeling our love and kindness, our pleasure and displeasure. When we enter a house the dog may be delighted, or he may recognize our displeasure and feel depressed; cats recognize our love, and so also do parrots and other pet animals of different kinds. Thus we see that the cat is vexed because another cat comes into the house, and we read how, when Joseph was in the well, it was a dog that brought him bread from a neighbouring town, and fed him during the time he was in the well. And in Arabian stories we hear about an Arab who was protected and guarded by his horse when he fell wounded on the battle-field; the horse became his protector.

In man love can develop still more, though sometimes man proves to be not only worse than animals, but even more dead to love than a rock. We would rather be with the rocks than with such a man. This is because he has developed selfishness with his evolution. He is more selfish than any other creature in the world, unless he wipes off the impression of selfishness from his heart.

It would be no exaggeration to say that the reason why a man cannot achieve occult and psychic power, and the intuitive and inspirational faculty, is because he has not developed the power of love; and this failure is caused by the selfishness which has kept him back from developing the power of love.

Man does not differ from animals in his passions and emotions. The human being differs from the animal by his human qualities; these are not eating, drinking, or seeking his kind. Human qualities can only be developed by the development of love. Man has fought in all ages with his brother on account of differences of religion, differences of faith, differences of belief, differences of Church, differences of community, not knowing that each religion, each time it was given, has brought only a message of love, taking a different expression each time. It has been given in different ages and to different people; they have received it according to their evolution; and yet there has really been only the one teaching, that of developing love. 'Love your neighbour; love your fellow-man; love your enemy', there has always been the same lesson given.

Christ told the fishermen to come, and he would make them fishers of men; that is to say, 'As fishes come into your net, so your heart full of love will become a net which will attract every man to it.' Rumi says, 'All who see me feel attracted to me, yet do not know what it is in me that attracts them'. Is it not the secret of the whole of life? If we could see to whom we are attracted in life, father, mother, sister, neighbour, or anybody that we feel drawn to, then it would seem to us to be a magnetic or psychic power. But there is no greater magnetic power than love. Its magnetic power is very great. It changes a person's voice, his heart, his manner, his form, his movement, his activity, everything becomes changed. What a difference between water and rock; that smoothness and that liquid state of being, the rise and fall of the surface of the water compared with the rigidity of the rock! The great teachers of humanity become streams of love. It is the first sign of the sage or holy man that he himself becomes love. His voice, his feeling, his presence, everything makes one realize that there is something open in him which we do not find in everybody; this something is his deep love.

The development of love is often hindered by different obstacles in life. The first obstacle is ourselves. We begin our life with selfishness, and all that we want is for self; and if there is a tendency to love, it is for one's own happiness, and one's own joy. When the question comes, 'How much do you love me, and how much do I love you?' it has come to be a trading in love. 'I love you, but you do not love me' is as much as to say, 'I have bid so much, and I expect a return of love'. This is trading in love, and trade cannot lead anywhere, because it makes one think of the self, and love is beyond that. To love is to give; it is not to take at all. The true lover never speaks of what he has done for his beloved, for he loves for love's sake, not for the sake of a return. If a person begins to love and makes it a love fed by the love of his beloved, then he seeks an impossible thing. If a person keeps waiting for the love of the beloved, he is bound to find that nature cannot grant that desire, unless both are traders in love. Then each takes the best of the other; each may think he loves, but neither truly loves.

Love teaches the lover patience, forbearance, gentleness, because he thinks, 'My beloved will be displeased; I will be as gentle as possible in my action and in my movements'. These thoughts are a correction to the lover. With every such thought that passes in the life of the lover he corrects himself. Hope is the only thing in life which keeps us alive, because it feeds on love.

Patience is fed by love. We can never have patience with anybody without love. How valuable is patience! As it is said in the Qur'an, 'Allah loves the patient'.

Another hindrance to love is its dependence on the beauty of the ideal, be it physical beauty, beauty of thought, of character, or of personality. Whatever beauty it may be, whenever love depends for its continuance or for its existence upon the beauty of its object, it must some day fail. Therefore true love does not regard the body, the external object; in point of fact love prepares its own ideal. For when a person says, 'O, I have loved you for your beauty', what will he say when youth has gone and the beauty is lost? Where will the love be then? The love will change too. And if love has gone with the passing of the beauty of the object of its love, what then? Another may say, 'O, I love you for your personality', and yet perhaps within a month the beloved may not show the same personality, the same attractive goodness. What then?

We think a flower is a fleeting thing, so soon does it change; and yet the human heart is liable to a quicker change than even the flower. A person may be very good one moment, very kind; and the next moment the contrary; calm one moment, and then restless; at one time so affectionate, at another indifferent; all according to the state of mind in which he happens to be at the time. So it cannot last if it is allowed to depend on the beauty of the ideal; such love is dependent and would sooner or later die. That is why so many hearts cannot keep the flame of love alive in them.

Often it happens that lovers grow cold just from lack of understanding that love must not be for an external ideal, but that the lover has to prepare the ideal in himself; they have failed to make the self-sufficient love within themselves. Not so the sages, the holy men, the wise ones. They know that a person who is kind today can be the contrary tomorrow. Therefore the wise lover expects both opposites in the external and inner beauty of the beloved.

Those who have developed the ideal love within themselves by the aid of an object to love, transform their nature into a more and more loving one in time. Their love for a certain person is akin to learning the abc, for by learning the abc one comes to be able to read not only the primer, but any book. By learning to love one, we gain a light, a torch, by the light of which we can read all things in life; it is as if in our nature we have developed something that we can give to everyone.

In the East there is a saying, 'A loving son is always a loving husband'. This is a true philosophy. It teaches the fact that he who has known from the beginning of life what love means, has laid the foundation of a whole life of being truly loving. A person who is faithful and kind to one friend can be kind to all, acquaintances, servants, neighbours, and strangers alike, because he has developed that quality. But when people pretend to love they are kind to one and bitter to another. This shows that they are not really lovers. The real lover will show his kindness, gentleness, sympathy, all aspects of love, to every one he meets.

When one thinks about occult powers, such as knowing the condition of other people's minds, their pleasure and displeasure, also the joy and pain of another's heart, knowing what is going on at a distance, receiving news from far away in the world, we find that all these can be gained without study, just through the power of love. It is all so easy and simple to one who loves. The traders with love cannot know this. The real lover will know such things without special meditation or concentration, for what can exert a greater concentration than love? If one's thoughts are scattered over pianos, chairs, tables, jewels, dress, one cannot understand such power; but if one has true interest in an ideal, the power is there before one seeks it.

Therefore all occult and psychic power is the power of love. But it is not only a matter of love for a living person. There is a love of art, of science, of music, of poetry, of all the different aspects of beauty. Love in every direction shows one the sublime vision of the beautiful. It is those who have loved the beauty of poetry who are able to enjoy its beauty and to express it to others; those who have love of music are enabled to give their music to the world and attract the lovers of music, as well as being able to enjoy its beauty themselves. Love's power ever shows its magnetism afresh through all the ages.

But love in its higher sense teaches us that there is a love, an object, a beloved that can last with us and prove satisfactory, compared with which there is nothing in life worthy of all our love; and that one object is God. But among those who say, 'O yes, I love God', very few tell the truth; very often that is a false pretence. How can we love the formless and colourless? It is impossible to love one whom we cannot confine within any particular beauty. It is only those who pretend to be spiritual because they are godly and pious towards those of their own sect that say, 'We love God'. It is as absurd to say this as to say to a beloved, 'O beloved, I love you very much, but I do not like looking at your face'. For God says, 'I have made man in My own image'. When man is prejudiced against man and still says, 'I love God', how can God be pleased with that kind of love? How can that be true love for God which refuses to see the beauty that is before it? If God said, 'If you wish to see Me, see Me in the face of man; that is My own image' this would show what true love is. Also, if a person claiming to love an artist were to say to him, 'I love you very much, but I cannot bear to look at your picture', what kind of love could that be? The artist has given all his soul and life to that art; his very self has, so to speak, become art, and his whole satisfaction lies in our appreciation of his art. How can those claim to love the Creator who do not love what He has created? For God could never have become known had there been no manifestation. So he who does not find sufficient beauty to admire in His manifestation cannot pretend to love God.

So, too, if someone limits his love to a single object, saying, 'I only love this and there is nothing else I need', surely he has not the right kind of love either. True love is limitless. Though it begins by being limited in such a way, yet it progresses and some day breaks out. Such a thing is constantly happening in life, but people do not understand the psychic law which underlies it. Eastern people say, when someone loves another person intensely and does not care for anyone else, 'There will be some mishap there some day'. There is always some breakdown, some danger waiting, some trouble in the future, when love is not allowed to flow freely and is limited. The Japanese and Chinese have called God jealous, because He does not allow two persons to be devoted only to each other. God cannot tolerate this narrowing of love. If one tried to put the whole sea into a little jar, the sea would break it. The sea of love breaks its limited channel. To speak of the jealous God means that the unlimited force of love cannot allow its expression to be directed towards one limited object. That is why the love of God alone is the culmination of love, for love is as vast as God. Verily, love itself is God.

There is a beautiful story which has been dramatized and acted in India for hundreds of years; the people never get tired of seeing it, so it is acted even today. It is called 'The Court of Indra'. Indra is the God of Heaven. His court is made up of Devas and Peris. The latter dance in the court, the Devas are to attend the pleasure of Indra. No earthly creature is ever allowed to enter, nothing of the earth is ever seen or allowed in the court of Indra. Once a Peri, the Green Peri, happened to fly to the surface of the earth, and she saw a prince of that country over which she was flying, whose beauty charmed her so much that she thought that if she could in some way or other take him to her high dwellings, she would be happy. She told one of the Devas about it, and he carried away Gulfam, the Prince, while he was asleep. He wakes up, and finds himself in a strange place, and breathing a different air. After great bewilderment he sees a Peri, a creature much more beautiful than the creatures of the earth. He looks at her and asks her how he comes to be there. She tells him he is in Indra Loka, that she loves him and will be happy to keep him there. 'I will do anything for your happiness', she says.

Gulfam forgets all about his kingdom, and lives with the Peri, most happy in her love. Every day she has to leave him to be at her duty, and every day she returns, never saying where she has been. This arouses his curiosity, but still she will not tell where she goes and what she does. Finally she does tell him that she has to dance before Indra every day. Then he wants to go and see. She expostulates, but at length consents to take him. She keeps him behind her, and hopes to conceal him with her wings as she dances before Indra. But one of the Devas sees him and tells Indra, who for a long time will not believe it possible that a human being could be in his court. Then he discovers him, and pronounces a curse upon him, while the Peri is to be banished until she has undergone the successive stages of purification through earth, water, fire, air, and ether. Not till then can she be allowed to enter the heavens again.

This story shows that in the highest dwellings, in that sphere which is Indra Loka where love conquers man, the King is Indra, the perfection of beauty. The highest love must be for God; it belongs to Him. In its development love should aim at that idea. The Peri is the human soul, Gulfam is the human body. The soul, which is heavenly, becomes interested in this earthly body; but when by the power of love it comes from the earth to the heavenly sphere, it brings to heaven an object which is destined only for the earth. The love of a limited being is not allowed to remain in heaven, and will be condemned to be purified and uplifted until it can nevermore find satisfaction in a limited object, in the love for a human being. Homage must be paid to the Lord of Heaven. True love must have free flow; and to learn that free flow the teachers have taught us first to love from the limited, and thence to advance in love till we attain to the love of God, the Unlimited.

INTUITION

INTUITION is a part of knowledge that is beyond man's personality, and above his knowledge of things and names. It comes at times when man becomes passive and exposes himself to that knowledge, consciously or unconsciously.

There are some who are more intuitive, and there are others who are less so; and if we study the nature of their character, we shall know the nature of their intuition. Those who are confused, who are constantly hurried, who are changeable in their nature, who are afraid of death, of disease, of their own actions, of their enemies, of their surroundings; those who have constant doubt, wondering whether they can trust this person or that, whether a friend may or may not prove worthy, and so on—it is all these who have less possibility of intuition. Those who can trust without troubling themselves, those who have few doubts, are usually clearer in their perception. Those who trust in the inner guidance, who understand the secret of the instinct that works through animals and all creatures, those who are pious, those who wish to walk in the light, who always prefer the right way of thinking and speaking and acting, it is these who often experience intuition.

Intuition is the first step, inspiration is the second, and revelation is the third. When revelation begins, it has arisen from intuition; for intuition is the first stage.

What is its way of manifestation? How is intuition expressed? Intuition is of two kinds: it may come without intention, without being invited, or it may come when one asks oneself a question. In the first kind a person may be sitting down, and the thought comes to him that a danger is awaiting him; in what way it may occur he does not know, he just feels it. Next day he finds that something was going to happen to him. Then he sometimes thinks that happiness is coming from a friend, that some one from whom he has been parted for a long time is coming to see him; sometimes he thinks an enemy is going to turn into a friend; and yet he had not been thinking of the subject. The thought comes to him suddenly. It proves true, it proves right. Without enquiry a thought comes to us which tells us of a coming event. People sometimes take this to be a spirit-communication; sometimes they take it to be thought-transference from someone else. Both ideas are possible, but intuition is a greater and higher thing than spirit-communication or thought-reading, because it is pure; it is our own property; it belongs to us. In this we do not depend upon a spirit, or upon another person sending a thought to us. In this we are perfectly independent; we receive the knowledge from within, which is far superior, greater, and higher.

The second kind of intuition is that of which it is said in the Bible, 'Knock, and it shall be opened unto you'. Knocking at the door is asking within one's own self, 'What will become of this particular business, or aim, or object that I am thinking of?' As soon as one knocks at the gate of God, which is one's heart, from there the answer comes, and it is a truer answer than any other person can give. There is no one who can know as much about our life, affairs, objects, motives as we do ourselves. And therefore nobody can advise us better than ourselves.

Mankind cannot understand this secret, and consequently begins by depending on the advice of others. This would be advantageous if one had the good fortune to find a better adviser. But sometimes the person from whom advice is asked is foolish, sometimes he is an enemy, sometimes he himself is in confusion and cannot advise. Therefore people keep themselves from their real and true adviser: the guiding faculty within.

Intuition begins in the form of impressions. As soon as we see a person we have an impression of him. His face, his features, his expression, his atmosphere have in a way made an impression on us of his goodness, his righteousness, his wisdom or foolishness, his being useful or not, his being displeased with us or not, his being our friend or enemy; whatever his condition may be, we receive it without knowing from any other source that these are his feelings. According to our own openness of spirit we get our impressions. We may receive a kind of impression as to whether we will be successful in our business or not. All these impressions convey to a man that his intuition is beginning. That is the first step.

After having intuition about individuals in their relation to ourselves, the next step is the intuition which occurs when another person is telling us of his projects. We have an impression as to whether they will be successful or not. We cannot give a reason for it; or even if we do we become aware that as we utter the reason it is not the real reason. For as soon as we begin to think it out, we at once descend from the higher, the spiritual source of information. To try and prove the basic truth of its spiritual source by means of reason, is to use earthly means to establish that which belongs to heaven. A proper reason for an intuition cannot be given.

The source from which this knowledge comes is not reason. People who are very good at reasoning can go on fighting all their lives, and yet nothing may come of it. Ultimately their reasoning turns into a play on words and terms; and as a word can be made to mean anything, they have always an easy way of escape from being caught by the person with whom they argue. It is just like wrestling; or just as in a court of law two barristers will each present their case as being the truth even though they may in fact know that it is not true. They fight with their reason and logic.

First of all, it is necessary to realize that when we see that our impressions are right and our doubts cannot destroy them, and we have been right in ten impressions and wrong in only one, then we know that the wrong one was not what we thought it was. When this realization has evolved, then we are able to know things intuitively. The difference between imagination and intuition is sometimes puzzling to define. Both come in the same way. When a certain imagination began to construct itself, we cannot say. The imagination came suddenly; but so also does intuition. That is why it is so difficult to discriminate between them. The truth is that if imagination comes with light, then it is certainly intuition. Every imagination is intuition until it has been corrupted by reason; and when the intuition is corrupted by reason it becomes imagination. But every imagination and every thought which is illumined by the intelligence is always an intuition; and therefore to an illuminated person any thought or imagination is intuition. To him there is never a thought or imagination which is not an intuition.

But it is difficult to keep these from being corrupted by reason, because as soon as they are produced we doubt whether they are right or not right. We doubt it until we have killed all the truth of our intuition. Our doubts are always the enemies of our intuition; and therefore practice is required in everyday life to keep intuition from being corrupted and finally destroyed by our doubts. We ought to build a fence round intuitions as if they were delicate plants, and protect them from being destroyed by reason and doubts. By doing so, in time we grow to be sure of our intuitions, and then we never fail to get things right. And when the intuitions become right then the dreams become right. We see what is really going to happen in every thought which comes to us; the truth of life. Then our life becomes a miracle; there is no need to look for wonders in the outside world. Our own has become full of wonders. To the illuminated one every night's dream becomes a book that tells the past, the present, and the future, both of himself and of all those whom he cares for or wishes to know about.

The next step is inspiration. Inspiration is not only the coming of a single thought, a single idea, but of a flow of ideas. One may express them in poetry, in music, in philosophy, in speech, in writing, in thinking. The inspirations come as many ideas. Inspiration is a developed intuition. The expression of inspiration is according to one's particular ability. If a person speaks a beautiful language, he can express his ideas in that language. All prophets and messengers have received the same message, but they have uttered it in different languages. Why? Because surely it is one idea, one knowledge from heaven, but it is expressed according to the language the receiver is accustomed to, seeing that he has no other with which to express it.

The angels are not as great as man, because though they are gifted with the higher knowledge and are in the higher spheres, they have no power of expression. Man gets his knowledge from the higher source, but expresses it through the means provided by the lower spheres.

The Qur'an tells that God said to the angels, 'I am going to create man, who will be the chief of creation'. They asked, 'Are we not a satisfactory army of servants who are always busy in Thy praise and admire Thy beauty and glorify Thy name? Why intendest Thou to create one who will do evil and shed blood, as he will do?' The answer was, 'Are you capable of appreciating all that I have made? Can you tell me what are the names of these things that I have made?' God asks man; man tells Him all the names of things, the things that are sweet or bitter, the names of all manner of things; he knows and enjoys all these things in nature. That is why God says, 'We have created him that he may be the chief of all creation, and enjoy all that We have created'. Therefore those who think that the heavenly knowledge is sufficient are mystical; but the joy of the heavenly knowledge and the full understanding of it come from being able to express it in this world's medium of expression. Therefore man can have knowledge both from within and from the external world. When the two come together, there is a perfect expression.

The last and most delicate degree of intuition is revelation. This comes to prophets and perfected beings. This is a full light thrown upon the human personality, full light from within. To their eyes, ears, sense of taste or touch, all things disclose their secret. Those who have received this knowledge even partly, have by receiving it come to understand the properties of this plant or that, to know that this bitter medicine is good for this purpose, this sweet one for that, this drug or that vegetable for another. The knowledge of the property of the names and forms of the world is understood by them to the extent that revelation has helped them. When they look into the mind, they know all about the mind. When they study the earth, they come to know it. Whatever they try to know, they succeed in knowing; such is revelation. Those who look in the higher spheres are prophets, those who look on the earth are scientists, musicians, soldiers, and so on. It is from the direction in which he has studied that a man receives the revelation. In the higher spheres all things become clear to those who direct their attention to these spheres.

A man even sees his future in the teacup, with limited light; similarly he sees it in cards, in the crystal, in the coals of the fire, in smoke. All these things have the future written in them; it is the same light that shines upon them and begins to reveal itself in them. It is not only books, but all things in nature which begin to reveal the secrets of nature to him.

Sa'di says, 'When the eyes open and begin to see with the divine light and divine sight, even the leaves of the trees become as the pages of the sacred Book'.

FAITH

WHEN THE question of faith arises, the orthodox always think that it is their religion which is being spoken of. To have faith in a religion, in the priests or clergy, in a certain dogma, ceremony, principle, or in a certain form of teaching, this is what is usually understood by the word faith. On the other hand, those who are intellectual and look at life from a different point of view say, 'Faith is blind; why should we believe blindly?'

To a mystic, faith is the unique power that works through the whole of creation. He does not mean by faith a belief in a certain religion or dogma or ceremony or book or teacher; he means trust, a trust even in the absence of reason.

Many people possess this quality naturally, while others do not seem to possess it. We may think that one person has brought faith with him and another has not, because he has or has not that quality. But when we study life minutely we find that there is no soul which does not possess faith. How true it is as the Prophet says, 'Every soul when born is a faithful follower; it is afterwards that he turns to the contrary'. This really means that every soul is born on earth with a simple faith, and it is only afterwards that he doubts. If it were not so, we should never have been able to learn the language we speak. Was it not learned by faith, from infancy? When the mother says, 'This is a tree', the child says 'tree'; when she says, 'This is water', the child calls it 'water'. And there are many things which the parents speak of apart from ordinary everyday matters, and the child believes them as they want him to believe. Whether the names given to the things are right or wrong, the child takes them as his guardians wish him to take them, for that is his natural tendency.

In the beginning every soul has faith. Then how is it that man loses this quality which nature has bestowed on him? He loses it by the knowledge of names and forms. As he grows he covers up his faith with the knowledge of names and forms, calling that 'learning'. At every step in his progress towards knowledge he compares things and considers some things better than others, saying of one thing, 'This is true', of another, 'This is false', 'That is what I can believe and rely upon', and 'This is what I cannot believe and rely upon'. The one thing he calls true, the other false; but in reality neither is true or false. It is only at the beginning of knowledge that man passes through this stage. Later, when a person has raised himself above ordinary knowledge, he arrives at a stage when he is able to say, 'All that I have called true is not true, and all that I have called false is not false'. He finds that whatever difference there is, is only a difference of comparison. This point of view is difficult and vague, and everybody does not perceive it.

The course of human life involves so many disappointments, so many failures, so many heart-aches, that no one can avoid doubting. There is a peasant saying, 'He who has once burned his tongue with hot milk tries to cool even buttermilk by blowing on it'. When a man has been deceived by one person, he distrusts ten people; when he has found one person unreliable, he may perhaps consider a hundred others to be so too. After failing in one thing he suspects he will fail in a thousand things. So many things take away that natural and powerful quality which was at first present, that faith which is the secret of the whole creation, the secret of all success that can ever be attained in life. This faith is broken by life's discouraging experiences. When confidence in others is lost, then confidence in self is lost also; and the more it is lost, the more failures one meets. A doubting person considers himself to be wise and one of simple faith to be a fool. Whoever he sees he suspects; whatever he hears he questions whether it be right or wrong. He will doubt even his friend in business, waiting for the time to come when he can trust him. But that time never comes. His very doubts create doubts in the mind of the suspected person; and often the doubts come true as the effect of the doubter's thought; or at least it creates an illusion which for the moment shows the picture of his doubts.

How truly the story of Othello demonstrates this! The more he doubted Desdemona, the more proofs for his doubt life created. His doubt was fed more and more by the illusory proofs, until in the end he could not possibly believe the least thing contrary to his doubts. So it is with our own lives. We doubt; and by that very doubt that which we fear happens, because it is created by us in the other person's heart. Whether the actions we see support our doubt or only seem to support it, yet our suspicion creates the desire in the doubted person.

We can experience the same thing with dogs. If we have the least fear of a dog barking or biting, he will bark and come up to bite us. If there is no fear in us, the dog will not come towards us. The fear which makes us suspect that the dog will bite is enough to give the dog the desire to bite, because we are looking for it to do so.

If we could only develop the quality which is called faith, about which so much is said in the scriptures, in the Bible, in the Qur'an, we should find what power it would carry. It is the secret of all success.

We are here to fulfil the purpose of our life. What is that purpose? Our desire, our inclination which is constantly at work in our mind, that is the purpose of our life. If we are unable to fulfil that inclination, we go from this world without accomplishing our purpose. As Omar Khayyám says, 'Heaven is the vision of fulfilled desire; Hell is the shadow of a soul on fire'. If the desires are not fulfilled the soul is naturally on fire. But there is no reason why the desire should not be fulfilled; the very existence of a desire promises its fulfilment. In the heart of man is the desire of God. The Qur'an says that without the will of God not even a single atom can move. This shows that every wave of thought and feeling, every motion and action is from God. Every thought that comes to our mind is God's thought, even if it appears to be a thought of everyday life in the world.

Once man realizes that every activity and impulse that comes into his mind is really from God, from that time he feels that it must be fulfilled. If it is not fulfilled, it is man's limitation that is the cause of its hindrance; he has allowed his weakness to hinder its accomplishment. It is man's lack of faith that generally causes failures. In faith is the secret of fulfilment or non-fulfilment of every thought. There is no doubt about the fulfilment of a desire if man's faith works with it. But when one's own reason and doubt come and destroy the hope, one generally meets with failure

What an important part faith plays in life! Can there be anything equal to it? In the Arabic language it is called *Iman*. The whole of religion is faith, however much people have called the separate religions faiths. Faith itself is a religion.

Does this mean that one is to believe and trust anyone blindly? Would not that be a blind faith? Would it not be obscuring the reason, the power of discrimination between right and wrong, between possible and impossible? Suppose a person says you are going to be a king, and you believe it, this would be a blind faith, since there is no possibility of its being realized; still more impossible would it be to believe if he said, 'You are a king', when you see no sign of kingship in your life, but rather the contrary!

But the point is that the first lesson to be learnt is to have faith in oneself. How many among us there are who have no faith in themselves! It is this very lack that makes them have no faith in others. Once a person has faith in himself, he can have faith in others also. For instance, if one feels a person to be good and spiritual, what does it matter if the whole world does not think the same? But if somebody says, 'I do not know, perhaps the other person thinks right, and I do not', then he has no faith. He does not know what faith is. He may have faith in a man, and yet as the days go on the time comes when he will lose it. A person who does not believe in himself cannot believe in anybody else, and is really an unbeliever. Faith must begin within. Belief in oneself should be so strong that even if a thousand people say 'no', one will say 'yes'. To look to others for every opinion, not trusting oneself to say whether it is day or night, is to end by not only distrusting others but by developing a kind of insanity.

Faith means self-confidence. The secret of faith is that it can be used as a medicine, and it will be better than medicine; it can be wealth, and greater than wealth; it can be a religion, and greater than religion; happiness, and greater than happiness. For nothing can buy or sell faith. If there is anything that can be called the grace of God, it is faith and self-confidence. It is something one can neither teach nor develop; it must be in one, and one can only strengthen it by loving it, by enjoying it. It must develop by itself.

Faith is in fact a power operating all through our lives, and imparted to us from the time of our birth. This power is obscured as soon as reason is developed, which occurs during the process of acquiring the knowledge needed for merely maintaining life; and then one loses one's self-confidence as well as one's confidence in others. This is doubt, which is the greatest enemy of the soul in its progress towards self-realization. It is removed as soon as one perceives that faith is really a power from God, by which He seeks to express Himself through the individual.

Confidence is assured, not by blind belief but by careful insight into the life which surrounds us. The higher self is then able to be like the rider on a horse, and direct all the affairs and actions of the lower self. Faith defends the innate desire of the higher self, and the more faith develops, the greater is its influence, through us, upon our whole environment. Faith breeds faith. Also, faith must dominate the reason and direct the reason; and it will do this the more surely when we realize that every thought, desire, and impulse that comes to our heart is from God, to be accomplished for some great purpose of His own.

Sometimes a person will say, 'I had great faith once, but in the course of my life I have met with people one could never trust. They deceived me, and since then I have lost faith in everybody'. That person is much to be pitied; he has lost so much more than anybody else. The good quality which was in him has been killed by unfortunate experiences. How important it is that the heart of the faithful should be kept unbroken!

In India birds are made to fight as a sport. It is called *Buttase*. Two birds are brought together on a table, while all stand round to see the fun. As soon as the birds see one another they attack each other. The owner of each bird thinks that his bird will win, the prize will be his. But as soon as it appears as if one bird will be beaten, its owner takes it away, saying to the other, 'You have won, we will not continue the fight'. This is because he wants to save his bird from being disappointed. The bird would then be without faith.

Those who have no faith in themselves, those whose faith is broken, are like the bird which is allowed to be beaten. However strong he may become, there will always remain the impression in his mind of having been beaten; and this he cannot bear.

It is like this with the elephant too, giant animal as he is. Once he is beaten, all his strength and power go. For years he will not forget it. In spite of all that power which is within him, he will never attack another elephant. The faith that really gave him his power has all gone.

There is a Hindustani saying, 'Failure and victory are both in the mind'. If there is failure it is in the mind; if there is victory it is also in the mind. As long as the mind has not failed a seeming failure may be a victory, but if the mind has failed a seeming victory becomes a failure. That great power which the mind has is nothing but the power of faith. People who have done great works have not done them because of their worldly heritage; for instances occur in which people began life without a penny, and yet have ended their lives the possessors of millions. They have had no help to encourage them in life, or to raise them in life; they have raised their position themselves.

So we see that reason has no part in faith. People may be called fanatics because they work only by faith, their critics thinking that faith only enables them to imagine things. But there are numberless people who are thinking and reasoning all their lives, asking themselves, 'Shall I do this? how can I do that? how can I overcome these obstacles? And all the time they are thinking of the hindrances, or waiting for suitable circumstances to arise, and they never do. Their whole life may be spent in the pursuit of something which reason prevents them from attaining.

It is quite otherwise with faith. When there is faith there is no thought about whether there are any means of accomplishing the desire that has entered one's mind, or whether there are no means. This does not matter when faith is there, to care for and to defend the thought, to rain upon the thought and make the plant grow and bear fruit, so that some day one may see its realization.

Ask those people who have led wonderful lives in the world. See what they have to say about it. What does Christ say? What does Mohammad say? Christ said to Peter, when he walked on the water, 'O thou of little faith, wherefore didst thou doubt?' If Peter had had faith, he could have conquered the waters.

In the different wars that the Prophet of Arabia had to face throughout his life, what do we find? From the beginning to the end there were wars. He was born an orphan, for his father was no longer alive and his mother died in giving him birth. There were no resources, either of money or of influence when the message was given, later the whole community rose against him; even his relatives were against him. What stood by him? It was his faith. His call to his people was to have faith.

It once happened that when the army of the Prophet's enemies had been successful one among them by chance caught the Prophet alone. He was kneeling on his chest, and wanted to kill him. But before doing so, he said, 'O Prophet, all your life you have taught the name of God. Now tell me where your God is. Where has he gone?' And the Prophet called on the Name of God, on whom he called night and day; and as soon as that Name came to his mind, the strength of the whole world came into the Prophet. With one bound he brought the man down, took his sword in his hand, and said, 'Who will save thee now, since thou art again in my hands?' And he answered, 'Thou, Mohammad'. And Mohammad said, 'O man of little faith, till now thou hast not learned the lesson. Now thou hast seen that my faith in Him saved me. He has just saved me. If thou takest the Name, He will save thee too. Ask Him!'

The strength of that faith and the hope it imparts, the power it gives, the might that faith can give, is there anything like it?

One person may doubt and doubt; one moment he believes that things will come right, and then he fears that perhaps they will not. Another person will trust, and he will be watching, and his trust will become bigger with every experience.

There is a story of a Sufi who was travelling with a caravan through Arabia. Among the travellers were some who had money with them for their expenses. They came to a place where it was said that robbers were likely to be and that everybody should take care of his own purse as many caravans had been robbed in that area. This young Sufi also had some money, but he thought to himself, 'I have no place to keep my money. I will find some man with whom I can leave it. To whom can I give it for safety?' He was wondering if there could be any village or habitation, but could only see a tent some distance away from where the caravan had come to a halt. So he went and found a man sitting smoking his pipe in the tent. He went up to him and said, 'I do not know you, sir, but I have heard there are robbers here and that many caravans have been robbed, and I am a poor man. I thought I should protect my money, if I could only find someone to whom I could trust it; having found this tent, I feel I should entrust it to you.' He left the purse, and returned to the caravan. When he arrived he found that the caravan had been robbed, and all had lost their money. He was very glad he had escaped. They were all moaning and lamenting about their losses. He thought that he at any rate was safe. Then they described the robbers, saying how many of them had come, how many had been there.

He returned to the tent to fetch his money again. He found the same man smoking there, but he was surrounded by many men, for he proved to be the chief of the robbers. The others were all sitting there, fighting and disputing what share each should take, and the chief was helping them to divide their spoil. So the young man was afraid to go nearer; and at the same time could not help thinking how foolish he was not to have kept his money, for while he was bringing it the robbers had come, and so he would have escaped anyway. The others had lost everything, but he had fooled himself. While he was thinking this, and was about to turn away, the chief called out for him to be fetched. He approached the chief trembling, because he believed that now even his life was in danger. The chief said, 'Why did you come here; why are you turning back?' The young man asked, 'Are you not the head of the robbers? Then why should I not wish to go? What use can it be to come?' The chief answered, 'Man, I received your money to keep; I did not rob you of it. You trusted me. The money is therefore in my trust. Even if I am a robber, I am not dishonest. I gain by robbery, not by breaking trust. You trusted me with your money, and your money is safe. Here it is for you to take back again.' So the young man was delighted, reflecting what a good thing trust is, inasmuch as one may have faith even in a robber, for he had proved himself trustworthy.

We can see this in our everyday life. A servant, a helper, an assistant, a co-worker, a partner, can be made either trustful or distrustful, trustworthy or unworthy of trust; this we do ourselves by our own faith. How true it is that when faith is beginning to fail, when doubts begin to come, the loss of faith goes on until a person begins to doubt his nearest and dearest friends. Husband can doubt wife; wife can doubt husband; brother can doubt sister; parents can doubt children. One can doubt one's nearest friend, and in the end one doubts oneself. That is the utmost limit; from then on life can be nothing less than torture.

The question arises, is it right to cover up our reason and act according to our faith? The answer is that it is not right. Reason is the servant of faith, and faith is the king of reason. But failure comes when reason becomes the king, and faith the servant. Success comes when faith is king and reason is the servant. If faith says, 'I wish to open a factory', reason replies, 'Yes, you can proceed with your factory in this way. You will be successful.' Reason is the servant; faith is the first thing. Faith says, 'I will succeed'. Reason says, 'These are the different paths you will have to take'. This is how faith is helped by reason.

It is very different when reason is king. When reason is king, it says, 'Open a factory? Why, just look at yourself, without a single penny in your pocket.' Faith says, 'Yes, you are right'. Reason says, 'You don't know anything about a factory; how can you pretend to carry on such work?' And faith answers, 'Yes, I will not think about it any more.' When reason is the leader of faith, the result is failure; it is when faith is the leader of reason that success comes.

With regard to trusting people a person may think, 'Is it right to believe in anything a person says? Is it right to trust everybody? There are many people who are not worthy of trust; shall we then trust everybody in order to develop our trust?' The answer is, yes. Perhaps we will have failures, but we will only trust another person when we trust ourselves; when we have faith in ourselves then we will have faith in another. Without faith in ourselves we can never have faith in another; to have faith in another is to have faith in ourselves. It does not matter if once or twice we are disappointed; but if we are afraid of being disappointed even once in our lives, perhaps we will doubt all through life, and so there will never come a time when we will be able to trust anybody, even ourselves. There are many things that can develop our trust. Sometimes an unworthy person can become worthy of trust.

The Hindus say that if one has faith in an idol-god, that god will listen and grant one's desires; but if one has no faith in the God of Heaven, even He is helpless to do anything for one. The Bible says that faith like a grain of mustard can remove mountains.

There is a story that a preacher was once speaking in a little village in India. The peasants he was preaching to could not understand philosophy or mysticism or the great problems of life. What the preacher taught was, 'Have faith in God; faith is such a great virtue', and he told them that if a person repeated the sacred word he would be able to walk on water. Everyone was delighted to hear this, saying, 'What a great thing! He is always talking about this same thing.' Next day an old man came and said, 'Sir, I cannot understand the deep problems of life, but I was very delighted with your idea last evening'. The preacher answered, 'What was that?' He said, 'I was very much surprised. Will you come and dine at my home? It will be such an honour.' The preacher said, 'Yes, with great pleasure'. A day was appointed. When the day came, the man arrived to fetch the preacher, and they set off together. On their way there was a little river which had to be crossed. When they reached the bank, the preacher said, 'Where is the boat?' 'Why do you ask for a boat?' the peasant replied. 'The other day you said that when you use that sacred word you can walk on the water. And I was very much astonished to find that it is so. Why take a boat when it is only necessary to say that word?' But the preacher could not do it; he was not a true teacher. So he said to the old man, 'You are my teacher. I have spoken, but you have acted; and if I had had your faith I should also have been able to cross the water.'

This shows us that things sometimes seem obscured, as if in a mist, as if seen through a dark glass. We fear beforehand that a thing will never come, that there will always be disappointment, failure, sorrow. Depression comes on; we begin to think the times will never alter, and the same conditions will always continue. The only remedy to clear these clouds away is to look for a better time, to hope for something better in life, to feel that every thought, desire, and impulse that comes to our heart is from Him, and that it is to be accomplished with all that power for some purpose. No circumstances in our lives, not even friends and advisors, nor our reason or our doubt should be allowed to prevent the realization of our thoughts. It is through that one thing, faith, that our thoughts are kept powerful and full of strength; it is by nothing but that one thing: faith.

THE EFFECT OF PRAYER

KEEN STUDY of life enables us to perceive that every individual is dependent upon every other. This is true of all aspects of life. The rich are dependent upon the poor, the strong upon the weak, the wise upon the foolish. When we see how limited man is even at his best, we see that it cannot be otherwise than that each one must depend upon another in order to obtain the needs of life.

It is evident that the servant is dependent upon the wages that are paid him, that the worker is dependent on the money he receives. But there are needs which money cannot meet, and then he who receives repays by love or kindness or care. Times come when money is too poor, when influence is powerless to buy or take. When this is so, the natural thing is to pay respect and give adoration to the one to whom money cannot be given and who cannot be influenced. It does not matter whether the respect and adoration are given with a selfish or an unselfish motive; in either case there is the same dependence. One is dependent upon one's beloved, or upon one's wife, or upon one's neighbour, even upon one's servant. How many troubles and difficulties begin if that servant happens not to be at home! Whether one pays money, or whether one can only show love and adoration, one is dependent just the same. From the time when one first opens one's eyes as an infant, one's life is nothing but dependence all through.

Those who watch keenly will see what is real dependence, and how far-reaching that dependence is in our lives. Those who need money, are they not dependent on people who have money? Those who desire position, are they not dependent upon someone who has position, such as a Secretary of State, a lord, a duke, a high official? The more a man reflects, the vaster does he find this web of dependence to be. It becomes more and more clear that all the sources upon which people depend exist for the use of the different individuals. One individual desires or needs wealth; and therefore there are people who have it, and he can be dependent upon them. Another may desire or need a rise in position; therefore there is someone who is in a high position, who can distinguish him or place him in a higher position. He will bow to this one; he will respect him; he will do anything to gain his favour and kindness.

When we discern that every individual has some different source of power before which he bows, to which he turns, on which he is dependent, we begin to ask whether there is any one source which is supreme above all these other sources of power. These various sources depend on one another; is there one which reigns over all? And the answer is that there is one; there is a source which reigns over all other sources of power, and it is this one source which we idealize and name God.

Those who idealize this source call upon Him, pay all their respect to Him, turn to Him in every difficulty, in every trouble, in every case of need. There is no one else who will suffice to console them, there is no means of assistance, no help to be obtained but this one ideal on which they fix their eyes, this ideal which is not known nor seen, yet is idealized in the mind. How poor all other sources are compared with that one source! Whereas all the various sources before which men bow and on which men depend are so uncertain that today they are kind and tomorrow they are not, yet that one source is all-sufficient, never changing, and almighty. From that source all things can be obtained. All other sources are only apparent powers; for after all, even if they do succeed in giving any help, it is still really the one source that has given them the power to provide our needs.

The Nizam of Hyderabad* was a great mystic and a very good man. He used to say to those who had obtained access to him and had made a complaint of not having yet received help, 'Have you got an order from There? If you have got one from There I will give you help, but if you have not got it from There, I will not help you.'

In the Qur'an there is a sura which says, 'God alone is rich, and all are poor'. The more we study life, the more we see the truth of this sura. People may live in palaces endowed with all manner of wealth and comfort, and yet they can still feel, 'If only I had that,

* H.E.H. Mahbub Ali Khan, † 1911.

I would never be unhappy again'. People may have their motor-cars, their furs, their wealth of millions, and yet cannot truthfully say they are perfectly happy. Can they say they have all that they need in life? Is there anyone who can say this? You are more likely to find such a one among the poor than among the wealthy.

This shows that God alone is rich. Whoever has need is poor. Poverty means need. As long as there is need there is poverty. Since man's life is full of needs, he must be in poverty. He is still in darkness if he does not realize that there is only One who is rich.

Undoubtedly we all of us have our needs through life. How often do we experience disappointment regarding them! How many are disappointed in love, in money, in help, in service! How apt is the heart to be discouraged, disappointed, broken, feeling, 'O, this is my brother, my only brother, and yet he has not helped me in this hour of need.'—'I looked on her as my sister, and yet she has failed me at this crucial time.' People meet so many disappointments in life. One depends, depends on limited sources, never reflecting that these sources can only sometimes be helpful, and that often they are quite unable to help, however much they may desire to do so.

There remains the one source which is always helpful, and can always help. It is only because man does not see Him, does not realize Him, that he doubts whether there is such a being as God. However religious or pious he is, he always looks to a material agent for help. However religious or pious, he cannot explain God; not even a mystic or philosopher can explain Him. The ideal of God is the first lesson that must be learnt; and it cannot be learnt by analysis. Therefore the intellectual mind which seeks for an analysis of God is always sure to be disappointed. The philosopher spoke truly when he said, 'To analyse God is to dethrone God'. Analysis can never portray even the ideal of God. That is why every messenger, Mohammad, Christ, Moses, Abraham, emphasized the one word: faith.

But one should not think that these seers and holy ones and teachers who had such power and realization, wanted the world to imagine that this faith should be blind. They themselves learned the first lesson that it is no use beginning with the idea that if one analyses God, one will come to believe in Him. Such a one will never believe. The first step is faith, and not reasoning or intellectual perception. Can one explain why it is that a diamond is worth twenty thousand pounds? Is there any reason for this? 'Yes,' a person will say, 'it is because it is sold in the market for that price. There is no other explanation; it is a precious stone'. But another may say, 'Yes, it is a bright stone; no doubt it is better than glass and it is certainly brighter than a crystal; but why twenty thousand pounds?'

The answer is just this, that it is worth twenty thousand pounds because our ideal has made it so. What we call an ideal is only another way of saying that there is no explanation. We have to accept it that twenty thousand pounds is its value. It is the same with every ideal, even with the ideal of God. An ideal is beyond explanation.

THE MYSTERY OF BREATH

TO A mystic the subject of breath is the deepest of all the subjects with which mysticism or philosophy is concerned, because breath is the most important thing in life. The very life of man is breath. He lives in the presence of breath, and in the absence of breath man is called a corpse. After death the organs of the body are just the same as before; the only thing that is lacking is breath.

Breath is that within ourselves which keeps all the parts of the body in connection with one another, working together, depending upon one another; it is that which enables man to move, to put his muscles into action, to keep the whole mechanism of the body always at work. There is no other force or power concerned in all this than the power of breath.

Mystics know that it is regularity of breath that brings good health; that irregularity of breath is the cause of all illness. Many teachers and students of physical culture know that it is not the exercises and practices of this culture that cause the muscles to develop, that impart strength and vigour to the body; they know, as did the ancient mystics in India, that it is a matter of the breath. To practise for one moment with the help of the breath will do more than a whole day's exercises carried on without considering the help of the breath. In the latter case the muscles cannot be developed, whereas in the former case the physical body is easily developed with very little physical practice. That this is true is easily shown by looking at the porters at railway-stations in India. If physical labour were the only thing needed to develop muscles, would they not all be veritable Sandows?*

In India we can study particularly well how men work with heavy things. Sometimes a man will carry on his shoulder a burden that it would ordinarily be impossible for a man of his physique to carry. Yet such a man cannot only lift it, but he will walk with it. And when one watches him one will find that the

* In India railway porters often look thin and underfed. For Sandow, see Vol. VI, page 266, note.

secret lies in his way of breathing. If he did not breathe correctly he could not possibly carry such a weight over the shortest distance. There was in India a man called Rama Muti. He could lift elephants and stop motor-cars running at speed. When this man, who was not extraordinary in build, was asked where he got this gigantic strength, for he looked like an ordinary human being, not like a monster, he said, 'You know, and yet you do not know. The secret lies in the breath, which is all power.'

As man cannot see it he does not believe in the possibility of breath giving power. He attaches importance only to the things he can see and hear and touch. He is so material that he cannot see anything beyond what his physical eyes are able to see. He is like a blind person who can only feel and not see. He cannot see that strength is something greater than a rock.

How difficult it is for a man to perceive the truth of the Bible saying, which says that faith will remove mountains. He thinks mountains are stronger than faith. He wonders how faith can be stronger than the rocks and the mountains. Man cannot lift the mass of a mountain; surely the mountain is stronger than faith! The idea is too subtle, too fine for him to understand.

And it is the same with all other fine and subtle things in life. So much more importance is given to the study of the material sciences, while the spiritual, the higher knowledge, is neglected. More importance is always given to the development of bodily strength. Therefore, when a man goes to the seaside, often the first thing he does is to weigh himself, so that he can find out how many pounds he has gained during his holiday. He never thinks how little time it will take to lose all those pounds again. The weight he has gained at the seaside he will lose again. He does not understand that it is energy that makes a person move and feel active and in good health, not the bodily weight. Is it not true that the addition of weight to the body makes him lazy and comfort-seeking, and often results in illness? And yet how pleased many people are when they have gained in weight!

Then when we consider the mind, we find that breath has to do with mind also. The mystic knows that the breath which we perceive by exhaling and inhaling through the nostrils is not the essential breath, but only the result of a current which runs not only through the body, but also through all the planes of man's existence. That which the nostrils feel is the result of the activity of breath. Were it not so we could not explain how the mind, which is so much vaster and finer than the body, and is a separate element, can possibly exert an effect on the body, and the body on the mind.

Every passion, every emotion has its effect upon the mind; and every change of mind, however slight, has its effect upon a man's body. Physicians in all ages have realized that consumption is often the outcome of constant worry.

What keeps mind and body connected? What keeps the mind always active? What gives the mind its vigour to create imaginations, to create thoughts, and not only to create them but to retain them by the faculty we call memory; to keep the knowledge gained by the faculty we call reason; to possess emotions which can sometimes be felt and sometimes not felt? Where does the mind keep all these things? What force can it be that is behind them all? Is it not the breath? That is why the mystic studies and realizes and masters the breath, in order to master not only the physical body but also the mind.

From the mystical point of view it is evident that there is some strength, some current, some affinity which runs through and binds together all the trees and plants in a forest, and which also causes the desert to be without them; which causes the coal-mine to have coal, the gold-mine to have gold, the sulphur-mine to have sulphur in them. This strength, or force, draws all these elements together.

So it is too with the tides of the sea. It accounts for the waters running in the same direction, whether at first they tended towards the south, the east, the west, or the north; it accounts for the surface of the waves keeping a rhythm. Wherever we look, be it the changes of the seasons, the changes of the weather, or even the constant circles which the earth describes on its journey, all these show the same underlying current, the current of the whole of nature, which is the real breath. The whole universe is going on with a certain rhythm; there is a current which keeps the whole universe going. It is one breath, and yet it is many breaths.

There is a tide which has a cycle of forty days, and a tide which has a cycle of seven days, and another of thirty days; and yet at every moment waves are rising and falling. There is a wave under the wave, and a wave over the wave. There is a tide that turns twice a day, and also a tide that turns once a month. So is it with breath: one breath, and yet many breaths.

Then consider how the trees keep together. One tree, and yet its branches and its fruits and its flowers all turn in different directions. Every branch takes a different direction, and yet all keep together. What is it that directs the vigour and the strength of one branch and not the others in that direction, for they are all attached to the same tree-stem? Is it not that life-current which runs through it that directs their ways? As long as it runs through a tree it produces fruit and flowers.

So it is with animals and birds and man. The same current of life runs through all. Man is the ideal being, as the scripture says. He is ideal because intelligence is given to him to perceive the secret of this breath, whereas from animals and birds it is hidden. The life of all creatures is mysterious and full of wonder, but man alone is blessed with the intelligence which conveys the power of understanding the secret of the breath. If there is anything more lasting than our transitory life it is this, the secret of our being. It is by this that man is able to master life both here and in the hereafter.

Having understood this truth, mystics have been able to teach that the religion of all religions is the knowledge of self, for the knowledge of self brings the knowledge of life. This life-current which runs through the centre of man's being, attaching mind to body and to all other planes of existence as well, it is this that is all-important. It passes from man's innermost being out to the body, which is the instrument whereby man is able to experience life on the surface. When he has knowledge of this a man begins to realize, 'I am not as small as I had thought, not as weak as I had thought; I am much stronger on other planes. I can live much longer than I could on the physical plane. I can see myself on all the different planes by means of that inner knowledge of the breath.'

Therefore to the mystic breath is like a lift, a lift in which he rises up to the first floor, and then to the second, and then to the third floor, in fact wherever he wishes to go.

The mystery of the Sphinx, and the mystery of Buraq, which is mentioned in the life of the Prophet Mohammad, has to do with this. When the Prophet reached the court, or gate, of God, the Buraq was sent. The Buraq was an animal with wings, and the Prophet rode upon it in order to reach the gate of the highest heaven. He passed through gate after gate as he passed the seven heavens. In the end he arrived at the gate of the highest.

What does this allegory mean? The body of the Buraq is this physical body. The wings represent the ability of the breath to reach far and yet retain its connection with the physical body. The Prophet mounting upon his back represents any soul who treads the spiritual path. Whoever has courage, whoever has faith, whoever has confidence, whoever has trust, whoever has patience and hope and perseverance, can tread this path and make use of the vehicle of the breath.

If we read the history of Buddha, who was a yogi, we shall find that without yoga and without spiritual meditation, which is accomplished by breath, no one in this world has ever attained spiritual perfection. The healing power of Christ, the magnetism of Mohammad, the miraculous power of Moses, the charm of Krishna and the inspiration of Buddha—all these were attained by breath. And how did they attain them if there were not a current passing between us on the earth and the source of energy, the source of power and magnetism?

Is it not plain that breath conveys even the words which go out from our lips to the ears of the hearer? The voice is breath. The word is breath. Without breath speech cannot be produced. And yet a person may easily accept this and acknowledge that it is true that it is breath that does this, but he will not willingly believe that thought also is breath. He can see the movement of the air which arises from speech, and he wonders if it is meant that thought also causes a movement of the air. This is because he does not understand that a life-current runs through it all, and that is breath. It is easily seen when it manifests itself upon the physical plane, but on the higher planes it is not seen; yet it extends higher than the planes. If there is anything that connects man with God, if there is anything that connects the mortal with the immortal, it is this bridge which we call breath. It is a bridge whereby to pass from the world of mortality to the world of immortality; it is the bridge whereby immortality passes down to mortality. That life which seems mortal is really the ray of immortal life. What seems mortal is only the shell. It is not life that is mortal, it is the cover that makes it seem mortal.

From the time when man first perceived that there was a secret in breath, he has wanted to use his understanding of the secret in order to be able to perform wonders and reach the spirits, to master the elements, read thoughts, convey thoughts, and to perform any psychic or occult phenomena. But to seek to do these things is to give pearls to buy pebbles. How wasteful to spend life in gaining these powers when breath is the rope that takes us from this mortal plane to immortality, that saves us from the struggles and worries of this transitory life, and leads us to the happiness and joy and peace for which every soul longs! If breath can accomplish these pearls, will it not also accomplish the small things, the pebbles, the worldly needs? Yes, it will. After all, to have performed a few wonders is nothing.

One man is perhaps striving all day to earn his own bread so that he may live in a comfortable manner; another is always worrying about how to maintain himself and his children. Another is thinking, 'What can I do to save my fellow-man from his trouble?' If we compare these people, in order to see who is the greatest, we see that he is greatest whose ideal is greatest.

When we consider the great heroes of the past and present, those whom we admire and to whom we look with hope for right guidance, we shall find that what has made them great has been the greatness of their ideal. The lower the ideal, the less the efforts; the higher the ideal, the greater the life. If we use all our intelligence and strength and wisdom to accomplish some little thing, it is only a waste of life. To consider what great things one can accomplish, to seek to do those things which will be most useful and valuable to others, that is the ideal life. The man who has earned money only to keep himself comfortable, what has he accomplished with his life? If he has just gratified his wish to roam about in a motor-car, to set up a comfortable home, to have people waiting upon him; he cannot be happy, because he has not accomplished anything with his life. He may possess many houses, he may possess much money in the bank, he may make a great name; but it will amount to nothing in comparison with the man whose power is greater than all wealth, position, or fame. Such a man will be much happier with the small things of the world; he has gained that peace with which the pleasures and transitory joys of this earth offer no comparison.

The one life is like the lips touching a cup of delicious wine; the other life is like drinking the whole cup full of heavenly wine. What a difference between just touching the wine with the lips, and drinking it! The pleasures of life are like touching the wine. The experience of these pleasures is only like a dream, a passing joy; it comes and goes again. One longs for the joy of that little pleasure to stay; but how can it stay? Even if one tried for thousands of years, one could not keep the happiness which is external. The only way to obtain the eternal bliss is to do as the mystics do, and to rise by the aid of the breath from plane to plane, finding the greater joy and the greater happiness.

It resembles the taking of a drug. A person may sit in meditation, and dream and imagine he is very happy. A materially minded person may easily say that a meditative person hypnotizes himself into thinking he is full of joy, but is it not hypnotism when a little word of flattery pleases one, when a little silver and gold produces such a change of expression in one's countenance? The materialist, not understanding this, will laugh at the mystic and call him a dreamer, but if the mystic is a dreamer, what is the worldly man? Is he not a dreamer too? What produces the joy in these things that are of no importance? If it is good to be hypnotized by silver and gold, is it not better when the mystic is hypnotized by his divine ideal of perfection? The silver and gold will certainly be snatched away; at least the mystic's ideal of God will last.

When we consider how this life and our environment can cramp and restrict us, we understand how it is that with all our hopes we still seek solitude, try to be by ourselves, and close our eyes to all the passing things. The life and activity which are directed to experiencing the pleasures of life, the transitory sources of joy and pleasure, all fade away before that which we seek in solitude, where we strive to reach the inner and enduring things. Even if our bed is comfortable, if our house contains all the comforts that the heart can desire, the mind still goes through all manner of torments, and sleep will not come. We may take a little rest, and sit still in order to obtain peace; but the real trouble never goes. It is to drown this trouble that people take drugs and intoxicants, and lose themselves in the pursuit of common things, however undesirable. Everybody strives to obtain some remedy which will enable him to realize the joy and pleasure and peace which his inner life unconsciously seeks; but he cannot get it. If he tries to obtain it through drugs or intoxicants, he only becomes a slave to them. If, failing these, he seeks to gain his desire through other vices, he will never find the contentment he seeks.

Come to the mystic, then, and sit with him when you are tired of all these other remedies that you have employed in vain; come and take a glass of wine with him. The mystic wine is the inner absorption, which removes all the worries and anxieties and troubles and cares of the physical and mental plane. All these are now done away with for ever. It is the mystic who is at rest; it is he who experiences that happiness which others do not experience; it is he who teaches the way to attain that peace and happiness which are the original heritage of man's soul.

CHARACTER AND FATE

WHEN A person hears that an influence is exerted on fate by character, he at once wonders how far this can be true with regard to those whom he sees to be well off and in favourable circumstances. He dare not think that their degree of rank and wealth could be attained by good character and its effects.

This is the first stumbling-block which man meets with. When he begins to idealize or admire a character, he has his practical benefit before his eyes. And when he asks himself, 'Shall I gain anything from a practical point of view?' the heavenly bliss is disregarded. The first thing he thinks about is his fate: 'If only I could have good fortune!' If he gets all he wants by having a good character, he is at once disturbed by the disappointment of finding that the actual facts do not agree. If it is in business, for instance, surely it is constant application which brings success, and not the personal character.

If we considered that good fortune lies in the achievement of worldly power, or of wealth or position, this would be the poorest fortune. However high a person is in rank, however great the wealth he possesses, and whatever position in life he occupies, these have nothing to do with his happiness and satisfaction of mind. It is fate that has to do with happiness and satisfaction.

Even if a person be living in a palace, his heart may still be in torment from morning to night. Is that enjoying a good fate? He has a thousand difficulties; his own longings are his enemies. Is that good fortune? Happiness may exist in a cottage. Yet one who suffers from lack of money says, 'What good fortune the rich man has!' But the rich man says to himself, 'All they want is to get what they can out of me. They are waiting till I close my eyes in order that they may inherit what I possess. Many minds are constantly working against me'. And is health good luck? Is a healthy man also the possessor of a mind at rest? Is his heart satisfied?

But if good fortune does not consist of these things, are they then desirable? Surely they are desirable; but can we say they are the only good fortune that we can attain? Can we say that they are the only things that can satisfy our need in life? It is only when we lack wealth or health that we say good fortune lies in them. Yet when we attain them we find we are still not satisfied. Therefore it must be something else that constitutes good fortune. It is not being very religious or pious. It consists in the attainment of what we wish, what we desire, and what we would choose to have.

What do we desire? All things that seem to us best according to our evolution; these we think we desire and wish to have and consider to be good fortune. But when it comes to giving away these things, we are not willing to do so. The whole secret lies there. If we could only grasp the fact that it is for us to give to others that which we expect them to give to us. We like to be in the company of a good or calm person, and our desire is to deal with such a one; in our profession or in business we always think, 'If I could have a righteous and just and reliable person to deal with'. But when we are put to the test, when it comes to being righteous ourselves, we fail miserably. When others expect us to treat them well, fairly, and kindly, and to be stable and reliable, we forget that it is for us to show these characteristics. We think so much of our own wishes that we forget what it is that we ought to do for others.

The seer, therefore, teaches that all the things that we desire and think beautiful, we ought to produce within ourselves instead of expecting them from others. What a task that is! What great self-sufficiency there would be if every country always itself produced that which it seeks from others; what an independent life it would be to produce within ourselves what we expect to obtain from others! Instead of depending on them for something we ourselves can give them, we should experience the joy of giving, the joy of being kind to others. What joy and freedom we should ourselves find in being kind to another. However natural it may be to have someone love and admire us, are we not dependent? The wife is dependent on her husband's love; the friend is dependent on the friend's love. But in the other case we would be free and independent; for our joy would lie in the love itself, and not in the person. We should enjoy life by doing kindness to others. Receiving kindness from others only makes the recipient expect more. He keeps saying, 'He is doing this for his own benefit; he is not considering me; he is blaming me; he did not help me; he did not deal fairly with me.' His life becomes full of grudges because he expects from everybody all the good that he wants, and he does not know that he ought to have it all in himself; that he should become independent. Therein lies the secret of character.

It is a wonderful thing that all that we possess in the way of character we transfer not only to our surroundings, but also to such animals and birds as may be pets in the house. If we could see exactly to what extent our character itself acts on our surroundings we should be surprised, the effect is so great. According to science we see that the law of attraction is such that it always attracts the same elements. When we emit goodness, we cannot receive anything else but goodness; and even those who have not that element know it to be of God. All attributes and all goodness that are in the original spirit of God are in man's spirit also. However wicked a man may be, however lawless, however degenerate, if we are quite the opposite our power will be greater than his; his power will not have any influence on us. The power of goodness conquers badness. Badness is weakness; goodness is strength.

A man who has the habit of losing his temper cannot control another person with the same temperament, because he has that weakness himself. Therefore the other person loses control also. If a man has control over himself, he will smile and be patient even if he is exposed to rages a thousand times. He will just wait. He who has spiritual control has great control; but he who has it not can control neither spiritual nor physical events. He cannot control his own sons and daughters, for he never listens to himself first. If he listened to himself, not only persons but even objects would listen to him. The self will never guide unless we allow it to do so. We always go astray when we are not guided by the intuitive self. Confusion always follows when we have disappointed our intuition, and failure always comes when the control has been lost.

A person's weakness spoils his affairs, for all the different spheres in which his affairs lie—family, daily life, business, profession, industry, and so on—are all affected by every lack in his character. Do not think that a person of high position is always an ideal character; he would have come to a ten times higher position if his character had helped him.

It is the character that is our teacher. We do not need to speak to people about being virtuous, kind, righteous, for our own righteousness is enough to make them so; our goodness is sufficient to make our surroundings good. People are for ever seeking psychic power and control when all the time it is within themselves. Our self is the greatest enemy we have. The horse wants to go where its rider does not; it is the self that will not listen to us and does not act according to our wish. It is not what another person says, or a priest says, or a Church says; the great teacher is both within and without. If we are willing to be guided, everything can teach us a lesson. If we wish to see the advantage of sobriety, we shall see it among sober people; if we wish to see the disadvantages of lack of sobriety, we shall see them among people who are not sober; if we wish to see the advantage of guidance, we shall see it among those who are guided. It is all a matter of experience and study; and our own guide towards our true ideal will never fail to guide us aright.

We should do all that we wish others to do to us; and we should not only do what we please to others, even if they do not wish for more. All that we expect from the world we desire for ourselves. But if we acted otherwise, we should become great personalities in the world; instead of being examples of selfishness we should give of our best in our dealings with our nearest relatives, children and friends.

Life in general is like a plant with thorns. Wherever we wish to take hold, there we find a thorn. The more our eyes are opened, the more, wherever we put our hand, do we get thorns, the thorns of selfishness; for every ego wants what is best for itself and is not ready to give. Yet if we tried out of curiosity to become a rose instead of a thorn, we would make our life worth while.

When we begin to see our own faults, then we see how much more we should deserve the name of human beings. Ghalib said,

'For man even to become man is the most difficult of all the other difficulties in life'. One day a *madzub* (that is, a man who has devoted his entire life to spiritual realization, living always far from the crowd, who think him crazy) was coming from one side of the market-place when he met another coming from the opposite side. They made a little bow to one another. And it surprised a bystander to see two crazy people greet one another thus. What brotherhood there is between crazy people, he thought. He then went to the place where the one madzub lived, and sat there waiting a long time until it should please the madzub to explain himself. At last the mood of the madzub became such that he would speak to him; and he placed his hand upon the head of this man, saying, 'My child, go into the bazaar, and look at it; and come back and tell me what you see'. So the man went back to the city, and looked at the crowd, and returned full of surprise. He was bewildered beyond expression, and said, 'Every face that I see has the appearance of some animal; not a human face can I see throughout the whole city, except that of the man to whom you bowed, and of your holy self; of only these two!'

It does not mean that the faces were changed; it does not mean that the features became different. It means that the garb of humanity, the appearance of the human beings, is not enough. If we can distinguish ourselves from other beings, it is only in the things that animals do not do that man can be different from them. When it comes to eating, do not both eat? Both sleep; both seek comfort. Man does all the things that animals do; man can only be greater than animals in things that they do not do. And what are those things? Building houses? Birds can do this. Ability to fight? Animals and birds fight. The showing of art and skill? Animals can show these things; think of the spider and how it weaves its web; it is wonderful.

Man was created in order that he might overcome that which animals have not overcome. And what is that? It is the ego. It is the ego that makes him selfish, that makes him try to get the best of his neighbour. This is the only real cause of all the disturbances of life, of all unrest, of all that we suffer, of all the harm that comes to us. The great enemy is the ego, the selfishness, manifested in husband, wife, son, daughter, friend, neighbour, or servant.

Seeing how man's selfishness is torturing the world, the greatest need is to understand that no one is better than anyone else, and that no one can rightly think or imagine he can be better than anyone else, or more helpful to children or family or surroundings until this one thing is achieved: the suppression of ego, of selfishness. Do we not fight with one another unjustly, all because of vanity? We say 'That is my thought; that is mine'. 'Me' is such that everything but 'me' is wrong; what I have, no one shall touch. This is the one thing against which all religious teachers preach.

Many people think it is very necessary to hold to self and self-interest. Yet even if man does differ from animals, he resembles them in this, that where there are two dogs and one has a bone before him, he does not want the other dog to touch his bone. Even though he is satisfied and does not require the bone himself, he still does not wish the other dog to come and touch it. 'This is my bone', he thinks, 'I will have it'. And as long as the other dog is afraid, it is all right. But if the other dog is bigger, he will come and take the bone, and bite the first dog too. That is the picture of life.

Yet we see that in similar circumstances one man will say of the other, 'O, he was so good. I went to him at lunch-time and he was so kind as to ask me to have lunch with him.' This is a man's feast; the other was a dog's feast. This is where man should be different from an animal. An animal will not recognize his mother, or father, or his birthplace, but man will. After he has grown up he will consider, 'My mother took care of me when I was an infant and was so kind to me; and now she is aged, so I will do everything in my power for her'. He dwells on all the respect he can show her, and how worthy she is of it. At once he shows himself to be man; the animal does not act in this way. Hence, in the case where a man does the same as an animal, and does not care for those who did all they could for him in his youth, he shows his lack of humanity. Forgetfulness and lack of appreciation of the care bestowed during childhood are characteristic of the animal.

Even angels bow to Christ, and Christ is the ideal man. Angels bow to the ideal man. Even when standing on the earth below, he is higher than heaven and the angels, if only he can be man, if only he exhibits humanity. Christ said, 'Ye are the salt of the earth, and if the salt have lost its savour, wherewith shall it be salted?' This explains that man is the ideal manifestation, higher than mineral, vegetable, animal, and other kingdoms, and even higher than the angels. If he loses the sense of humanity, who is to come and teach him? He is the one who is able to teach.

Man is the father of humanity. If the father loses his way, where will the children go? How much depends on the preceding generation! It is to this that we always look for prosperity, for success, for the future of the nation, country, race, or family.

The real welfare to be sought is not the keeping of so much money in the bank, so many houses built, such and such an education at the university; it is the benefit to the future that is the guide. Parents should think of the welfare of the child even before it is born. The child will show what he has inherited; but how few parents think of that.

Our rest, our peace, our harmony, our tendency to all good and beautiful actions and things are the wealth that we can reserve for the child. The parents should know what psychic influences they can transmit to their children. The father and the mother are just like the planet which controls the souls and the spirits of that planet; but they are the living planet, their influence is much greater upon their children.

The father thinks that if he does a certain thing, the child should do the same. 'I must make my child follow in my footsteps', he thinks. This is fate. Is it not the fate of nation, race, family, or the individual, to consider that which belongs to their generation as ideal, believing that that is the best fate for the next generation?

People give their lives for the new generation, for the new hope. Should one not see that what matters is that the lives of the children should become better? The leaders of a town, of a country, are looked to as an example which the people may follow. How can one prove oneself fit for all these positions? The position of leadership can only be filled after training oneself, and not someone else.

What an atmosphere one can create by one's character; what influence one person can have on another's character! 'Where are you going?' asks a father; 'I am going to the library', says the son. His answer expresses truth and conviction. But another who is going where he knows his father does not want him to go replies with hesitation, and he falters out the same words; 'I am going to the library'. The same words are used, but there is no strength in them, no effect.

What power character gives; what power truthfulness gives; what power is lost when the character of the prospective act is in doubt! What fear the murderer goes through! He is himself half murdered before he commits the act, and after committing the act he is in a worse condition than the one he has murdered. His fear, his conscience, his kindness, his justice, his reason, all are in conflict.

The power of character is like the power of an army. With Christ there was an army of angels. With Mohammad there was also an army of angels. He stood, while thousands of people were running away. When an enemy came near to the great Khalif to behead him, the enemy was afraid. But this fear was simply a result of the Prophet's power of control. Personality shows what has been sown in it. One cannot pretend to be righteous and good unless one's spirit has practised it and that strength has really come. One's appearance and one's atmosphere can tell what one is, because man is the picture of his thoughts. Whatever he thinks, whatever he is about, that speaks in his atmosphere, in his voice, in his movements. In everything he expresses himself as he is, how far he has evolved, and how far he has not evolved. Whatever he is, he shows.

How great an influence can be! There is the story of a boy who was sent to Baghdad across the desert, after his mother had sewn a few gold coins in his blanket, telling him to keep it safe and not open it till he reached the city. This was a precaution against robbers, for there were no trains or cars or caravans; it was necessary to travel alone and on foot. When this lad came to the desert, robbers met him. Thinking he would not have much money, being only a little boy, they asked him all the same, 'Have you any coins, any gold, any silver?' Having been trained to tell the truth, he answered, 'Yes, I have'. His conscience would never permit him to answer 'no'. 'Where are they?', they asked. 'They are sewn in this blanket', he said. But the very fact of his telling them won the robbers' hearts and made them act rightly themselves. They said, 'We would have stolen them had you not told the truth', and they let him go free.

If a person thinks that God is all, but the whole world is vile, he does not worship God, for God is all and God is beautiful. 'God is beautiful and He loves beauty', the Prophet said. And as His being is in us, we are supposed to love beauty also. What is beauty? Not only the external beauty, but the beauty of personality, the beauty of character, that is the real beauty. If we did not worship it, we should not admire it in other people. We cannot appreciate anything without beauty of character.

All gains, whether material, spiritual, moral, or mystical, are the outcome of one's own character; and if we have gained nothing, it is only by reason of our own character.

Truth comes to man's soul, and yet truth is not the exclusive property of creed, caste, or race. We are all the children of God, the Father-Mother Spirit of all that exists. And we ought to have such a feeling of brotherhood that we exchange helpful thoughts with one another all the time. We can take love and guidance from one another. Speech is not as great a help as contact; but the privilege of meeting one another is great. When souls meet, what truth they can exchange! It is uttered in silence, yet surely always reaches its goal.

When God wants to destroy a thing, He gives it into unworthy hands.

GAIN AND LOSS

TO THE view of a mystic a gain is not a gain nor is a loss a loss; for that which appears to be a loss at one time may appear at another to be a gain. The more deeply we think about it, the more we see that in every gain there is a loss, and in every loss there is a gain. That which seemed to be a gain yesterday may prove to be a loss tomorrow, and that which is a loss at one time proves to yield a gain at another. Consequently the mystic realizes the joy of the gain and the sorrow of the loss in their right aspect; he discerns what it is that turns a gain to a loss, or converts a loss to a gain. The more deeply we consider the subject, the more do we discern that there are certain gains which are only transient, because material, and that to attain them we may have sacrificed a greater gain. Of course if we do not see that greater gain, we do not mind the loss. We can only see what we have lost or what we have gained after we have discovered whether the gain we have sacrificed really was a greater one or not.

Every experience in life has three aspects: that in which it is in the state of a motive; that in which it is in the process of achievement; and that in which the experience is an accomplished fact. In the first aspect, where the experience is as yet only in the form of a motive, we can have no clear conception as to whether it is a gain or a loss. We start out, for instance, with the thought, 'I wish to start a business; in this business I shall make a profit'. That represents the initial motive. The next step will be the actual building up of the business. It is now that the gain or the loss becomes more clearly perceptible. But the gain or loss is most clear after the business is accomplished. The experience is now realized. Hitherto the person has not realized the benefit or otherwise, but in the final stage he is able to form a true estimate as to whether the idea of his life has led to gain or loss.

In life we discriminate between two things: the real and the false. We think more of the real and less of the false. We discriminate between imitation gold and real gold; we pay more for the real gold because it is more lasting. The two samples of gold may be equally bright; hence it is evident that the value we attach to things is in proportion to their lasting power. Similarly, if we could see what things in life are lasting or passing, we should discriminate between real loss and false loss, real gain and false gain. The gain or loss which is momentary is not real. So, too, joy or sorrow is a momentary state; the joy over a gain today may tomorrow prove to be a sorrow. If we knew the realities, we should never grieve over the loss of things which experience shows to be only of a transient character.

On the one hand we are working for our own individual benefit and interest; but on the other hand there is a universal power which is more mighty than ourselves, and more just in its working. When these two powers, the Kaza, or universal, the Kadr, or individual, are working harmoniously, things come right. But when they clash, that which is thought right by Kaza will happen without regard to what Kadr may think right or wrong. Those who know this, and harmonize their will with Kaza, the universal Will, begin to experience divine impulses, and they begin to feel every time what is and what is not harmonious in the Kadr also. To such as these there come fewer failures in life. Life is easier because they swim with and not against the tide.

Our sense of justice is partial, because it is obscured or shadowed by our likes and dislikes, by our personal interest and lack of interest in people and things.

In the Bible it is written, 'Where your treasure is, there will your heart be also'. If our gain is only in objects of a passing nature, our heart will find no gain in this life or in the hereafter. Those who trust in transitory gain must accept the inevitable disappointment, both here and in the hereafter. Everybody in this world is selfish; for is it not true that the sages who renounce that which is valued by worldly people, after all only take up that which they understand to be really the greater gain? The only difference between their action and that which seems entirely selfish in those who are not sages, is that they sacrifice what they perceive to be a false gain. For anyone to do otherwise is to be like the dog which was running after its own shadow.

The privilege of having life on earth in this delicate human vehicle is too great to risk wasting it on something which will leave one the loser in the end, however rich and ample the false gain may appear. What gain is it to have the object we have gained snatched from our hands in the end? What gain is it to have an object which has to be constantly guarded and watched against the rapacity of others? Everyone is on the watch to take our gain away and make it his; and this he can do with any transient gain. We always desire dependable objects and friends. It is our nature to long for something we can depend on for life. Our own nature teaches us that if we realize our life's desire, that which we consider important, we realize only transient things. Has not this war shown us how artists lose their art, poets their poetry, kings their thrones and many a man falls from his heaven to the earth, all in a moment's time? What, then, is there in this world that can be depended upon? Have we not seen how parents have even sacrificed their lives in order to give the desired happiness to sons and daughters? Have we not seen that friends whom one relies on, in their turn depend on someone else and are disappointed?

When we really think about these things we are bound to see that after all we are only like children in understanding. We think ourselves clever and wise, and yet we do not really think deeply about life. Some day we begin to think, and then we see ourselves as a parent sees his children's acts. The child thinks its sand and toys are such important things, things that we grown-ups attach no importance to. And we too begin to see how childish our own life is when we can assess at their true value these actions and desires which seemed so important to us yesterday. We think little things so important: dignity, ill-treatment, insults, reputation; and what do they matter in the end? Do we not see people praised and raised up high in vanity and greatness one day, and next day they are quite forgotten? Before the revolution every shop in Moscow had a picture of the Czar in one window, and of Jesus with the Virgin in the other. Within three years, what a change there was! Even a whole race will change its attitude in a moment's time.

Praise, honour, love, kindness, are they lasting, are they dependable? Are we not seeking after wealth, or fame, or love, or kindness, or some help from morning until evening? However evolved we may be with our education and experience, yet what are we really seeking? Things from which we cannot derive any lasting gain. From these false things we gain the experience that the things to which we have hitherto attached importance and which we have valued are things that do not last. We learn at length that it would be wise to remember that all these objects and ideals and aspirations which we have in life should be judged according to whether they are dependable or not, lasting or not. After we have perceived the truth that this or that is not to be depended upon, we find that it is not necessary to renounce them all, to give up everything in life. We can be in the crowd just as well as in seclusion in the wilderness. We can have all good things, wealth, friends, kindness, love to give and love to take, once we have learned not to be blinded by them, learned to escape from disappointment, learned to escape from repugnance at the idea that the things are not as we would want them to be. A man can still attend to business, he may attain wealth, he can carry out all those things, but now his eyes are wide open; before, they were blind. This is the teaching of life. Thus it is that when we study life in the East, we will find that a Sufi may be a king or he may be a faqir. A Sufi means a seer; and a Sufi may still be a king. It is not the actual literal renunciation which counts, it is the personal abandonment of belief in the importance of transient things.

A person who pretends to be unselfish is generally foolish-selfish. It is the wise-selfish who are right; they are selfish, it is true, but they are selfish with true wisdom. They think out what it is in life that will benefit them most. The foolish-selfish man never puts money by, and thus never has any to give away. The wise-selfish man will obtain money in order that he can express his generosity with what he has collected. He who remains a pauper all his life has never achieved anything for anyone. Therefore he is wise who not only understands what is real gain and what is false, but also understands the price there is to pay for the gain. What determines our success is weighing whether one's gain is of more value than the price one has to pay for it, or whether the price one has to pay is greater than the gain one can obtain. He who perceives this clearly has learnt the true business of life very well.

For every gain, however, there is a need for sacrifice. To gain anything we have to sacrifice something; to pursue two gains is to lose both. Therefore it is necessary to decide once and for all what is false, and then to follow the real and leave the false.

If there is such a thing as saintly renunciation, it is renouncing small gains for better gains; not for no gains, but seeing with open eyes what is better and what is inferior. Even if the choice has to lie between two momentary gains, one of these would always be found to be more real and lasting; that is the one that should be followed for the time. When we take the torch of wisdom to show us our faith through life, we will end by realizing what is really profitable in life and what is not.

STILLING THE MIND

BEFORE one can understand the use of stilling the mind one must consider the discrepancy between advising that the mind be stilled and advising that the body be not stilled. Life is nothing but an activity in all things. Inactivity of the body takes away its vigour and strength; the muscles do not have a chance to develop; the lazy, inactive person is always suffering from indigestion or some such ailment. How then can it be that when the mind is made still it will not suffer loss of vigour and strength? Would not stilling the mind stupefy a person? If the voice is to develop, it must be used in singing exercises and in carrying out certain practices; if the muscles are to develop, they must be used. How then can stilling the mind create power of mind?

There is great truth in this objection. Stilling the mind would stupefy and render it powerless, did the person not understand life's secret, life's law. It is true that in life on the physical plane our exercises and activity of the day must give place to rest, comfort, and sleep during the night. If our body does not receive that rest, it can never flourish. We need more rest than activity; we need more comfort than toil; and if we do not get it our health becomes unbalanced. So it follows that just as it is necessary for the body to have comfort and rest after toil, so is it necessary for the mind to have rest and peace after thinking and working.

Indeed, the mind is composed of finer elements, whereas the body is made of grosser elements, and that makes a great difference in activity. The higher the plane of existence, the more active one is; the lower the plane, the less are the activities. That is why the mind is naturally more active than the body. Therefore, if after toil rest is necessary, how much more does this apply to mind than to body! We usually rest our body at will whenever circumstances allow us to; we recline on a couch or in an armchair after coming back from the office or work, and at night we rest and go to sleep; but when do we give the mind a rest? Rest for the mind is as necessary as rest for the body, and yet we always keep the mind in action. It is constantly at work even if our body is resting. Even if the body is sleeping, the mind is producing dreams, and is constantly at work. Many people stand at their work the whole day, during which the mind is no less busy with the work on the physical planes than is the body, for mind works with body; and yet they work with the mind the whole night long. The body is having rest and comfort, but not the mind. Even in an armchair they are still imagining, still working with the mind.

The mind has no leisure; it is perhaps worrying, or planning, or thinking over the struggles and anxieties of which life is so full. There is hardly ever a time when the mind is at rest, except when nature gives it a rest because it is too exhausted to work any more. The mind says, 'I will have a good sleep'. And if it has two hours' sleep only, still one wakes up with such joy and strength that all the world seems new. If there have been dreams, one can only say that one has been asleep, but one does not feel rested, because that part of the being has not had any rest.

All this shows the great practical need for the mind to be at rest, for the mind to be stilled. Those who make it a principle that work is always an advisable thing are one-sided. Balance lies in perceiving that work and rest are equally necessary for good health, both physical and mental.

The work of the body is sometimes kept under a man's control, but he does not keep the work of the mind under his control. This is not because he cannot do so; it is because he never thinks about it. Does one ever stop to ask oneself, 'Why was I thinking? Was there any purpose in those anxious, worried thoughts? Was it not that the mind was just allowed to go wherever it wanted? While sitting quietly in a chair, were not the thoughts active with things that have nothing to do with my life, with things that do not matter in the least either to myself or to anyone else? It was just a waste of energy.'

The more the mind is allowed to go on without purpose, the more likely it is to become a vehicle or machine, which all manner of influences around it of other human beings or spirit obsessions will employ instead of its owner. If the user of that mind is a sensible person, then it may perhaps act properly, but otherwise the work of the mind is wasted. In any case it would not be a fulfilment of the purpose of his life. This purpose is to learn mastery, not to be a vehicle for others to use. He who does not direct his own mind lacks mastery.

All this shows that the very first lesson that the mystic learns in life is the training of mind. It is not stilling the mind; stilling comes afterwards. The first thing is to train, to check the activities. This is illustrated in the words 'imagination' and 'thought'. Sometimes we use the word thought when we should use the word imagination; sometimes imagination when we should use thought. Both are different forms of activity of mind. In the first case the imagination, the activity of mind, is uncontrolled, without our intention, and is not directed towards a certain purpose. A person may be imaginative, and his imaginings may appear like beautiful flowers. But if there is no purpose, the flowers are of no use to the plant; that beautiful things have been produced is no credit, because no one knows from what source the imaginings have come. But in the case of thought, this is directed imagination; it is a controlled activity of mind. That is why we cannot call a thoughtful person imaginative, nor can we call an imaginative person thoughtful. He is thoughtful whose mind is directed by his will, whose mind fulfils his intentions, whose mind is under the control of his intention.

Imagination may be very beautiful or just the opposite; it may be right or it may be wrong. Many people who are praised as being imaginative may really be in the first stage of insanity. Only those who have controlled the activity of their minds have given deep thoughts to the world. Those whose minds are working mechanically like a machine, or just reflecting the activity of those around them, may appear to be living beings, but the mystic would say differently; for it is not till a person has gained mastery over his mind, till he is above this activity, that he is a ruling power, a true person.

When we think about it, we find that all the things that are accomplished in this world are accomplished by the power of mind. As it is written in the Vedanta, 'The world is the creation of the mind of Brahma'. That is, it is the thought of the Creator which has created the world. And if it is the Creator's thought that has created this world, then we ourselves are not far from Him. The soul of man is the spirit of the Creator, and therefore has within it the same power of creating by the power of mind as his Creator has. Whatever man creates in science, in art, in phenomena or wonder-making, in poetry, in music, in pictures, in everything that he brings into being, is all achieved by the power of mind.

What is man? Is not his soul divine substance? The very word man is from the Sanskrit *Manu*, which means mind. Man is what his mind is, what he thinks. 'As a man thinketh in his heart, so he is'. Even the future, as well as the past, is what he thinks, because he himself becomes the image of his thoughts. God created man in the image of his thoughts. If there is any self of which one can say, 'This is man', it is the mind. The three Sanskrit words *Mana*, *Manu*, *Manusha* show that man is his mind, is the product of his mind, and is also the controller of the activity of mind. If he does not control his mind, he is not a master but a slave. It lies with his own mind whether he shall be master, or whether he shall be slave. He is slave when he neglects to be master; he is master if he cares to be master.

Mastery lies not merely in stilling the mind, but in directing it towards whatever point we desire, in allowing it to be active as far as we wish, in using it to fulfil our purpose, in causing it to be still when we want to still it. He who has come to this has created his heaven within himself; he has no need to wait for a heaven in the hereafter, for he has produced it within his own mind now.

There is a story of a murshid and a mureed. The mureed said, 'O, Teacher, I should like to see heaven'. The teacher said, 'Yes, this is the way you should meditate in order to see heaven'. So the mureed went and did so; but the vision of heaven which he had was not as described in the scriptures, a place where one enjoys nothing but comfort and luxury, milk and honey, marble halls and white robes, beautiful gems and jewels, garlands of flowers, and the waving of palms. He could not see any of these, and he asked himself, 'Has the murshid perhaps shown me a wrong heaven, or have the prophets given a wrong message in the scriptures?'

So he went back to his teacher saying, 'Now I should like to see hell'. The murshid said, 'Yes, this is the way you should meditate in order to see hell'. And then the mureed did this, and he saw in a trance that there was certainly such a place, but there was no fire or snakes or serpents or thorns or tortures or imps or flames such as have been described to people throughout the ages. So he could not understand whether his vision was right or wrong; and he went back to the teacher, and said, 'I have seen in this way: I have not seen in heaven the things that are promised, nor have I seen in hell the things which are foretold as being there'. 'O, the teacher said, 'all the things promised for the hereafter you will have to take there from here. They are not kept ready for you; you will have to bring them with you. If you take sorrows with you, you will find them there; if you take hatred, you will find it there. Your mind is like a gramophone record, and if you use a harsh voice, the instrument produces a harsh note; if beautiful words and tones, it will sing beautiful words and tones. It will produce the same record that you have experienced in life. Indeed you have not to wait till after death in order to experience it; you are experiencing it even now'.

Everything is reproduced before us now, if we would only listen to it and perceive it. Every good or bad word or deed is reproduced before us, though it seems as in a dream.

If we watched life keenly, we should see how true this is. Joy, sorrow, love, all depend on our thought, on the activity of our mind. If we are depressed, if we are in despair, it is still the work of our mind; our mind has prepared that for us; and if we are joyful and happy, and all things are pleasant, that also has been prepared for us by our mind. It is only when our mind works without control that unhappiness, sorrow, trouble, pain, or whatever we experience comes without our intention. No one could wish to create hell for himself; all would create heaven for themselves if they could; and yet how many allow their minds to create these things for them, regardless of their own intention.

The control of the activity of mind is called concentration in the language of the mystics. The meaning of this word is often not rightly understood. People are apt to think that concentration means only closing the eyes. But one may close one's eyes for hours, and still the thoughts keep coming like a moving picture. People are never at rest, never at peace; anxiety and sorrow do not disappear just because they close their eyes. It is concentration that does that. Concentration is activity of mind in the direction desired; our desire dictates in which way the mind is to be active; the mind acts according to our wishes.

How difficult it is to do this is best known by those who have tried. As soon as the mind is still and inactive it begins to jump and run away from control. It runs in every direction but in that which we wish. We hold it; it slips away. Not till one begins to try and concentrate does one see how uncontrollable and unruly the mind is.

This truth is pictured very well in the story from Ramayana, the great Hindu scripture, which tells about Rama's two children Lahu and Kusha*. The myth explains the condition of the human mind as being like that of an unruly horse. Is it not always running hither and thither; is it not like a wild horse running from place to place, farther away every time we think we are able to touch it? When a person says to himself, 'I will not think of anything', do not a thousand thoughts come? That shows that its nature is like that of the unruly horse, which needs skill to control it.

The key to the problem of controlling the mind, the key to concentration, is given to us by our elder brother, the murshid among the Sufis, the guru among the Hindus, who is a teacher with experience of the horse, having trained it and mastered it. He says, 'If you are without the right friend, you will perhaps succeed in catching the horse, and perhaps you will not. But if you know the right way in which to go about catching it, you will not be long in doing so'. That is why it is so necessary to have a method of concentration. Mystics, yogis, faqirs, ascetics, have a method; and by learning that method the concentration is easily obtained. When the mind is controlled and made into a vehicle, absolutely in our hand, working as we desire, then we can still it also.

The benefit of stilling is even greater. If one only grasped the benefit of perfect stillness, even of only the body! We see a symbol of that stillness in the statues of Buddha, or of Krishna, or in other idols. What an effect that has! Compare it with the effect of a person who comes into our presence and is always active, rubbing

* See p. 63.

his hands, moving about, raising his shoulders, making grimaces, tapping on the table, scratching, fidgeting in some way or another. Does he not make us fidget too? The whole atmosphere becomes disturbed. Why? Because there is an intense activity of mind having its effect on the body. The body and mind are both in an unrestful state, which affects everyone present, for it produces unrest in the whole atmosphere. We may not be conscious that this is so, but unconsciously we feel disturbed.

The great comfort that one finds after waking from a deep sleep cannot be compared with anything in the world; but more than that, the mystic sees in sleep the symbol of a great mystical state. Rumi, the Sufi teacher of Persia, says, 'O sleep, in thee I find the divine bliss. Thou makest patients forget their illness; thou makest kings forget for the moment that they are in a palace; thou makest the prisoners forget for a moment that they are in captivity. What bliss, what joy of bliss when the soul is freed from these limitations, from the presence of the different aspects of life that are keeping it captive!'

Sleep is the time when the soul is free. That is why deep sleep is so important a state to the mystic. In the East they say: when a person is asleep do not wake him; it is a great sin to do so. Of course in the West they cannot say this, because if he does not go to his work in the morning, what then? It would be a great sin if we did not wake him.

As there is such comfort and joy and so great a secret of heavenly peace during sound sleep, so there is a greater joy and peace and inspiration when the mind is stilled. The mind is so like water that our poets always call it the sea, the ocean. The nature of water is that as we look into it we see a face reflected there, our own image. If the water is not still, the face is not clear; when the water is still everything reflected in it is clear. So it is with the mind. When the mind is stilled it hears what another person says, it can ponder upon anything that it sees; and when one is sufficiently developed the mind can hear even what is said from the other side; even what God says from heaven.

Therefore it is those who have first accomplished stillness in their life, who have enabled the ears of their heart to listen to the Word of God. And what an atmosphere such persons can produce, what effect their presence has! It is more than healing, more than medicine. A man with a perfectly stilled, comforted, and rested mind will at once raise up another who is going through distress, or restlessness, or pain, or ill-temper, or worry, or anxiety. The very presence of one whose mind is stilled gives such hope, such inspiration, such sympathy, such power and life. All the heavenly properties flow so smoothly and freely from the person whose mind is stilled that his words, his voice, his presence, all react upon the mind of others; and as he stills his mind, so his very presence becomes healing.

MENTAL CREATION

SO ABSORBED are people in this visible creation that they very seldom think of the value of that other creation which exists within themselves. Those outer things that tempt, that attract attention, that are of interest, are all pursued by so many persons, who therefore become limited and unaware of that other creation which goes on unconsciously within.

In reality every man is a world within himself. But how little he reflects about it! He is always conscious of being just like a drop in the ocean, whereas he does not know of the other state of being, in which he is the ocean and everything else a drop.

There is a passage in one of the sacred books relating how God created the earth and then created the heavens. What does this mean? Was heaven created after the earth? The meaning is that this creation which is around us is first impressed upon the mind, and then the mind creates its own world, its own heaven. It is the creation of mind, a higher world, yet within ourselves; and this world may be heaven, or it may be the opposite. As Omar Khayyám writes, 'Heaven is the vision of fulfilled desire, and hell the shadow of a soul on fire', which shows that the desire is the source of heaven and its fulfilment. At the same time it is mental fire and disappointment, or worry, or anxiety, or torture that is the shadow of the soul on fire.

Centuries ago Zoroaster taught that there are three kinds of sin, and three kinds of virtue: those of thought, speech, and action.

A person always takes virtue to be virtue in action, sin to be sin in action, never thinking about virtue and sin in speech or thought. Sometimes man's thought is stronger than his speech or action. It is the experience of every mystic and every person who has trodden the path, that the power of thought is much greater than that of speech or action. In our everyday life we often find that if we think of a person bringing a certain book or flower we desire, he comes to see us, bringing this book or flower with him. We had not expressed the desire, and yet it has been fulfilled. Such is the power of thought, the creation of mind. 'Thoughts are things', it has been said. But they are more; thoughts are beings. They are as much living beings as we are; they work as we work; they have life in them. The body can generate, but the mind can generate too, it is the generation of the mind which we call thought or imagination. Thought is controlled, whereas imagination is not.

There is a saying in Sanskrit, 'There are numberless gods, and yet there is one God'. This means that as every planet is a world, so every mind is a world; it is a living world. The question is, if we make our world and mould our life, why should we have unhappiness, why have troubles in life, why have failures in life? The answer is that it is neither the fault of the Creator nor of the world; it is the fault of our ignorance; it is our lack of knowledge. Buddha pictures this lack of knowledge in this way: it is as if you are clinging to the branch of a tree in the thick darkness of night so that you cannot see what is beneath you, whether it is land or sea; so you are all the time afraid of falling. You keep on clinging to the tree and suffering with the fear of how long it will be before you have to let go, thinking, 'How long can I cling to this branch?' Yet under your feet there is nothing to be seen. Such is life until light comes. Then it is like the coming of the sun. When the sun rises you find there is no water, and hardly any space; for the ground is just beneath your feet.

The land of immortality seems so far from us. But when the sun of knowledge arises we see that it is near, so near. Once man knows that, he need not be taught morals or virtue; he knows what is best for him, whither to go; he knows his own creation. He knows that if he creates hideous spirits in his thoughts, they will become monsters which will work against him and will ruin his own life. But if man creates the spirit of love and kindness, others will help him in his need, and he will always be surrounded by love and kindness.

Once people realize this their life becomes different; they become the healers of men; they sympathize with the trouble of another; they serve in the difficulty of another; they seek to know if they cannot do something, cannot help in some way. A word may help; a thought of kindness and of sympathy will help. Whatever they do to others they do to themselves, because every thought of kindness or goodness or sympathy has generated a world of sympathy around it; and such persons cannot be without it. Even if they go to a land where no one knows them or understands them, they can still attract sympathy and love, if they have created that within themselves.

This shows how important it is to be careful of what one says. If one acts under the spell of anger, says such things as, 'I don't wish to see his face', or any evil words, then the speaker wishes he had not said or done such things after the spell has gone; not even about an enemy would he wish to have said these things. But at the time he did not realise that what he created lives. That which he has created he will be afraid of, and it will become his own enemy as well as the enemy of the person against whom his wrongful thought was directed. Not only that, but he will generate many more of the same kind. Once one bad thought is created, in the spirit of anger or annoyance, a thousand other spirits are created out of it. A world may be created by giving an outlet to one single weakness.

All that we collect and gather in the external world for our happiness and comfort is limited. Not even a thousandth part of this world that we possess can we really call our own kingdom, our world. But our mind can create and can collect numberless thoughts and impressions, which all make up its real world. All our possessions, all that we collect in life, all these things which we shall have to leave one day are transitory; but that which we have created in our thought, in our mind, that lives.

A person thinks, 'Some day I should like to build a factory'. At this time he has no money, no knowledge, no capability; but a thought came, 'Some day I should like to build a factory'. Then he thinks of something else. Perhaps years pass, but that thought has been working constantly through a thousand minds, and a thousand sources prepare for him that which he once desired. If we could look back to all we have thought of at different times, we would find that the line of fate or destiny, *Kismet* as it is called in the East, is formed by our thought. Thoughts have prepared for us that happiness or unhappiness which we experience. The whole of mysticism is founded on this.

If thoughts can accomplish this, so can love or imagination;

even a dream can accomplish it according to the impression which it makes. Some thoughts are like things, like objects, other thoughts are like beings. Some thoughts are like angels by our side, and some are like devils. They are all round us, either helping us towards the accomplishment of the objects before us, or drawing us back from those things we wish to accomplish.

One person may think, and perhaps the result of his thought is very feeble; another has a thought today, and tomorrow the desire is fulfilled. Why is this? It is because of the power of thought. In the thought of one person there is more life, in that of another there is less life. The difference between an object and a living thing is that there is more or less life in them. But where there is consciousness and activity we call that life, and we call that which lacks intelligence and consciousness an object. Yet in reality both are alive. A person with a weak will has no strength in his thought. If he thinks a thousand times, it has no effect, because he has not that vitality or energy which is necessary for thought to live.

What is the vitality which gives life to the thought? It is the same in man as in the vegetable or in the mineral kingdom. In one case the life is on the surface, in the other it is hidden. That is why we call them things in one case, and beings in the other. So there are dead thoughts, and there are living thoughts. To which class a thought belongs depends on the power called will-power. When there is will-power, the word is both spoken and done.

This idea is expressed by the words *Kalpa Vraksha*, the tree of desire. The story is that whoever happens to sit down for a moment under this tree will have his wish fulfilled; yet nobody knows where this tree is to be found. The tree is the mind; its root is the heart. That which gives power to thought, gives spirit or life to thought, is feeling. A man without feeling is as though dead; with feeling he is living, and so is his thought. Thought with feeling is a much greater power than thought without feeling. Merely to say, 'I like your picture so much' will have no effect when there is no feeling behind it. It is just a string of words. There is no life in it. But when these words are uttered with feeling they go through your heart also; the thought becomes living.

There have been great people whose living thoughts could make anyone live; they could impart life and heal. They have left their thoughts behind them, and people have treasured them as scriptures, as holy books; they have taken them for a religion. Such thoughts can never vanish nor die, such a long life has been given to them. Whatever form their thoughts have taken, whether music, prose, poetry, aphorisms or precious sayings that will never die, they will live for ever. There are others who have not known the value nor the immortal character of this creation of the mind; they pass through life without realizing its value. Such persons are foolish, stupid, grumbling all the time about people, and criticizing others.

A Hindustani poet has said, 'Beware before you speak a word; you do not know that this world is a dome, and that in a dome there is an echo'. So, in this world, whatever one utters is re-echoed. If a good thought is sent to a person, he may not know of it; yet we have sent a good thought, a thought of kindness, sincere sympathy and love. We may not tell him; we may not see him; but after even ten years we will find something was prepared for him; something has made the friendship closer. He will know that we have thought about him. The secret of this is that life is one. In it all these phantoms live and move; and we think that everybody is a different life, and yet there is only one life, which the mystic calls God, who cannot be divided.

The Sufi says that man is not a part of God, for how can God be divided? Can one divide space? Since space cannot be divided, how can God be? How can this one life be divided? There is no division. There is no wall between any two people in this world.

Whether the thought be of bitterness, or sympathy, or love, or kindness, it reaches the other person. When the thought has feeling behind it, it has life, whether the feeling be of bitterness or of kindness. If it is bitterness it will destroy. But the consequence of such a thought will be that it will return to the giver; it will surely rebound; it will surely return to him who sent it. Whether it was bitterness, or whether it was kindness it will return just the same. But more than that: this thought generates as surely as do germs and worms. One thought of love gathers a thousand beings of love and kindness around one.

There is a prophecy in the Bible that when the next Teacher comes, he will bring ten thousand holy ones in his army. What does this mean? Does it mean ten thousand visible people? No, there will be numberless thoughts of goodwill and service to mankind which will become his army.

Externally we are a single being, but internally we are a world. As vast as is the world around us, so vast is the world within. Asif says, 'The limitation of the sky and land cannot be compared with man's heart. If man's heart be wide, there is nothing wider than this'. All can be accommodated in it; heaven earth, sun, moon, all are reflected in it. It becomes itself the whole. This world becomes as one chooses to make it. If man only knew that! But since he does not know that, the world is not heaven, but has become its opposite. We blame others for our sorrows and misfortunes, not perceiving that we ourselves are the creators of our world; that our world has an influence upon our life within as well as upon our life without. For instance, if a person is blamed by the self within, he will be blamed by everybody else, and if he is admired by it, he will be admired by all around; if the self within feels guilty towards someone in the external world, he will feel guilty, and if it feels doubt about the right spiritual path, he will go through the world in that spirit of doubt.

We read in the scripture how Moses spoke with God on Mount Sinai. The angel Gabriel brought a message to the prophet. What was the angel? What was Mount Sinai? Mount Sinai is the mind of man; God is within it; it is man's feeling that builds a bridge from man's mind to the mount of God.

Rumi says so beautifully, 'There is a flute, one end of which is between the lips of God, and the other end of the flute is in the heart of man'. What a wonderful metaphor! When man's heart is awakened, when the thoughts have become living beings, then whenever this feeling comes its current runs from infinite to finite, from the objective world back to the world unseen, from God to man. A current is established. It is man's thought which is the bridge to heaven.

Whatever the thought of man has built, it becomes his heaven, with the singers, the Upsaras and fair ones. This is the true heaven. A man with an army of beautiful thoughts is in the Garden of Eden. He has produced a garden within himself. There is a verse of Bedil, 'These beautiful gardens and flower-beds, if you wish to have them round you, you need not go and see them in the external world. You need only open the gate of your heart to see them there, and you will enjoy them.'

People think such a world is only imagination, only exists in thought; but really this world is the only one that will remain in the hereafter. There will not be any other world, for this physical world will not remain. Every soul is creating a world. However vast a planet may seem in comparison with the mind of man, in reality the mind of man is vaster. There is a world in this planet. As the Hindus have said, 'Our planet has a god, and man is the god of his planet'.

First one must know what one needs and become the master of oneself and of one's thoughts and one's life. Then one's personality will become agreeable and pleasant to others, and one will become a blessing to all one meets in this world.

THE ATTAINMENT OF POWER

THE POSSESSION of power brings with it the desire to attain more. We can attain everything that we desire if we only know how. No one attains a higher position unless he follows some hidden trend. The tendency to arrive at some perfection is that which causes one to attain a greater perfection. Even if he attains wealth, a man is tending towards perfection. Napoleon attained something hidden which was great and wonderful, if we could only understand it. So a merchant may perhaps have begun by selling empty bottles, and ultimately becomes wealthy enough to be able to found colleges, libraries, hospitals, and so forth, which proves that there was an inclination to a certain perfection. Even though the ideal may not be so high, the very inclination to attain power is a great force.

There is a spiritual, psychic, occult, telepathic power. How are we to attain to that? The soul feels, 'I am a king, but in this mortal casket I have become a pauper', or as Rumi expresses it, 'I was created free, but in this flesh I am in captivity and have become weak'. From an almighty state of being we have become helpless beings. When we become conscious of spirit, we become conscious of a mighty power hidden; and our spirit is then the expression of the Almighty Power.

The power is in unity, but is lost in variety. Thus, for instance, if we hold a thing in our hand, we can hold it with strength, because all five fingers have united to hold the object. But if we try to lift it by one finger, this one finger may drop it, even though the finger belongs to the same hand. In all aspects of life unity is power. All religions show that power is in unity. This is the secret of philosophy.

There are two aspects of unity: firstly, the unity of variety; secondly, unity realizing itself. One is earthly, the other is heavenly. One cannot serve two masters. Unity is the only source of happiness. Unity in realization is far greater than unity in variety.

'When two hearts unite, they can break even mountains'. As two fuse in love, the more does intuition grow, the more does one understand whether the other is happy, or pleased, or displeased, whatever distance may separate them. This is nothing but just the unity of the one person with the other. It is clairvoyance. The mother knows the condition of her son at the battle front. She can see him in her dreams. Hearts which are united in love perceive the state of mind of the loved ones. They do not have to study mysticism or concentration, for they have natural concentration. The mother does not pretend to meditate; love teaches her more meditation than a person who pretends to study it can attain. One cannot, however, hold an object in mind when the heart has nothing to do with the object. Pebbles are not made to eat, and therefore one cannot eat them. The mind is never so satisfied with either an object or a being which it does not desire; therefore it is no use to concentrate specially on what the heart does not desire. The heart which does desire needs no special concentration.

Nothing gives greater power of confidence than love. If one loves a person, one has confidence in that person. Hence the mother is as a god to her child. The hen is the most timid of birds until she has chickens; at that time she is under the spell of love, and would not hesitate to fight even an elephant if he were endangering her brood. This shows the power of love. Can any charm or amulet be more powerful than this? The one with a loving heart will travel furthest.

Power can be attained artificially, by magic, or by the different laws of the power of sound, of words, or of concentration. Such power can make a person ill, can make a person run away from the country, can make two hearts separate; many wonders can be performed by the power of concentration.

We do not exist only as body; we exist as heart, as soul. If the heart is kept dead all our life, and we give the body all the things it wants, soft cushions and comforts, is this all we need? The heart is still hungering. The heart wants to see that it is living. The heart longs to be alive. It has been created to love, and it is not loved; it wants to melt. But though it wants all the love and kindness to come to it, it withholds giving when the time comes for it to give.

We accept love when love is offered to us, but when the time comes to give, we do not give. But can love really be given? Is love trade? Until this is known, it is impossible to understand love.

To love is to possess a heart, but not as a demon possesses a human being. When a person 'comes alive', this means that he has become the possessor of a heart. Whose heart? Heart is that factor of our being, of our thinking, which feels within itself a longing to express love; it is an awakening of love and to a feeling of love. This is the factor which produces thought; this is the factor which produces feeling; in this lies the creative power. All the power which one can possibly wish to attain throughout life is reached by this means.

How can power develop in the absence of unity? Suppose everyone had magnetic power. They would make all the money they could from their clients. Would it be just for some to possess the power of making money, and for others to be perpetually their victims? No, and that is why mysticism was kept hidden for the protection of these others. Those who are not worthy of the hidden knowledge would use their power for selfish purposes, for themselves and for those who belong to them. If ordinary people had this power, one could not even compare them with the devil. Rishis, saints, and sages have experienced the selfishness of man. They know it would be bad for the world if this hidden knowledge were revealed. And who deserves to be illuminated with this knowledge? He alone deserves it who develops his soul in the thought of unity; and he alone receives it.

The progressive steps of enlightenment in the use of power are shown when a man transfers his ambitions first to his family and then from his family to his city, from his city to his nation, from his nation to the whole world, and from the whole world to the whole universe. When the joy of every person he sees is his joy, when the pain of every person is his pain, then he becomes a conqueror and attains power.

WHAT THE POWER OF BREATH CAN DO

BREATH, being the secret of all being, is the most important of all things. Whether we have a fine body or not has nothing to do with it. If we gain in weight, we are only getting a heavier coat; but our true being is the breath. When the breath has left the body, the body is useless. Therefore the importance of our being lies in the breath.

Breath is God. If God is manifest in anything, it is in breath. The activity of our physical being depends on our breath. This keeps up the rhythm of the pulse and the rhythm of the beats of the brain. The centres are kept up by the rhythm. If the rhythm stops, the centres stop. As the tick of the watch, so is the swing of the breath. According to the rhythm, so is the condition of the body. Disorder in breath means illness.

In anger the rhythm of breathing is much quicker, even so much as to make speech impossible. The saying, 'speechless with anger' is proverbial. Therefore the breath acts on the mind as well. The lion, the leopard, and other fierce creatures have a very irregular breath; there is no rhythm; they are short-lived. The cobra never becomes excited; it breathes slowly, and attracts its food from any distance by mere concentration of will. It is very long-lived.

Breathing is the effect of breath. It is really a vibration rising and falling. There is a vibration in all things, in life and birth, and consequently all things have rhythm. It is the activity of God and nothing else. There are different rhythms for the day, the hour, the minute, for forty days. There is a connection between this rhythm and the life of the universe like so many candles and lamps.

Word; light; creation. The breath is the Word. We cannot utter a word without breath. But a word is double as it consists of breath and sound, and breath stands by itself. The sense comes before the sound.

Athletic exercises are basically exercises of breathing. A porter does not become physically developed because he does not use his breathing for that purpose. He has had exercise without benefit. If the breath did not manifest through the voice, it would manifest in some other way, as the absent sound of thought. Wherever it is directed, it will go. If you do not speak and yet think the same thought, the breath will travel silently. People think they cannot hear except with their ears, they are so attached to their physical body. But as soon as a man is convinced that he can hear without ears, he will do so without speech. One can tell that a person is angry without his speaking, because he reveals it in his whole vibration. The very way a person says 'yes' tells you whether he is willing or not willing; it depends on the character of the breath at that moment.

People who live a material life, reveal it because the breath becomes material and makes a noise. It has become so dense that it actually makes a noise. In refined persons the breath is also fine. Cows and camels and buffaloes make a noise when they breathe. This at once shows the fineness or coarseness of the individual. Those who perceive these things can see them clearly.

All the different moods that we are in—inclination to laughter or crying, heaviness, exaltation, or meditation—all result from the breath. It changes in activity so many times during the day and night. As it changes, it expresses a certain element, earth, water, fire, air, or ether, and it makes one feel inclined to do certain things in accordance with the element.

All the different desires originate in breath; even the character of a person, even his luck, all depend on the breath. Those who know the mystery of breath can read the soul. Breath is a link from God to man. Breath is purified by prayer. Fire-worshippers keep a fire before them in order to keep their breath in rhythm.

The science of breath is only transmitted by word of voice from the teacher when he sees someone worthy to learn. There are three stages: *Jelal*, force of breath; *Jemal*, the gentleness of breath; *Kemal*, perfection of breath. The latter stage culminates in miracles.

A book is a dead teacher. People continually send their breath into undesirable centres. It is essential to have a living guide, and not to try and study from books; a pure and good life is far better for the breathing. Do not let tranquillity be disturbed, and the rhythm of the breath will keep regular; the mind will keep in good condition, and the body healthy.

Do not be too attached to anything in the world; do not be a slave to anything. Be beyond all desires. Observe the law of cleanliness, the law of balance, doing good to others, having good wishes, good thoughts, keeping a high ideal, and always wishing to attain the ideal. By doing these things the breath itself will become fixed in the same mould.

THE KNOWLEDGE OF PAST, PRESENT, AND FUTURE

'WHAT NEED is there of effort in life, if the future is already settled?' asks one. Says another, 'There is no predestination, for everything that happens is caused by ourselves'. A person may be trying to do good, and yet may always find it turning to bad. Such a one comes to ask, 'Is there any interference by spirits?' The Sufi studies what darkness is in order to understand the light; that is Sufism.

The artist paints a picture in three stages: preparatory; stage of action; stage of completion—past, present, and future. The first stage is the design of the picture; that is predestination. We all begin with this. We are the manifestation of the eternal Sun, and therefore all the attributes of the Creator must be in the creature. Before doing anything do we not plan it? In our mind we have created it. The Creator acted thus, and so do we. We do it with a pen; He does it with nature. His art is nature. The Qur'an says that Allah taught man by the pen of His nature. It is our nature to create and by creating our art in harmony with nature we can prove our skill. The art we produce is according to the nature of ourselves, for we are the creator.

Secondly, the picture appears on the paper; this is the present stage. Thirdly, the picture itself inspires the painter. As it progresses he sees that in a certain place there ought to be a different colour; this is not right, that is not right, and so on. And as he looks at the picture, he sees its faults, and so he alters it here and there. So it is with each life. One stage of our life is predestined, the next part is that which we perform, and a third part of our life is that which is the effect of our actions. As we sow, so we reap. All that we do, we see in its reaction, and the reaction changes our life. The painter sees he must finish the picture differently, and so our actions tell us whether we ought to act differently.

A man always wants to know things he does not know; this

dates from infancy. Children break things to see what is inside. But man does not know how to know; he expects too much. When he knows how to know, then heaven and earth are both revealed to him. If we want to see what is on the seventh floor, we must leave the ground floor. If we are on the first floor and cannot get to the higher floors, it means, as mysticism shows, that we certainly do wish to go up, but are captives on the first floor. That is the captivity.

Rumi said, 'The bamboo flute, what is it that the flute says that makes you like it so much? Why does it mourn? Why does it so attract your attention? What is it that appeals to you? It mourns for the separation that it suffers; because it has been parted from its home, and has lost its original plant, the bamboo. It was cut off from its proper place. It mourns for the days when it was one with the whole bamboo tree; it mourns for the joy and the peace which it has enjoyed, but can never receive again. It is the parting for which it mourns, and through which it appeals to you.'

So has it been with man. Man wishes to know about God, about heaven, about the things unknown, and about the world unseen, and he thinks he can see them from the first floor. He is not ready to believe there is anything on the seventh floor; he thinks there is no such thing as a seventh floor, nothing but the first. If he were freed from this delusion, and if he were allowed to go to the other floors, then he would be able to see what the fourth, fifth, sixth, and seventh floors contain. And then he would know there is something through which one can gain a knowledge of past, present, and future.

Suppose on the third floor there was a machine which produced instruments, one would know that on the first floor there must be a store of materials, and on the second floor they must be assembled in groups; on the third floor they are turned into usable appliances; and one can guess what is likely to be on the fourth floor.

Thus it is said in the Hadith that God sent His servant the Prophet in the middle of the night to the sphere of heaven, where He showed him such signs as He desired to show him. In other words, God wants the one who wishes to realize Him, to know life; it is His desire that he may see the signs that God previously makes and arranges, and also the things which can be seen by rising to the third and fourth floors.

The floors represent planes of existence. We do not exist only on the earthly or physical plane. Being absorbed in this plane makes us awake to it, but blind to the others. Language fails to explain the things of heaven. Those who have the experience of such things are bound to be silent, because there is no language to express them.

As a matter of fact all the floors are really here; but as long as we are not able to see these floors, we are only on the first. Then, too, this mortal part must die; but we can die in this respect now, and pass on now to a perception that is beyond. The several floors are nothing but clothing. In this life the light is hidden under a bushel; the bushel is the physical body. The light cannot be disclosed until the mortal part is removed.

If we depend on our eyes for sight, and our ears for hearing, and our mouth for speech, we are still dead. But we sometimes experience in life that which we see without eyes, hear without ears, and express without speech. If we have once seen without eyes, does it not show that we can see without eyes? Can we not see in a dream without eyes? Therefore the faculty of seeing and hearing is in us; but as we always depend on the physical body, on the physical eyes and ears, we become helpless and subject to death.

The teaching of immortality is to awaken. We must rise above physical and material conditions if we are to live at all. We must aim at being independent of physical sight and hearing. We know that if we really want to understand a thing, we close our eyes because we can see it better. If we are thinking in this manner, it means that we are listening to some thought coming from some other plane. At such a time we want to cut off and stop outward sound or sight. All the meditations and concentrations of the mystics, as well as their dreams, are their journeys to the inner planes. It is necessary, if the soul has the desire to know the past, the present, and the future, to satisfy its desire by a contemplative life. The more tired and exhausted the mind, the more is meditation needed.

Sages, such as St. Francis, have spoken with rocks, birds, and animals, not as we talk, but by means of an insight into things; and every object expressed itself to them, speaking to them about its past, its present, and its future.

How wonderful that the animals and birds also know the future! Horses, dogs, cats know when someone is going to die; and yet man does not know it. Why should he not know it? Because his soul is so absorbed in the earth plane and in earthly things which the birds and beasts and animals are free from; for they sit quietly, and meditate and concentrate. Man never sits quietly; and therefore the animals and birds, through their silence, are capable of knowing what man does not know. All man's activity brings death and decay much sooner; intuition is stifled.

The soul has a tendency to look forward to what is going to be, or at what has been in the past. It is the light of our soul, the intelligence, that does this. Intelligence working through physical means is no greater than intellect, but intelligence working freely and independently from physical means is wisdom. And wisdom is not cleverness, but infinitely superior to it. Wisdom works independently of the physical means, and therefore requires intuition. The clever person works by means of his physical body, but the wise person works independently of it.

Palmistry, astrology, and the like, are they the best means of knowing the future? All these means are right, none is wrong. There is always truth everywhere. The eye must look, and at whatever it looks, the seer will see. It is not necessary for the vision to be in a certain symbol or tea-cup; it is as open as a book wherever the seer looks.

The master knows everything that goes on in a factory, but the workers only know what goes on just where they are working. The master sees all. One person sees a square, another a street, another a house, another less still. But the one at the top of the tower will see all of these. The seer will see all in his consciousness, and wherever he casts his glance he will see still more clearly. As Sa'di says, 'Each leaf of a tree becomes a book of revelation to the one who sees; and he reads the whole of nature as a book'.

SPIRITS AND SPIRITISM

SPIRIT in its true sense is the essence. The spirit of anything means its essence. And when we consider the true essence there is only one. When we consider the true spirit there is only one spirit.

But of course in the world of variety one life is many lives and one thing has many manifestations. This manifestation makes us see many forms and many names of a one and only Being; and when we overlook the oneness of that Being and direct our attention to the variety of manifestation, we see that the spirit of each thing is its essence. The spirit of jasmine, the spirit of a rose, and so on; each has its own individuality, its own essence.

Spirit, as understood by the generality, is the remainder of man's existence. After man's body had died, what remains of him is considered to be spirit, which has a very beautiful name in Sanskrit: *Bhut*, that is, 'the one who has been'.

The spirit world distinguishes itself as different and distinct from the spirit experiencing the world through the body. The spirit of camphor is not the colour or form of the substance, but the odour of camphor has existed in its spirit. The spirit of cinnamon is the fragrance and the effect that it has. The effect is still left after its form and substance have gone. Every object in this world, after it has vanished, leaves a mark of its essence just like the flower. When the essence is taken from the flower its external form is ruined, but it has left something which is its own. Both body and spirit are man. Man is a double spirit. Man in his cloak, his physical body, is more complete than a spirit alone. When the flower is living and its spirit has not been taken away from it, both the flower and its spirit are joined. A person whose sense of discrimination and feeling is well developed may find that a visitor coming into the house brings with him a certain influence: good feeling or bad feeling, an irritable feeling or a blissful feeling. There is something with him besides his knowledge, besides his beauty; when he leaves the house his body leaves, and together with it his strength and beauty, all that is material in him; yet there is something left in that room for a certain time after he has gone. The whole atmosphere is charged and we feel that there is something left there. The more keenly we watch life, the more wonderful it is. All the miracles and phenomena are before us; our everyday life is a miracle. If we are only absorbed in things which are material and not in things of a delicate character, we do not see this because we blunt our sensitivity. It is then that we think that what we do not see or perceive does not exist. Consider, for instance, how infectious yawning is. This shows we can never say there is nothing beyond what the eyes and flesh can see.

Influence goes out from a living person and affects others in the vicinity. If the influence is so strong during life, shall it not exist after he is dead? Only the influence remains after he has left, yet how much greater must it then be! The light of the moon is the light of the sun.

There are two actions of sense, which are in fact two actions of the whole being: expressiveness and responsiveness. The whole universe works on these two principles. As soon as the expressing spirit expresses itself, the responsive spirit receives its impression, just as a person whose picture is taken by a camera yields his impression when the camera is properly adjusted. If the camera is not rightly placed, there will be no image on the plate. If a spirit has a fondness for someone and desires to be in the thought of this beloved one all the time, always near him, then, just like a camera taking a photograph of someone, this unconscious spirit of man naturally takes the impression coming from that spirit.

Child prodigies may be the result of influence; under this influence they may work, speak, write poems, dispute, and so on. If someone dies with the thought of revenge that he could not accomplish, or had not the courage to accomplish, he may find a living person, a youth perhaps or a child, who performs the act for the spirit without even knowing why. Murders may even happen in this way.

The brain may be deficient in thinking power; the body may react on thought, and sometimes the thought may react on the body. Could not the mind produce decay in the brain, or is it true that it is always bodily strain that brings strain of mind?

Or does anger bring a strain on the body? The trouble usually comes from within.

Hallucinations sometimes arise from thought and mind, either in the same person or in some other person. We call it obsession when it comes from without.

Sometimes the living person can be the expressive one while the spirit responds. We cover our spirit under our body. We cover our light under a bushel. We never allow the spirit to become conscious of itself.

We are not doing spirits any good by calling them back when they have no body. Why not let them forget the experiences of this world of illusion rather than attract them? What good will it do to them? One should only trouble others when one needs them very much. We should use ourselves as the vehicle of all experiences. We can communicate much better with another person who is clothed like us than we can with a spirit.

Is not God enough for our souls, and is He not sufficient to inspire us and to illuminate our wills and guide our souls? Is He any less than a friend here or in the spirit life? He is the great well-wisher. In Him mercy is complete. He is the Soul of all souls. When we devote ourselves to the thought of Him, all illumination and revelation are ours. God-communication is the best communication that true spiritualism can teach us.

If we give all our wealth to the universe as a whole, no single person receives much. But it is a great accomplishment actually to realize God; it means that a very high degree of spirituality has been attained. It is most difficult to attain such a conviction of God that there is not the slightest doubt; but if someone does reach it, even the thought of him will bring blessing; it becomes a privilege to be his friend. It is a privilege because he is the friend of God.

A person possesses the knowledge which he has attained as he possesses the wealth which he has acquired. And so when the soul is illuminated it will desire to find some other soul illuminated in like manner, and will find great joy and bliss in its society. Such a one will surely find others who are on the verge of illumination. Even a drunkard will find others to drink with; and so it is mystically. A very little light can be turned into a flame, and that flame into a very big flame.

Why is it better to become a mystic than to remain a drunkard? As a matter of fact a drunkard will never be satisfied. The mystic will look for what Omar Khayyám calls wine, the wine of the Christ, after drinking which no one will ever thirst. He will always seek the wine whose intoxication never wears off. It is the only wine: the intoxication of the divine love.

THE MASTER MIND

IN THE first place what is the mind? Is it the intelligence of the brain, is it the activity of the brain, or is it something else? When a person limits the word mind to brain, he certainly puts cause and effect on the same level.

There are two ways of looking at things: one looking from the cause to the effect; the other from the effect to the cause. The first is like looking from the top of the mountain to the foot; the other is like looking from the foot of the mountain to the top. The one who looks from the foot often fails to see what is going on at the top. Therefore the mystic follows the other way. He perceives that a person who investigates a higher truth by standing at the foot of the mountain may sometimes succeed in seeing what is at the top, yet sometimes he will not; and even when he does see, he does not see fully. It is different when a person looks from the top of the mountain to the foot; and that is why the mystic goes to the cause, and sees from the cause to the effect.

But the great thing is to get to the cause. It is easy to agree with the teaching of Jesus Christ, 'Seek ye first the kingdom of God, and all things shall be added'. This teaching may be applied even in the investigation of human life, for as soon as one reaches the root of the cause one can see the light, and the light guides one. But what is difficult is to get in when one is on the outside.

Humanity has striven after truth for ages; and yet there is no period in the history of the world in which some of mankind have not realized the truth. The only difference is that one says, 'I have discovered something', and the other says, 'There is nothing new under the sun'. The mystic's view is, 'What I have known today has been known before, and will be known afterwards'. It has never been known by all, and will never be known by all; but as the sight becomes keen, so man will be able to see.

In the first place, what the master mind is, is really explained by the power of spirit over matter. When man sees that mountains are pierced through by the effort of man, that man has crossed the seas, and that he flies in the air, that in itself shows that he is the master of creation.

But what is man? Is man a physical being, or is there something else called man? If the physical being is man, then what of the elephant, who is twenty times bigger? Then the elephant would never have listened for one moment to what man says, and yet when he says, 'Sit down', the elephant sits down; 'Stand', and he stands; 'Walk', and he walks. At the same time the elephant is conscious of his heavy body, and the strength that he has. Then not only the elephant, but the tiger and the lion—the kings of the forest as they call them in the East—we can see them mastered in the circus by one man. Although these most brutal animals keep killing other animals, and live by the terror they evoke, so conscious are they of their strength, yet man has mastered them. Evidently there is something hidden in man. The word man means mind, and when the time came for mind to develop, man came into being; the physical being had been developed as long as the animal being.

There is also the question as to whether every man can really claim to be human, or as to what a human mind should be. This is shown by the story that one day Diogenes went searching in the market-place with a lighted lantern at midday, and when they asked him what he sought, he answered, 'A man'. And Ghalib, a Hindustani poet of Delhi, has said in his verse, 'There seems to be a difficulty in all things; it seems difficult even for a man to claim to be a man'.

The question is, what is the difference between man and animal? Is it not in the form of the man? But if only the form is man, strictly speaking all natural forms in this world gradually change into the human form. The more we study the life of birds, insects, creatures, or even the vegetable kingdom, the more plainly we shall see how the face of man has emerged, step by step, from the primitive preparatory stages, through all the different manifestations, until it has appeared as man. Thus if it were only the form that makes man man, he would never have been called mind; so it is something beyond form that makes man.

The whole matter is explained by Rumi in his Masnavi, 'Our

life on earth is as a captivity, an imprisonment'. An imprisonment in what? In a physical body which covers the light of the soul. And the mind is also helplessly attached to the body. It is the bodily desires, passion, anger, appetite, all the different desires and needs, that make the mind helpless and make man hold on to them. All the worries, anxieties, depressions, and despairs arise from them. There is not a single moment in which the mind is able to stand aloof so as to reflect the light within, the light of the soul, so limited has it been made by the limited existence on earth. In reality this is the whole tragedy of human life.

The one and only thing that hinders man from advancing spiritually, or at least from advancing towards the goal for which he is destined and which he is longing to attain, is this: that the mind is so absorbed by the demands and wants of the physical body that it has hardly a moment to give itself entirely to the reflection of the light of the soul.

A person may say, 'I do not even believe in such a thing as soul, since there is no evidence of such a thing; I do not believe in a hereafter; I do not believe in anything spiritual or higher, only in what I see or enjoy in this worldly life'. But what then? One could answer, 'You believe at least in being happy; you believe in happiness being something worth attaining in life; you also believe in living; you do not wish to die. Not only do you believe in these two things, but you believe in being left alone when you are tired, in being left in peace and having rest. You believe in understanding things you cannot yet understand'. So he believes in four things. He may not believe in inspiration, revelation, or some higher spirit coming and instructing him, yet he believes in trying to understand things that puzzle him; in seeking to remove that cloud of confusion which veils the light that would guide him to the understanding of those very things which at present confuse him. So there is a longing in him to find out about something he does not know.

In every person, therefore, whether spiritual or material, whatever his outlook, there are these four inclinations or desires: to live, to save his life even to the extent of risking it in order to defend himself against being killed; to be happy, enjoying the theatre, music, dancing, singing, a game, sport, something that pleases; a desire to know; and a desire to have peace, to rest, to be left alone. Whether he believes in God, in spirit, in heaven, in a scripture, in a hereafter or not, he certainly believes in these four things. They develop gradually. As one studies more and more the way to acquire these things, that study itself becomes a form of religion; and attainment to the root of the four things is spiritual perfection. The difference is only that one takes a religious path, another the path of wisdom, another the path of devotion, and another the path of the form or ceremonial of worship. Whichever way it be, the constant pursuit of these four things brings the attainment of the same goal in the end, the goal for every soul. Some paths lead there sooner than others, that is all.

If we think more about the desire for happiness, we see that although every soul seeks after pleasure, or wealth, or position, or power to become happy, he finds that everything in life is changeable. Whatever pleasure, or success, or achievement he gains, are all forms of desire for happiness, and these can only be held like air. How long can one hold that? Is it not always slipping from one's hands, be it wealth or position? The most difficult thing in life is to hold it when one has it. It is true it is difficult to acquire, but how much more difficult to keep! Thousands of people are after it. 'How can we get it from him?' they ask. Relatives, friends, enemies, thieves, everybody is contemplating his wealth; while he holds it tight, more and more worried about it every day. So on the one side there is the happiness of holding something which is not his own, and on the other the strain of keeping safe that which does not really belong to him, and which is changeable and temporary. This takes away his happiness.

All the things that give happiness seem so great a prize beforehand; but, however much pleasure and comfort they may give, when it comes to paying the cost of having them one begins to understand that there is no comfort or pleasure that is really worth while. As Omar Khayyám says, when man is seeking for happiness, all pleasures and comforts seem to be a blessing for that moment; but in the end everything is dust.

There is a beautiful story illustrating this idea. In the palace of a Moghul king there was a housemaid, and once when making the bed she was overpowered by the sense of the beauty of the king's room, the fragrance all round, the windows open allowing the cool breeze to come in, so grateful when the summers are as hot as in the East. She felt she would like to sit on the bed a moment and see how it felt. How very soft and nice and how very fragrant, she thought. And she sat there, and then felt she would like to lean back on the cushions. But unfortunately she fell asleep. Then the king and queen happened to come in. He said, 'What impertinence', and the queen was very displeased too.

In a moment a whip fell on her back, and she got up in horror, and looked hither and thither and then smiled. And the king and queen were astonished to see her smile on receiving the whip. Said the queen, 'Why do you smile?' She said, 'O, it was a thought'. The king said, 'Tell me the thought'. She said, 'The thought was that it is so fragrant in this room, and the cool breeze so balmy and this bed so soft and comfortable, I thought I should like to see how it felt, and I slept; perhaps I did not sleep for more than half an hour and you came, and I received the whip. By sleeping there for half an hour I receive the whip, so I do not know what you will receive. You have been sleeping here for years together!'

This is a lesson. There is no pleasure to be gained without a cost; it may be at the cost of wealth or of time; it may even be at the cost of life. Man, absorbed as he is in the pleasures and comforts of life, thinks very little of this, and goes on until the time comes when it is too late to think of it. Life has been nothing but a captivity to this constant longing for happiness and pleasure, which when it comes he finds himself unable to enjoy.

So this teaches that the source of real happiness lies somewhere else. It is not in a building of sand that comfort can be got. The building in which one can get comfort is in oneself. Having discovered the nature of pleasures one may well think, 'After all, these pleasures were just like lips touching the wine and not drinking it. The wine is somewhere else.' But in the end even the pleasure-seeker comes to the same goal, that of the truth.

The third thing is the constant desire to live. Every bird, every animal, even the smallest insect in the world, as soon as we try to touch it, it wishes to save its life; it runs away, it wants to live;

even if it lives in the dirt its desire is to live. How dear life is to every creature. How much everybody wishes to live! At the same time there is this force of destruction in the form of diseases and death, which sweep away so many; yet still the desire in every heart is to live. This thought teaches that it is not believing in God, in spirit, in religion, that is the secret; it is the desire for life in every heart. This, too, man can find by searching within himself. The life is hidden within him, and when he begins to find it then he feels he is safe.

If we think about the desire for understanding, we notice how everyone wishes to learn, to read, to study, to learn about things in every possible way. But the desire cannot be satisfied until the light within is disclosed by which he may understand. We come then to the truth that all things can be accomplished by mastery of mind. And so the question arises, 'How can the mind be mastered?' The answer is that the mind cannot be mastered until a man is master of the body. The difference between a master mind and a person without mastery is the difference between a man sitting on a saddle horse, holding the reins in his hand, and a man trying to ride bareback while the horse is bucking and going wherever it likes, and there is the fear that it will throw him at any moment; he is not able to control it.

A person may realize all the various weaknesses in himself, and be very sorry about them, and he would like to give them up if he could; but he finds that whether he likes some little weakness or not, he cannot hold himself back from doing certain things, whether it is weakness of mind or weakness of action. This shows that though the desire of the soul is always to direct man on the right path, on the path of virtue, on the good path, yet at the same time he has lost his control, and he is led away by some force he cannot control. This weakness of character is shown when a person says, 'I do not wish to be angry; after being angry I am very sorry, but at the same time I cannot help it. I do not wish to hurt others, but when the moment comes I cannot help myself, I am abrupt.' Then even vices such as drink, or thieving, or any weakness, are all caused by weakness of mind. When the mind has no control over its thoughts and feelings, when it is not mastered, all these things come to pass.

From all this it is plain that man has two aspects of being: the servant aspect and the master aspect. When only the servant aspect is nourished and the master aspect is not, then the master aspect of his being longs to be master, and cannot be; and the whole conflict in life depends on that. When a person is interested in the master aspect and wishes to be master, then he becomes master of himself; and he becomes not only master of his thoughts, feelings, and actions, but he becomes master of his affairs. Then the key to what we call fate is in his hands; he becomes the king of the kingdom that has been given to him from God; and when he has arrived at that stage, then comes a still greater and more exalted stage which may be understood in the following way.

Sometimes we notice that a person is guided by someone, or listens to him, or gives in to him. Why does he do this? The answer is, that the one who does not give in is the one with the master aspect alive in him; the person who gives in has the servant aspect alive in him. To understand this secret is to understand the secret of the spiritual hierarchy. It is the secret of the coming of the prophets and of the master mind, of what is called the superman. The picture of this is shown in Hindu symbology, where the Devatas have four hands, two hands for the body, and two for the mind. The four make a perfect man. When there are only two external hands, material hands, and the other hands are not yet attached to the mind, the mind is not active and cannot control. There are these four different forces: the two physical arms and the two arms of mind, which make life complete; the four arms that make the perfect man, the master mind.

Having these, he becomes responsible for his affairs as well as the affairs of others; and the people who have been leaders of nations, leaders of humanity, and have led humanity to the spiritual, the right, the religious path, have not done so just through their intellect. No, there was some other power behind.

There are many intellectual people who from morning till evening spend every moment of their time in using their cleverness and polish of mind. But this is only an activity; it is not the power of mind. The power of mind is such that without speaking words the mind speaks. Without the help of words, the mind reflects what is in this mind or that. Things that the outer arms cannot accomplish the arms of the mind can. Means are procured for the accomplishment of every object. In the ancient fairy-tales about the jinns it is said that one day a village teacher was teaching a class. Among them was a jinn, and he had taken the form of a boy. But the village teacher did not know that he was a jinn. One day he wanted something at a distance, and he asked the boy to bring it. This boy, instead of getting up, just stretched his hand and got it. And the teacher was so frightened that next day he would not admit him to the school.

This story tells us of the master mind. It is not necessary to be of a certain age to have this mastery. Sometimes a child may have greater mastery than a grown-up, and greater will. Therefore it is not dependent on age. 'Where there is a will, there is a way.'

For a man to say, 'Beware of me, I cannot keep a secret; I cannot control myself, I must tell it; I cannot manage this; I cannot remember that'—all these weaknesses denote lack of mastery of mind. The master mind shows mastery in everything: in speech, in listening, in understanding, in doing all things.

Is this to be attained by contemplation, by concentration, by meditation? No, actually it is in our everyday life, in our simple everyday actions that we develop the power of mind by this simple law: when we are doing some work and the desire comes, 'No, I must go and rest and sleep', and we go and rest, we give in to our desire. We go and rest, but the work is not accomplished. Then a person may say, 'I must not be abrupt, inconsiderate; I must have consideration from now on'. Next day something happens in which he should be considerate and gentle, but he thinks, 'In this case it does not matter; it is a small thing; it is a very small thing', and gives in. The excuse comes to the rescue; but as soon as he gives in to a slight weakness, next time he falls down again because the weakness wins every time. So every person seeking to attain mastery will find some weakness waiting for him; if it is not one weakness, then it will be another.

The one who does not think of this law is neglectful. He may think it does not matter; it is only a little finger. But if the finger fails, next time his hand will fail; and in time he will be in the mouth of weakness until he is swallowed up by it. Then it has become too late. And when his power has gone, there is no strength.

So what is the religion of a sage? Every religion is his religion, and yet no religion is his religion. His religion is that of wisdom. He masters the mind not only by all these things, but at the same time he practises this mastery by means of contemplation, by learning how to concentrate, and by learning how to live; for if he does not master his mind, concentration will not help him. If the small things are not controlled, how can he manage contemplation? How many people say, 'When we sit down to concentrate our minds go to a thousand things; we seem to be sitting in a chair, but our mind seems to be jumping all over the place'. Where is the concentration?

Therefore it is helpful to concentrate, and it is helpful to be guided by someone who knows the path of concentration; but at the same time if a person will not practise the law of mastery in his everyday life and in everything he will not be able to accomplish this great work.

THE DESIRE OF NATIONS

IN THE works of a great Sufi teacher we find the words, 'In order to know God, know yourself'. It follows that in order to know the desire of nations or of people, we should first know our own desire. Until we know ourselves, we cannot know about others. As long as we are ignorant of our own life's needs and wants and of the secret of our own nature, we can never understand the needs and wants and the secret of another person's nature.

In reality we ourselves are a nation within ourselves. More than that, we are a whole universe within ourselves. Therefore, if we study the self, we shall find we can study not only a nation, but this whole world and even all other worlds. To study our self means also the study of the primitive condition of man, and this again means the study of life in all its forms.

We must also learn about the inclination of life in all forms. What is this inclination? There is a verse in the Bible which explains it, indirectly giving a hint of its secret, 'For in Him we live and move and have our being'. We live to move, and we move to make our being in God. Without moving we are not living; without making our being we do not move, nor do we live. Therefore it is the condition of life that if we live we should move and progress, and attain that state of being for which we are destined.

We can see this inclination in every being. A little plant, a tree, if we suppress its growth, if we erect a fence round it, if we cover it with glass, it will not flourish, it will not produce flowers; in time it will die. Why is this? It is because its life cannot express itself when it is covered, it cannot express itself when there is a fence round it. It is not enough for it to be alive, because life does not want only to live; to realize itself life must be able to make progress, and progress is only made when there is free movement.

We find the same inclination even in worms and insects. An ant has the same desire. We try to touch it, but it does not want us to touch it. We attempt to keep it in a certain place, but it does not want to stay there. However much we may say we will take great care of the parrots and the sparrows and the beautiful birds we keep in cages, saying we love them so much, it is no pleasure to them. Of course they will eat in their captivity if they are hungry; they will drink water when they are thirsty; but this is no sign that they enjoy themselves or that they are happy.

Why should they be happy when it is not their life's inclination to be restricted? Life did not give a bird wings in order to stay in a cage. Wings were given as the means to enjoy life, to make a nest where the birds can live, to make the acquaintance of other birds, to enjoy the life of the jungle, and to find water and food for the comfort and ease of their family. It is in this way that they make their being; it is the same with animals and birds as it is with plants. For them also life means to have a being, to move; it is what life demands.

When we come to human life, do we not find it the same too? However much we love our child and say, 'Sit here, I would so much like you to be here', it will only stay there for a moment, and then it will say, 'No, let me play'. We say to it, 'You should be sitting here', but it answers, 'No, I don't like sitting here'. Then we give the child a beautiful toy, and say again, 'Sit here'. Yes, for the sake of the toy it will sit for a moment; but the next it will take the toy and go away. 'Let me have my freedom', it says. Does this not show that the purpose of life is freedom? As long as man is ignorant of this he is ignorant of the secret of his own nature and the secret of any other. Neither he nor anyone else can be happy, however much wealth or property, grandeur of position or palaces he may possess.

Interdependence is a law of nature. We make our life by sharing the joys and pleasures and sorrows of another, but it takes us a very long time to understand this one thing. Our observation and study of man's nature show that his life demands freedom; and yet on the other hand we find that selfishness develops naturally in man, more than in any other creature. The demands of his life are so much greater, and he becomes so absorbed in satisfying these demands, and possessing and enjoying them when he has them, that he really forgets the secret of nature; he forgets the secret of his own happiness as well as that of others.

Not only does individual man seek freedom, but also the nations and races and peoples throughout the whole world have been absorbed in the pursuit of freedom. Whenever wars have occurred, whenever there has been bloodshed in the world, whenever there have been revolutions and upheavals in life, all the various disasters that have taken place are due to these same causes: on the one side man's selfishness, and on the other his lack of understanding of the law of nature and the law of happiness.

Ignorance of this law exists in the human soul from childhood. When a child sees anything that is attractive and beautiful, it at once wants to have it, never thinking whose it may be. 'No one shall touch it; that shall belong to me', it says. 'I shall only be happy when I have what that other child has'. Even if it already has a beautiful toy, it still wants to have what the other one has. This is human nature, which goes on developing regardless of the secret happiness which can only be disclosed when the veil of ignorance has fallen from man's eyes.

He never understands what justice is, even though he may speak of it. Real justice cannot be perceived until the veil of selfishness has been removed from the eyes. The least spark of selfishness will prevent man from being just; he will continue to have a partial interest, because he will be looking after his own interest; whatever furthers his own interests, he will call his right and his justice.

The prophets and holy ones have all recognized the justice of God as the only real justice. What is the nature of the justice of God? It cannot be read in scripture; it cannot be learned from a book; it can only be learned from the self within after selfishness has been removed. Our limited self is like a wall separating us from the Self of God. God is as far away from us as that wall is thick. The wisdom and justice of God are within us, and yet they are far away under the covering of the veil of the limited self. Whoever has arrived at that realization of the nature of God's justice is able to see all things in a different way from others. His whole outlook on life becomes different.

From the most ancient times teachers have come as messengers, one after the other, in order to instruct man in this law of God's justice, the law of co-operation, the law of love amongst men. That which Christ taught, they taught; for that has always been their work. But it is the way in which education and new reforms have worked out in modern civilization that has covered the real spirit of religion; the nations gradually unlearned what true religion was, and became more and more depraved. Christ came to re-awaken the ancient truth. And then Mohammad formed not only a nation with his spiritual message, but also a school in which love, co-operation, equality, and democracy could be learned: the truth that on the dependence of men on one another the happiness of humanity depends. Hence it is written, 'Every Muslim is a brother of another Muslim'. If a king and a prime minister are offering prayer, a poor man can stand beside them and offer his prayers with them.

How was the original spirit changed? For at first Islam taught the world both directly and indirectly; directly to the followers of Islam, indirectly to humanity at large. Before the spirit changed the religion was given by the Prophet, but afterwards the religion was used as the instrument for forming a nation. Instead of a nation being the protector of religion, the religion became the protector of a nation. The desire to attain a God-ideal was degraded into a desire to attain a national ideal, in order to satisfy a selfish motive. No sooner did that spirit enter Islam than the whole building tumbled down.

In the history of the world this lesson has been taught not once, but a thousand times. As long as a nation works for the interest of God and humanity it will always be prosperous, but as soon as it uses religion in order to exalt the national ideal, then it falls down like a house of cards. We can see this in the history of Hinduism, in the history of Islam, in the history of the European religious sects. If there is the wish to rise, the ideal must be high; if there is the desire to fall, let the ideal be low. It is the love of the earth that will attract man to the earth; but it is the love of heaven that will attract him to heaven. It is as the Bible says, 'Where your treasure is, there will your heart be also'. When the whole of man's ideal in life is his degree of education, his success in trade, all towards exalting the self, the individuality, then he is descending and not ascending. He is selfish as an individual, he becomes selfish as a nation, then as a race, and at last there is warfare; the racial ideal expresses its selfishness in great wars. Even people of the same nation will fight one another.

The same thing develops further when it appears between classes and parties, between labour and capital, the higher against the lower. All of them have a wrong ideal; selfishness is allowed to rule instead of the higher ideal.

And even that is not the end. The next thing which develops is disharmony of sex. Families become inharmonious because of the selfish ideal; the husband wants his own way; the wife wants her own way. The husband thinks, 'As long as I am happy, that is all that is necessary'. In whatever direction you may journey in life you will meet this tendency. Selfishness may begin with the thought, 'As long as my country is benefited, that benefits me'; and then it will narrow down to, 'If my family is benefited, if we become wealthy and have desirable things, that is sufficient for the present!' And then it narrows down again, 'For my father, or mother, or wife or children,' until it ends in, 'Nothing matters as long as I am happy myself'. Man has now become cold, ignorant, and blind to the law that life depends on the happiness of those with whom we live. The whole of life is one. In all these different names and manifestations life is one. The true thought is, 'If my wife is not happy, if my children, my neighbours, my servants are not happy, how can I ever be happy?' An insult given to someone will one day return.

How simple it is; yet how difficult for man to understand! It is simple to him who observes life keenly; it is difficult to him who is absorbed in himself. Life is nothing but this. Life is not a particular philosophy, not a particular faith, not a particular religion, not a particular code of morals. Life is that dependence upon our surroundings, upon the life of our neighbours, upon the life of the nation, upon the life of the whole world. That is what keen observation and a wide outlook on life teaches man.

How the peace of the world has suffered during the past few years! Do not think that the effect of this suffering has not been felt by all the other nations, even though they were not actually engaged in the war. The effect has spread both directly and indirectly throughout the whole world. The whole of humanity has gone through this pain. Even the fishes of the sea have suffered with man in the catastrophe. The invisible beings have also suffered. It is all one life. How could it be otherwise? If a wound in the foot has an effect on the arm, even though the arm is not wounded, if the pain has its effect upon the whole body, how can it be otherwise between nation and nation?

We can see the operation of this law even in our own circle. When there is someone among our own acquaintances who is poor, someone among the servants or relatives depending on us, who is helpless or in distress, suppose we cause him trouble or do him some injury, even though we may not know of it at the time, some day later on we shall discover it; it will return to us. It may return through some other channel. We may be too blind to see that it has originally come from that source; we may not see if we are in Africa that the harm has come from someone in China; but life is nevertheless all one.

Similarly when we bring joy and pleasure and happiness, it is never lost any more than is anything harmful or injurious, or of a troublesome nature. Good deeds, kindness, forgiveness, tolerance, acts of love, none of these are ever lost, and some day they will return to us. Even if the recipient appear ungrateful or heedless, it is all the same. There is no need to be disappointed even if he proves to be unworthy of our kindness or our love. When we realize that all life is one life, we discover that it is to that life that we give our love and kindness and mercy. Then it is bound to return to us, if not today, perhaps next week; if not next week, perhaps next year; if not here, then somewhere where we never expected it could possibly come. 'Thou shalt find it after many days'.

Though there may still be time to awaken to a true understanding of these things, it is often too late by the time that sufferings, troubles, and misery have come to the individual or to the multitude. If someone has so far failed to understand them before they actually came, perhaps he will never understand. When there is some little pain or he feels bad in himself, he may think he has some illness; but if he does not think about it, if he takes no notice of it, something worse may come. And so it has been with the world. The worst evil that has ever been should show man that it is time now to awaken and understand that it is not a study of national or social problems, not a study of religious questions that will bring an everlasting peace; but it is the insight into life which is the real religion and which alone can help man to understand life.

What is that religion? It is nature's religion of freedom, the religion that will liberate man. When man sees that the ideal of every soul is freedom, and that he cannot enjoy his own freedom unless he has shared his freedom with others, then and only then can troubles and unhappiness cease.

A Hindustani poet says, 'It is for sympathy that we have created man, not that he should worship God'. There are so many angels in heaven who constantly worship God. Therefore man, being the final manifestation, is supposed to do something different from the angelic world. God says, 'We have made man to sympathize with his fellow-man, to be serviceable to others, to give joy and peace to others'. Until he does that he is not really man.

The animals are all selfish; they all seek their own life's demands, and the satisfaction of their passions is their life. Their understanding of happiness is that it is just this gratification. Birds make their nests; animals have their holes. Therefore, if the only ideal necessary for man were that he should attain comfort and wealth and position, he would be no different from the lower creation. The great difference is that man has the power of sympathizing. He it is who can say, 'My mother has taken care of me; now she is old; I must listen to her; I must tolerate her hard words; perhaps she has only misunderstood. I was very disagreeable at one time, and yet my mother was always patient and kind and attentive through it all.' If one's father has become old, if our friends are in difficulty, in every case we must have sympathy. Not like the animals who bite their aged ones, and forget their mothers and fathers when their own needs are satisfied, but like him who thinks gratefully of his aged mother and of the wife to whom he is united to share in sorrows and joys, and to find in what way they are able to serve one another.

He is a man who thinks, 'Though in business we have to make

money and profit, yet by proving ourselves sincere and true in heart, by proving ourselves honest and earnest, the business will increase still more and remain secure.' He is a man who in national, social, and racial ideals, in the ideals of the whole of humanity, looks at nature with wide open eyes, and can perceive that the whole of life is one, that all individuals are one embodiment of life.

He who perceives this realizes, 'What I have taken from another, I have lost; what I have given to another, I have gained. Whatever good I have done to another is my gain, and whatever good another has done to me is my loss.' The kindness, the service, the love and sympathy that another has given are all lost when the giver is gone; it could only be there so long as he was there. But deeds of goodness, of kindness, of consideration done to another, will remain with him who does them both here and hereafter.

DEMOCRACY

THERE is nothing new under the sun, said Solomon the Wise. Man thinks that democracy is something which has been developed in the spirit of man, and which he had never known before. He thinks the democratic way is not only right, but new. But when we think deeply, we see that life is the same, the ideals are the same, nature's laws are the same in all ages. And therefore these two aspects, the spirit of dependence and of independence, have always existed and have always manifested in their time. For instance every soul knows that in its own life the very first aspect to be experienced is the aspect of dependence. The infant is dependent on its mother and father; in whatever way they direct him, he acts and works. Then comes the time when he is old enough to understand his own affairs, and he says, 'Yes, Father, that is what I want to do, and I *will* do it'. The father and mother say, 'Yes, our child has grown up, and he understands his own way; we should not interfere with him'. Thus we see that in everybody's life there have been the two phases: the phase of dependence and the phase of independence.

It is exactly the same in the lives of peoples, of communities, and of nations. It is always the same: at first dependence, then independence; at first autocracy, then democracy. The life and evolution of the individual and of the multitude are alike.

As freedom is the nature of every soul, so the child, even from infancy, seeks freedom. We want the child to sit in our arms, but it prefers to go and play. An animal, a dog, or a cat, which depends so much on the sympathy of mankind, still does not wish to be deprived of freedom. This shows that at every stage of development life is trying to become free. That is why it is true to say that the spirit of democracy is not a thing just of today; it has existed in all ages. Sometimes its appearance has been timely, and sometimes untimely.

When we trace the cause, the reason for the spirit of democracy, we find that it lies in idealism. The human race first developed a thought of idealism in itself; religions, learning, education have all emerged from this one human tendency. And what is this idealism? It is the silent consideration, the recognition of affection and attachment which we even see in beasts and birds. We see that deer recognize their mates, and pigeons and doves have a kind of attachment for them. Sparrows and other birds share the responsibilities for their young with their mates.

This all shows us that this ideal has only culminated in man. Call it religion, wisdom, learning, whatever one wishes, the only really human thing is idealism. As soon as a man begins to think, 'These are my parents, and I would like to take care of them, so that they may not have the cares and struggles of life', he shows idealism. Then the ideal extends to his neighbours: 'When I was young I could not help them; now I can help them, and I will look after my neighbour's home and protect him from robbery'. Then comes consideration for his life's partner, the queen of the home. As man then sees the beauty of life, he begins to develop his thoughts and imagination, making beautiful forms which shape themselves into beautiful ideals. He expands the ideal and becomes capable of higher ideals. Motherhood is regarded by everybody with veneration, fatherhood is regarded by everybody with respect. Neighbourliness is looked upon with friendly feelings. The elders, chiefs, or kings in the village or town, who have given all their thoughts to the welfare of that town or village, how are they regarded? The people say, 'Here is our father who has looked after us all when we were helpless or ignorant'. In this way the idea of a king or raja came into being, through the development of a certain kind of ideal. The civilization of every age or time always originated in idealism. The whole source of civilization is idealism and nothing else.

In ancient times the religion and the nation went hand in hand; and there is no doubt that there is a great advantage in this when we compare it with later times, for no nation without religion or spiritual ideal, and based only on material values, can suffice the needs of a world that seeks lasting peace.

However developed or learned a person may be, if he is not in touch with the spiritual point of view he remains selfish. His outlook on life is not impartial; his justice is self-made. How can he claim to be a just ruler?

The two things originated together. The history of Khusru, the old king of Persia, who was both prophet and king, shows this. His feeling was, 'My subjects are my children; more than my children, nearer and closer than my children; their interest is my interest, for them I live, for them I was born. My whole life is for them.' The whole life of the country was based on that example, that king's ideal. He was the instructor, the preacher, the ruler; he ruled according to the spiritual law. Solomon was also prophet and king at the same time, and so was Rama, the Hindu king. Think of the impression they have left; it is so many centuries ago, and yet however many kings have come and gone since then, the impression made by Rama still remains in the Hindu race. There are temples and shrines, and in them an image of the king whose life was spent for the welfare of the subjects.

A figurehead or leader is always the ideal which the people will follow in every age, and is it not so today? When the President shaves his beard everyone does the same! Man keeps saying, 'I will get rid of this idol', but he can never get rid of it; it is human nature. From infancy man wishes to imitate somebody's walk, or movement, or expression, or way of talking.

'God is beautiful, and He loves beauty'. He loves beauty through every soul, expressed in movement, word, in whatever way the beauty comes. He cannot help following beauty, whether it be in democracy or aristocracy.

There is a story of a Persian king and a dervish. Now a dervish is a self-educated man, but one who knows and understands things. He is a free-thinker; he does not abide by the law of society; he touches the depth of the truth, and ignores all the superficial and artificial rules and laws of society and religion; he leads his life freely in thought and action; he is so happy in his philosophy that if he is clothed in rags and tatters it matters nothing to him.

This dervish was standing in the street along which the king was about to pass. In the front of the procession were the pages, and they called out to him, 'Get out of the way, the procession of the king is coming'. He said, 'That is why'. He went back a few steps, and when the pages had gone past he came forward again, and sat down in the same place. Again came the cry, this time from the courtiers, riding on beautiful horses: 'Away, away, the king is coming'. He said, 'That is why', and went a few steps back, and then when they had passed he returned to the same place. Then came the chariot of the king. When the king saw him standing in the middle of the street, he gently bowed his head to the dervish, who smiled and said, 'That is why'.

A young man who was watching this could not help laughing. He was curious about it too and asked the dervish, 'Why do you say to everybody, "That is why?" ' He answered, 'It is plain. The gentleness of the king was the reason why he acted so towards me; the dullness of the courtiers was why they were curt to me; the rudeness and crudeness of the pages and the bodyguard was why they were rude to me'. For in the East they pay respect to holy men, even to a dervish. It is inevitable that the culture and education and thought that have been cultivated for centuries among families, communities, and peoples should manifest its effect.

If one asks whether one person's mind is equal to another's, or different, the answer is, it is never equal; there is an immeasurable difference between minds. One mind may be developed more than two, another more than ten, another more than a hundred, another more than a thousand persons. One person whom we meet and talk to and sit with makes us feel as if we had been in heaven, so full is he of gentleness, knowledge, response, and goodness. With another, however open-minded we may be, we find that his manner, his point of view, everything, is repulsive, and we cannot help it.

This shows that the root of civilization is idealism. The seedling was in aristocracy, the plant of civilization grows in aristocracy, and the climax comes in autocracy; for it is comfort and power that have always blinded men. We always find people who are without money more thoughtful and considerate than those who have wealth; blinded with wealth they have no time to think of another person. Even helpless people will have sympathy and share our pain, while those who have the power to help do not.

This aristocracy on one side, and on the other side the authority of a Church with temporal power, both reach a climax when they are blinded by the power of wealth. The aristocracy which was the virtue and culmination of civilization turns into autocracy;

and once that autocracy begins, whether with king, president, elder, or head of a family, there arises a bureaucracy: what the king does the officer does, what he does the policeman, the constable and everybody else does. As it is said in Sanskrit, 'As the king is, so becomes the subject'. Everybody values the leader. An autocratic leader produces an effect on every person, making him an autocrat himself. If the king is fond of luxury, the man whose duty it is to wait on the king also becomes fond of ease and comfort. He is too lazy to get up in the morning because the king is lazy also.

When this is so it means that the time has come for another form of life to appear. That is why there come wars, revolutions, floods, strikes, rebellions. These are all signs that life is going to change. It is not only today; it has been so in all ages. Such signs always mean the change from autocracy to bureaucracy, and then the new era begins, the era of democracy.

By the time that this new period has arrived, the spirit of independence has become ready to meet it. When this spirit is understood wrongly it becomes a time of great trial to the world and humanity at large. When violence comes, rudeness and crudeness predominate in social life and disregard of the true spirit of religion, and of consideration for others; these are the degradation of democracy.

Human nature is just like goats and sheep: where one goes, twenty will follow, and fifty more want to walk behind. So it is with man: one comes and seeks democracy, and the others follow without knowing what democracy is. Democracy is not a craze, not lunacy, not a spell; it is the maturity of souls; that is the real democracy. The soul now feels the responsibility, the value of its own power, the latent power and inspiration which it possesses. It does not necessarily mean breaking with Church or religion or law, nor a disturbance. These would be a degradation of civilization.

Where can this spirit, this true spirit, be learned? From socialism? Only a little. From politics? Only partially. The view of the politician is a partial view. In the law-courts the pleader may tell the truth, but the other side also may tell the truth. Politics may give education, but the perfection of democracy can only be learned from the real science or religion, from the spiritual ideal.

Real spiritual democracy we see in Jesus Christ. According to their law the Jews wished to accuse the people who had sinned, but he told them to let him who had never sinned throw the first stone. That was the outlook of democracy. In that Christ suggested that human nature was everywhere. See the picture of the Master washing the feet of his disciples!

Then in the life of the Prophet we read of a negro slave whom the Prophet's grandson called by his name. The Prophet said, 'That is not good manners; call him "Uncle", he is older than you'. He taught his followers that in the house of God there is no distinction between king and servant; the place of prayer should not be for rich people only. All can pray together, shoulder to shoulder; the sultan and the beggar can meet and pray thus. That is democracy.

Whence did it come? It came from the depth of religion; it came from spiritual law. However humble and low a person may be in occupation and evolution, we are none the less interdependent and require his help and service as he needs ours. However much wealth or power or rank we possess, we still depend upon the humblest and poorest person in the world.

The realization that the whole of life must be give and take, is the realization of the spiritual truth and the fact of true democracy. Not until this spirit is formed in the individual himself can the whole world be raised to a higher grade of evolution.

SPIRITUAL DEMOCRACY

IN POINT of fact democracy is always spiritual; there cannot be a material democracy. People call any system democracy which appears or which claims to be democratic, even if it proves upon examination to be only a shadow of democracy. There cannot be two goals; there is only one. The birth of true democracy is in the spiritual ideal, and as long as there is no spiritual light to guide man's life, he does not know the real democracy.

There are two stages in the life of every individual, in the life of a nation, of a community, of a race, of the world: the minor period and the major period. The minor period is when a man realizes that there are others who have experienced life more than he, and that is the beginning of his career; he then accepts the help and advice of those who have more experience than he. This is the preparatory stage which leads to democracy. No parents think it wise that from the moment the child is born it should be permitted to act without any direction or advice. What really happens is that when the minor, the preparatory period is despised, then instead of democracy anarchy comes and takes its place. True democracy means rising from the lower stage to a higher stage, and false democracy is pulling those at a higher stage down to the lower stage.

In some respects a man shows childishness all through his life. Very often, too, he has the same characteristics that one sees in sheep which flock together. None of them knows where they are going, but one leads and the rest follow. One man cries democracy, and no one knows where it goes, what it will become, or what the result will be. As every moment in the life of a human being is one of growth and development in which he learns something of every kind of experience, so in every period civilization takes a certain direction, develops in a certain way, builds up something. Then spectators of this civilization can have two attitudes: the one who thinks it is not his ideal of civilization and wants to break it all to pieces, and the attitude of the other is that before wanting to break anything he first wonders what is good, what can be preserved and what should be discarded. This person can do a great deal of good by his attitude. He sees what is beautiful and valuable, and the whole that can be made of the existing parts. The tendency to destroy all the beauty and culture of life is not real democracy. Whatever nation or race has that tendency will destroy the beauty and culture of centuries. The right tendency is the one which comes from a spiritual ideal; the wrong tendency springs from man's egoism. What today is springing up as the democratic ideal comes from a material ideal. Men, revolting and agitating against others who have some culture, beauty, power, possessions, want to crush and destroy all these; but democracy born of a spiritual ideal is different; it teaches the true human brotherhood; it teaches the true equality of man, recognizing it in the source and goal of every person which is always the same. A real democrat is the God-realized man for whom the world is an open page. It is not he who destroys beauty for selfish purposes.

It is the realization of the beginning and the end, where we come from and whither we go, which is the real spirit of democracy, the realization of the one life. If there is not that idea of spirituality then there are only parties of democrats fighting for political aims, for business interests. This is no real democracy; it is a pretence. When a person has not yet come to that stage where he can give his whole life for his ideal, what is he? Selfishness is a lock that closes the door to democracy. Today democracy is laid claim to by those who are working on a basis of selfishness. Man, however, should consider not only national interest, but the interests of the whole of humanity. This should be his sacred duty. For a long time nationalism has existed, and the war* has proved that nationalism cannot solve today's problems. There is a great good that man can do by this example in life, by an example of the absence of egoism. If any nation can do good, it will be by working not only for its own interests, and then others will follow, for it is the nature of the soul.

How can this spirit be awakened? No doubt every activity like the League of Nations, every institution of this kind is good, but

* First World War.

not sufficient. What is needed is religious awakening; the awakening of that religion which is of every soul, not of a particular section or faith. If the spirit of democracy is born, it will only be born in hearts awakened to spiritual life. Every faith and belief has its principles, right or wrong, good or bad. Some follow these, others do not. They are given to humanity for a particular time, when a message is given for that period for a certain race. Whenever a spiritual wave has come to the world, in the time of the prophets and great teachers of humanity, it has always been a great spiritual ideal to awaken democracy. In the scriptures of Zarathushtra, in the Bible, in the Qur'an, in the Kabala, it is always the same voice teaching the equality of man and love for one's brethren.

Whenever there has been a wave of social reform, however good the service it has performed it has never been able to kindle the spirit of universality. This shows that a reformer is the child of civilization; the prophet is the father. One ideal comes from the heart of an intellectual man; the other from the spirit of God, expressed by man.

The message of God is not a system which is only given for a certain period, after which the world is deprived of it; it is Alpha and Omega, and has pronounced softly or loudly the same words at all periods. Advancement or progress is not standing still and stopping at one ideal or principle. Progress is life; standing still is death. When a person becomes hardened in his feelings, when his only interest is for the family or the nation, he does not go further, he is dead. But as long as he is advancing from a family to a nation, to a race, he is alive, he is progressing. The great disaster that has come upon humanity in recent years is caused by this death: the feeling confined in nationalism has burst out in conflict.

This is not only visible in nations, but also in religious forms, in communities. Destruction is always the result when man does not progress. The mystical explanation of this is found in the Bible, where it is said, 'In God, we live and move and have our being', and as it is said also that God is love, we can say that we live and move and have our being in love. When selfishness eats up that divine spirit which is in man he is dead. His heart is dead; he is only seemingly alive. Many people seem to be alive, but only rarely do we meet one who is really alive.

The greatest progress is a constant expansion of the divine spirit, expansion in any direction so long as the ideal of unity is applied; this is the ideal of the Sufis. It is not the desire of the Sufis that all should become members of the Sufi Movement; but the ideal of its members is to invite humans to become members of humanity. Sufism is not a new religion or community; it does not want to add a community to the world. It is an attitude of life, not taught by any particular principle or dogma; it is to tune oneself to a certain pitch, so that the heart can become tuned to the Lord. This is the only religion that exists; this is the only message that Christ gave.

There cannot be two religions, truths, or Gods, if our mind is clear. But to understand this religion it needs tuning; and to fight in order to make people believe this, is not the ideal. What is necessary now is understanding another person's point of view; to see with two eyes instead of one. Why is there so much misunderstanding? It is because of using one eye instead of two.

There is another side to religion: the esoteric side, that part of religion which prepares man by prayer and other forms of worship to receive the blessing of God from within. Without that blessing it is difficult to become illuminated. There comes a stage in man's life when he begins to enquire, 'Is this all? or is there still more to understand?' And that is why he starts looking for a teacher. It is this need in man's life which the Sufi Movement tries to help. It is the contact with the teacher, study, meditation, silence, repose, which makes one understand one's own religion, the inner side of religion. The Sufi's idea is that man in time may arrive at that stage of understanding where he can hear the voice of God from all sources, all sides, all things, all beings. There is a saying of Sa'di: 'Every leaf of the tree becomes as a page of the sacred book, when the eyes are opened and the sight is keen!'

THE FREEDOM OF THE SOUL (1)

FREEDOM is such that it is desired by every creature. From this we see that it is the soul's tendency and the spirit's longing to become free. Animals and birds, however carefully educated and tended by us, still have the instinct to avoid being confined.

Where does the desire for freedom begin? Its beginning is explained in a very beautiful way in some of the ancient stories. The stories from the Hebrew and Arabic scriptures tell us that when God made Adam He commanded the spirit to enter the body of Adam, which he had made out of clay and water. When the spirit was commanded to enter, it refused, saying, 'No, I will never become a captive in this dark prison, I who have always been free, dwelling anywhere without bondage, without barrier. I will never become captive in this place'. Then God said to the angels, 'Sing'. And when they sang, the spirit fell into ecstasy, it became intoxicated by the beauty of the singing. While in this state of intoxication it did not know whither it was going, and thus it was that it entered the required place. So when Adam opened his eyes, the spirit was there; Adam was alive.

Rumi said, 'The bamboo flute, which appeals to you so much mourns over its separation from its home, the original bamboo'. In Persia and in India the reed flute is taken from the tree; so it says, 'I am taken away from my source, my home; made into a piece instead of the whole which I was at first'. And this pain in its heart is the only thing that appeals to the heart of those who listen. It touches them and moves them to listen to its longing. There is a very beautiful truth in this.

When we inquire into the tragedy of life, the very first of all causes is this separation from freedom. This tragedy can be seen in all kinds of people. From rich to poor, from the most illiterate to the most educated, every one has this grudge. Maybe one confesses it while another does not, but the grudge is in everybody's mind just the same: that he has entered this objective world. For this entry seems to be the cause of all the tragedy of life, the tragedy that man's spirit cannot be satisfied in life, cannot have lasting happiness, as long as he stays in it.

But if you ask someone you meet what the cause of his life's tragedy is, he may say, 'O, that I long to have more money; I am very poor, and without resources I am so unhappy'. Another person may say, 'O, I have everything I want, but my relatives are quarrelsome and very unkind to me'. Another says, 'I have everything I want but good health'. A fourth says, 'I have everything, but I long to have a certain peace'. Another, 'I long to accomplish this art; that big purpose in life; not having done so makes me unhappy.'

And if you were to supply to each his life's need, giving money to the poor man, harmony to the man without harmony, position to the man who has not got it, a beautiful palace to the one who longs for that, health to him who has it not, then see how long he would remain happy! It would be only for that moment when his desire was fulfilled, and then he would again feel the hunger for he knows not what. He asks his mind, 'What more do I want?' and his mind says, 'You feel so unhappy'. And as soon as he asks, 'For what?' his mind answers that he cannot have that which he seeks.

It is in this way that all through his life a man runs after things which are not the real desire of his soul. Sometimes he thinks it is his bodily appetites and passions which demand satisfaction, sometimes that it is his intellectual powers; but even if they were satisfied he would still find himself unhappy. 'Perhaps', he thinks, 'it is wealth, position, or honours that are lacking'. Or he thinks, 'It is not that I have not got the things I need, but I have not enough of them'. If he has a motor-car, he is unhappy because he has no chauffeur.

His mind, his reason, always puts forward some other cause for his unhappiness rather than the real one, in order that he may be kept in illusion all his life; in order that all his life he should run after things which are not the real aim of his soul. Throughout his whole life he seeks after things, trying first this, then that. One day he buys this, another that, and after getting these things he still thinks, 'O, there is still something else, that is why I am unhappy'; and as long as he has not got it, he considers that is the cause. If he has ten things he wants twenty; if he acquires twenty he seeks thirty; if he has thirty he desires fifty; and so on. Indeed if he had thousands and billions, he would want a kingdom; after that a whole universe; and if the whole universe were given him, his heart would not be satisfied, because the demand of his soul has still not been understood. He goes through life mourning and sorrowing for things he cannot get, not understanding in what lies true gain and true loss.

Therefore, when a seer or one who has realized life looks at this world, he sees that however old a person may be—aged, young, middle-aged—he is still like a child. Children become very unhappy because they have not got, or cannot get a toy, a toy to which grown-ups would not attach any importance. To the seer, the desires of ordinary grown-up people are also like toys. The things that matter to the world do not matter to him. This is the sign that he has realized the aim of his soul.

For the aim of his soul is freedom. Freedom is the soul's true nature. It is a captive in mind and in body. The whole tragedy of the soul is its captivity. Words such as *Nirvana*, or *Mukti*, salvation, or liberation—all these names are those of the one aim or ideal of the soul throughout our whole life; yet hardly anyone knows what it is he aims at. All that he does know is that there is such a longing, that there is this hope constantly there.

Everyone wakes in the morning as if he were expecting something. Everyone goes to bed with the thought, 'Perhaps tomorrow or the day after tomorrow I shall obtain my heart's desire'. With some the desire is for a position, or a friend; with others it is a hope. Everyone is looking out as if waiting for that something to come.

There is a familiar saying, 'Wait till my ship comes home'. Every soul is waiting for his ship to come, not knowing what that ship will bring, or what sort of ship it is. Still, every soul is looking for 'my ship'; every soul is unconsciously waiting for the coming of 'my ship'. One person thinks it is the prospering of trade, another of business, another thinks it is the coming of power or position, but everyone believes the ship will come!

The ship is different according to whether it is pictured by the mind or the body or the soul. The ship of the soul is its freedom.

Indeed, freedom is the real object in all aspects of life; if the desire is for wealth, that is nothing but a desire for freedom from poverty; if the desire is for power, that is nothing but a desire for freedom to act as one wishes; the ideal of every soul is freedom, freedom to work, freedom to act, freedom to think, freedom in every direction.

Not knowing that this is the heart's real desire, from the first day of his creation till today, man has always neglected the true freedom, because of his pursuit of freedom in the external life. That has been his mistake. In spite of the little freedom he has thus gained he finds himself a captive still; he has still failed to gain that complete joy and peace which his soul longs for.

Freedom for the body would be the freedom of walking in gardens, of moving about wherever it wished. But that would not be freedom for the mind. The mind would still be captive. Suppose the mind has freedom, freedom of thought, of understanding, of imagination, of actions, even then the soul would still be captive. But if the soul is free the mind is free, and the body also is free.

How do we attain to this freedom? In the Sanskrit language there is very expressive word for freedom: *Taran*, which means 'liberation', 'swimming', or 'floating'. And it is such a beautiful idea that both these things, swimming and liberation, are alike in their nature.

How true it is, as the Eastern poets have always said, 'Life is a Bhavasagara, an ocean into which all things are drawn, fall and are absorbed'. It sweeps away all the plants and trees, animals and birds, and all that lie in the path of the flood; all are borne away into the ocean. Such is the force and power of the ocean. Similarly, this life sweeps away all the trees and plants, animals and men. Everything that we see is here only for the moment, and then is swept away. There is always a certain period after which the things that seemed so enduring have all disappeared. Our ancestors, if they came back, would not recognize the country, the houses, the trees, the manners; everything would be different. All that was familiar to them has been swept away. That is the story of this life. That is why it is called Maya, the illusion created before us like a dream in the night. In the morning, it has all gone.

All the happiness, unhappiness, pleasures, horrors, whatever we experience in the night, we perceive in the morning to have been a dream.

The whole of creation, when we come to think of it, is not in the end what we have thought it was: manners, customs, faces, everything changed. That is the condition of life. It is just like the sea. The tide comes, and it sweeps all before it, flowers, fruit, and all. Therefore life is pictured by the thinkers of the East as an ocean into which everything is swept.

The miracle of Christ walking on the water is understood by mystics as teaching a mystery. Walking on water expresses the same idea which in Sanskrit is called *Taran*—to float or swim. To float or swim one must have one's head above water. The water which sweeps us away we avoid, to preserve that existence which our soul longs to save. Our body is alive as our mind is alive and as our soul is alive; and it does not want to be non-existent, but it desires to continue to exist. However unhappy or feeble a man may be, his life is too dear to him to sacrifice. Suicide is only possible under great stress of emotion. All work, all struggles are in order to live. All fights, all disagreements, all money-seeking, all comfort-seeking, are in order to live. All through life it is one struggle to live, yet the true life is not realized.

Christ, from first to last, teaches the reality of eternal life. His only lesson was 'life'. It is the desire of the soul to live; and that life is the real life. Man keeps imagining that his life is for eating delicious dishes, for making merry, or for being comfortable for the time being. But when the body has gone, how will he live? What will become of his comforts? When the mind is not there, how will he satisfy the mind? To live in the body or the mind is to live in vehicles upon which one becomes dependent but which must pass, and be no more.

Therefore the lesson that we must learn is how to swim, how to float, how to prevent ourselves from sinking in the flood of death or mortality. How shall we avoid that? The answer is found when we understand that man is travelling in a boat; and the boat is heavily laden. The storm comes on, and the one who is rowing says to the man, 'The storm is severe, your luggage is very heavy; the best thing will be for you to save your life by throwing one of your bundles into the water'. The man says, 'O, that bundle contains things I have collected all my life, and I cannot throw it out'. 'Well,' says the boatman, 'if you cannot throw it out you will drown'. And when he has thrown out one bundle, perhaps the storm becomes greater, and maybe then the last bundle has to be thrown away as well. And he says, 'O, this one I can never part with; it contains things I have collected all through my life; they are souvenirs, and you want me to throw them away; things from my grandfather and my great-grandfather, do you really want me to throw them away?' The other says, 'If not, you also will go. If you want to save your life, throw that last bundle away too!'

That is what death does with mankind. It says, 'You are so interested in your vehicle which you call your body', and so first of all he sends disease. The person who thinks so much of his body is always ill. That is the first step. He is very conscientious about his body, saying, 'This is the one thing I must keep well-preserved'. He goes on thinking of it too much. And so he feels ill, and in the end he has to throw both bundles away, body and mind.

Others will say that they do not care for their body, but only for their mind. They take care of their own imaginations, their own standards of thinking, 'What you say is wrong, what I say is right'. They are occupied with thoughts, with pursuits, with arguments, saying, 'Am I right? Are you? Is she?' And they are all the time in doubt and constant worry of mind; all the time occupied in a struggle about something which is really nothing. To the seer it matters nothing. And then the tide, death, comes, and they are swept away; the mind goes, the body goes, and the soul returns to its own source. This is a picture of mortality when mind departs from body with the impression of death.

There is a story which explains this subject very well. It is of a king who had a parrot which he loved so much that he kept it in a golden cage, and always attended to it himself. The king and queen both paid such great attention to the parrot that everyone in the palace was jealous of it.

One day the king was about to go into the forest where the parrot came from, and he said to it, 'My pet, I have loved you, and kept you with all the care and attention and fondness that I could; and I should like very much to take any message you wish to your brothers in the forest'. The parrot said, 'How kind of you to have offered to do this for me. Convey to my brothers in the jungle that the king and queen have done their very best to make me happy, a golden cage, all kinds of fruits, and nice things of all sorts; and they love me so much. But in spite of all the attention they give me I long for the forest, and the desire to dwell among you, free as I used to be before, always possesses my mind. But I see no way out of it, so pray send me your goodwill and your love. One only lives in hope. Perhaps some day my wish will be granted.' The king went into the forest, and approached the tree from which the parrot was taken and said to the brothers of the parrot, 'O parrots, there is one whom I have taken from among you to my palace; and I am very fond of him, and he receives all the attention I can give. This is your brother's message.' They listened to the message very attentively, and one after the other dropped to the ground and seemed dead.

The king was depressed beyond measure. Spellbound, he could not understand what it was that he had said that should have affected the feelings of those parrots so much. The loving parrots could not bear his message. And he thought, 'What a sin I have committed, to have destroyed so many lives'. He returned to his palace, and went to his parrot, and said, 'How foolish, O parrot, to give me such a message that as soon as your brothers heard it, one after another they dropped down, and all lay dead before me'.

The parrot listened to this, and looked up gently to the sky, and then fell down too. The king was even more sad. 'How foolish I was! First I gave his message to them and killed them, and now I give their message to him and kill him also'. It was all most bewildering to the king. What was the meaning of it all?

He commanded his servants to put his dead parrot on a gold tray, and bury him with all ceremony. The servants took him out of the cage with great respect, and loosed the chains from his feet; and then, as they were laying him out, the parrot suddenly flew away and sat upon the roof.

The king said, 'O parrot, you betrayed me'. The parrot said, 'O king, this was the aim of my soul, and it is the aim of all souls,

My brothers in the jungle were not dead. I had asked them to show me the way to freedom, and they showed me. I did as they told me, and now I am free.'

There is a sura in the Qur'an which says: *Mutu kubla anta mutu*, which means, 'Die before death'. A poet says, 'Only he attains to the peace of the Lord who loses himself'. God said to Moses, 'No man shall see Me, and live'. To see God we must be non-existent.

What does all this mean? It means that when we see our being with open eyes, we see that there are two aspects to our being: the false and the true. The false life is that of this body and mind, which only exists as long as the life is within. In the absence of that life the body cannot go on. We mistake the true life for the false, and the false for the true.

Dying is this: when there is a fruit or something sweet and good to taste, the child comes to its mother and says, 'Will you give it me?' Although it would have given pleasure to the mother to eat it, she gives it to the child. The eating of it by the child is enjoyed by the mother. That is death. She enjoys her life in the joy of another. Those who rejoice in the joy of another, though at their own expense, have taken the first step towards true life. If we are pleased by giving another a good coat which we would have liked to wear ourselves, if we enjoy that, we are on the first step. If we enjoy a beautiful thing so much that we would like to have it, and then give that joy to another, enjoying it through his experience, we are dead; that is our death; yet we live more than he. Our life is much vaster, deeper, greater.

Seemingly it is a renunciation, an annihilation, but in truth it is a mastery. The real meaning of crucifixion is to crucify this false self, and so resurrect the true self. As long as the false self is not crucified, the true self is still not realized. By Sufis it is called *Fanà*, annihilation. All the attempts made by true sages and seekers after real truth are for the one aim of attaining to everlasting life.

THE FREEDOM OF THE SOUL (2)

MAN SEEKS freedom and pursues captivity. There is not one single person whom the word 'freedom' does not touch; and there is not one person who does not long for freedom.

At the same time, if we look closely at human life we see that man pursues captivity in some form or other, whether he seeks freedom or not. The soul of man is a dweller in heaven; it is able to see more than the eyes can see; it is able to hear more than the ears can hear. The soul is able to expand further than man can journey; the soul is able to dive deeper than any depths that man can ever touch; the soul is able to reach higher than man can reach by any means. Its life is freedom, it knows nothing but joy and sees nothing but beauty. Its own nature is peace, and its being is life itself. It is not intelligent; it is intelligence itself. It is spirit; its nature is not human but divine. It is for this reason that the soul feels a limitation, continually all through life, as a fish would feel when it is out of water and a bird when its wings are clipped.

If someone asked, what is the reason of pain, the answer would be that if we were to summarize in one word the reason of all the pain we see in the world, it is limitation. And where does this limitation come from? From a heavenly being turning into an earthly being. There is nothing to be surprised at, when we see that hardly anyone seems to be perfectly happy in life. A rich man has his tale to tell, a poor man has his story; a wise man has his complaint to make, a foolish man has his own legend. And so everyone has something to say; and what they all have to say is the same thing and that is: limitation.

What one pursues, what one seeks after, is a feeling of freedom; and yet nearly everyone pursues freedom wrongly. The nature of life is such that whenever a person thinks, 'that will make me free', that in itself makes him more captive, though he cannot realize this until he gets it. As long as he has not got it he believes it will make him free. And so life goes on. Man goes on in the pursuit of freedom and what he gets is captivity. With all the talk about freedom today life is more a life of captivity than ever before. Man lives in captivity because he does not think enough about the real meaning of freedom. The more he thinks the more he will find that as he pursues the path of freedom, every step brings him closer to captivity.

Today in this world of science, where materialism mostly prevails, there are fewer every day who believe in such a thing as the soul. They say, 'The only thing we know about is the body; if there is a soul, we have never seen it'. It is true that nothing comes out of nothing, but their idea is that as the human being is the flower of this tree of manifestation, intelligence must have developed gradually through the mineral, vegetable, and animal kingdoms until it manifested more fully in man. But how can matter develop into intelligence? It is intelligence which is the source of all, but it is the captivity of intelligence in matter which we see; that is why it seems to us that manifestation begins from matter, and as it manifests in man we think man is a development of matter. In reality man identifies himself wrongly with the material part of his being, for the body is only a cover over the real man. Real man is soul itself. And when one says, 'I do not see the soul, I see my body,' my answer is that the eyes can never see themselves, though they can see all other things; and as the soul is intelligence it can see all other things but it cannot see itself.

The very fact that it cannot see itself makes it the real self. Besides, all things that we can point out, which are intelligible to ourselves, we call 'mine'; and so we call our body 'my' body. Naturally the body is not the self; but as man does not know himself he thinks it is. If an actor were to play on the stage with a mask on, those who saw him would recognize the mask, but they would not know what was behind it. So it is with the soul. The manifestation of the soul is only seen through the body; therefore one identifies oneself with the body, and this keeps one ignorant of the soul.

If the soul is intelligence, where does it come from, what is it in essence? All the scriptures of the past agree, as well as most philosophers, that the source and goal of all things is the

Intelligent One. But if it is the intelligence itself, why call it the 'Intelligent One'? Because it is a being; it is not a thing, nor is it a condition. It is first a being, and then it is all conditions and all things. It is a great mistake when a man considers himself as a being, a person, recognizing his own personality, and when it comes to the source and goal of all things he calls it a force, an intelligence. People want so much to get away from the idea of a Person behind all, that they prefer to say 'gods' instead of 'God'. Instead of calling Him the divine Being they say 'forces'; they would like to turn into plurality the source and goal which remains one and the same through the whole process and all stages of evolution. The oneness of the Spirit is so great that even in this world of variety there is one spirit and one being.

In all ages prophets and masters, thinkers and philosophers, have taught that the ultimate aim of philosophy and mysticism is to attain to the freedom of the soul. This truth is disclosed in many different ceremonies, sacred legends, and philosophies. Whatever be man's longing in life, whatever his life's pursuit, his object of attainment, behind it all there is only one pursuit and that is the craving of the soul to become free from all bondage. Man does not want to think about that which will make him free when he is absorbed in getting things in life; he does not give a thought to freedom but only to what he pursues for that moment. Perhaps if he gave a thought to the real condition of life he would become different, his attitude would change, his outlook would become wider, and he would not attach so much importance to the things he usually thinks important.

If one asks what kind of captivity it is, the answer is that for a spider the thin threads of the web are a captivity, and for an elephant iron chains are a captivity. The stronger a person is the greater the captivity; the greater power he has the greater are his difficulties; the stronger the soul is the heavier the load it has to carry. Therefore in captivity we are all equal. When a person sees only the surface, it appears as if one has an easy life and another has to toil all day; as if one has a gay life and another is miserable. But that is the outside. When we look deeply into life, in some way or another, whether a person looks cheerful or sad, some captivity is always hidden there. We do not know. In order to understand their life's situation it is not enough to cast a glance at people from the outside. We only see the prisoners; if we saw the prisons we would be shocked.

I have met numberless people who do not know what they want to do next week; they only think of today. Life is becoming uncertain, and its burden greater. They say that we are progressing. But towards what? Freedom? No, towards captivity. A greater and greater load of duty and responsibility is put on our shoulders. Perhaps it is worse in the West, perhaps it is worse in the East; but the cause of it all is the lack of understanding of freedom. One must look in another direction to see the sun or the moon; one must not look at the earth. How to die before death is something that man today does not know; and he does not care to know. The central theme of life today is self-assertion. When a person speaks about himself he wants to make himself ten times more important than he is. He cannot help it; if he does not do so the others will not understand. I even heard one man say to another, 'Your modesty is your greatest misfortune'.

Every man has to be self-asserting, continually guarding his interests in order to live. There are many who toil from morning till evening, guarding their self-interest and thinking about nothing else. And what is it all for? In order to exist. But even germs and grubs exist and enjoy life much better! Birds fly in the air and are quite happy; but man is loading his heart with a thousand troubles, making his responsibilities greater and greater. And in the end he gains nothing; his health is spoiled, his spirit wrecked. He does not know any more where he is, nor where his spirit is; and if he has nothing here he has nothing in the hereafter. Many die without ever having given a thought to the deeper side of life. Not that they did not care for it; but they could not find time for it; they had too much to do in life.

One might ask, why is this condition so tragic, why can it not be improved? The answer is that it is natural. What is man? Man is a process; manifestation is a process through which the spirit goes from one condition to another condition, from one pole to another pole. And through this whole process the attempt of the spirit is to find itself. In that process the spirit first loses its freedom; freedom is lost in order to arrive at freedom. That is the tragedy.

Yet in the end there is happiness, for the whole of creation was intended for the fulfilment of this object.

To every thinking soul, to every feeling heart, tragedy appeals. Why? Because tragedy is going on continually. Man would like to get away from tragedy, but it appeals to him because the soul is always in that condition; it is longing for freedom though it does not know what it is.

The highest perception of freedom comes when a person has freed himself from the false ego, when he is no longer what he was. All the different kinds of freedom will give a momentary sensation of being free, but true freedom is in ourselves. When one's soul is free, then there is nothing in this world that binds one; everywhere one will breathe freedom, in heaven and on earth.

THE FREEDOM OF THE SOUL (3)

IN THE East it is said that the reason why an infant cries immediately after its birth is because it grieves over the loss it experiences, and this loss is the loss of freedom. The soul which was once free and could float into the spheres higher than the birds, and could expand and live as light and life, has become captive in this limited body of flesh and bones when it came to earth, a sphere which is quite new and strange to the infant. Neither has it yet made any connection with earthly beings nor with the earthly atmosphere. That is why the first thing a soul does is to cry. The Sufis, all mystics, have recognized this fact and have founded their philosophy on this theory, that through every condition in life man is consciously or unconsciously seeking for freedom.

It may be that one is seeking freedom from having to work; another may be seeking freedom by getting away from some influence which surrounds him; perhaps another seeks freedom from a national point of view. But they each and all strive continually for freedom, and what gives the incentive to strive after freedom is the unconscious craving which the infant feels from the moment of its birth. That is why man is continually striving, knowingly or unknowingly, to attain to that freedom.

Our despair, our depression, our sorrow, our worries may have innumerable causes. But at the back of all these is one and the same cause, and that is that our soul is striving every day for freedom, which is something that perhaps only death will give us. People very often commit suicide hoping they will obtain freedom by it. Sometimes people think that getting away from everybody will give them this freedom, but they do not know that whatever effort one makes to get out of a situation, one will still not be free, for it is one's own self which is in captivity. Apart from all outward situations which give us the impression of imprisonment, even our own self is captive; we are a captive in ourselves.

The relation between the soul and the body is that of the spark and the charcoal. When the spark of the fire touches the charcoal then it is caught by the charcoal. The saying 'it has caught fire' means that the fire, which was apart from it, has been caught by it; and so the soul is caught by the body. One can also look at it in another way: that the body is caught by the soul, or better, that the body is used by the soul. And as the charcoal turns into ashes, so the body in the end is destroyed. But the fire is not lost, it has disappeared to its own element, which is heat.

It is the sun which is in electricity and gaslight and in all forms of heat; it is the sun which manifests through different processes. It is the same with the spirit which, like the sun, has appeared through different processes as souls. One has become many in different forms, although it is not many in reality. Light appears as a fire in a room, or as six or as a hundred different lights, but in reality it is one light. It is only in appearance, because there are so many globes, that each light is limited. In the same way each human body has absorbed divine light and shows it as a separate light; and all these lights seen in many globes are called souls. But we may call them the light itself, for it is one spirit seen in different globes as different souls. All human beings are part of one consciousness, they have one source and one goal, although the spirit is caught by different vehicles.

The condition is that the body holds the soul and the soul holds the body. The soul holds the body in order to accomplish its purpose, and the body holds the soul because when the soul leaves, it will turn into nothing. Therefore the body is continually striving to keep the soul, because it is made for the soul and lives for it; it is the body's continual desire that the soul should live in it. That being so, it is only when the soul feels it has finished its work and should no longer exist in the body, that it leaves the body; or perhaps the body has become so feeble that it can no longer hold the soul. This is the way it happens, and as a result there is death.

Very often there are people who wish to die and do not die. The reason is that it is the mind which wishes death, but the body is still clinging to the soul and the soul is still using the body for its purpose, although the mind is against it; that is why death does not come. Sometimes one thinks that the body is too feeble, that it can no longer hold the soul, and yet the mind says, 'I have not finished; I have not seen my friend, or my husband, or my daughter, I would like to live until I see them'; and it goes on living because the soul, having the impression that something is not finished, keeps holding on to that body which can no longer hold the soul. It holds on as long as that particular desire lasts.

After the soul has been caught by the physical body, there comes a time when the soul awakens. As long as it is asleep it is in a kind of dream in the physical body. That is the condition of the average man: a kind of dream. The mystic is the one who is awakened. The amusing thing is that the average man will call the mystic a dreamer, whereas in reality it is he himself who is dreaming! During this dream the soul knows nothing except what appears before it, for instance desires, habits, wishes, experiences, environment, actions, thoughts, and impressions. All these are like a dream which a soul dreams. One person will perhaps dream all his life; there is another who will wake at an early age or in his youth; but there are souls, as in the case of Jesus Christ, who from childhood begin to manifest their awakened condition. Therefore it does not depend upon a certain age; even an infant may be awakened. And it may be that a person will live all his life in a dream and may leave this world in the same dream; yet though there is a subconscious awakening when something begins to say, 'You are dreaming; there is something else for you to know!' often one does not listen to it.

But sooner or later that time may come in our lives when we waken from the dream. And as soon as we wake from this dream our first thought is, 'What is it all about? Why are we here? What are we doing here? Where are we to go? What is the purpose of our life?' And when this thought comes, then a person begins to feel a little less interested in the things of daily life. This does not mean that he is less capable of doing them, on the contrary, an awakened person can accomplish greater worldly things than the one who dreams, and in a better way. If our politicians today, and our great merchants and wealthy men, educationists and scientists, were spiritual persons, the world would become different; and they themselves would not be any less than they are; indeed they would accomplish greater things.

Do you think if the generals of today and the politicians and statesmen and business people were awakened souls, we should have had wars? By this time we should be past those days of stupidity when people killed one another; we are in a different stage of evolution, and today there should be no need for war. Humanity is grown up, it is no longer an infant. But even after a war there is no security of peace. We do not know what will happen tomorrow, and that shows that there is something missing. And what is missing is the realization of the dream; people think they are awakened, that they have common sense, and yet they are still asleep. We must be wakened from this dream we are in; the soul must come to the realization of what it is; then a better day will come for us.

The first sign one notices after the awakening of the soul, is that one begins to see from two points of view. One begins to see the right of the wrong and the wrong of the right. One begins to see the good of the bad and the bad of the good. One begins to see that everything is reflected in its opposite. In this way one rises above intellectuality which then begins to appear as a primitive or elementary knowledge. One sees the dark in the bright and the light in the dark, death in birth and birth in death. It is a kind of double view of things. And when one has reached this, then reason has made way for higher reasoning. No doubt one's language will become gibberish to others; people will not understand it. They will be confused by what one says. To some it will be too simple, to others too subtle; too simple for those who only hear words without meaning, and too subtle for those who strive to understand the meaning and do not reach it.

The third aspect is that in failure one will not feel such disappointment, and in success not such a great joy. In adverse conditions one will not be so dejected, in favourable conditions not so conceited. And these continual changes we experience in this world, such as friends turning into enemies, love sometimes turning to hate, sense to senselessness, these little surprises that we experience every day in this world, when things are different from what we expected, all these shocks will not be felt so deeply. Life in the world is full of shocks; there is no end to them. At every turn we find some surprise, all the time something new; but when the soul is awakened we do not feel these shocks so deeply. They come but they do not hit us so heavily.

At the same time, in spite of all this there comes a deeper feeling. An advanced person is more susceptible to hurts than the one who is not advanced, because his heart becomes tender and he feels acutely; he is living. A rock would not feel it. This awakening of the soul gives fineness on one hand, and strength to sustain shocks on the other.

And then we come to another stage that develops after the awakening of the soul, and that is the desire for freedom. People think they can attain this by retiring from the affairs of the world. No doubt that is a temptation; a spiritual person regards it as temptation. An awakened soul no longer considers the dream important, and yet he will say, 'When I retire I shall still work, because I shall still be able to be useful.' That is the thought when one is less selfish.

The ultimate freedom of the soul is gained by concentration, by meditation, by contemplation, and realization. What concentration is needed for the freedom of the soul? The concentration on that object which is prescribed by one's spiritual teacher, that by the thought of that particular object one may be able to forget oneself for a moment. And then what contemplation is necessary? The contemplation that 'this, my limited self, is no longer myself but God's own instrument, God's temple which is made in order that the Name of God be glorified.' What meditation is required? The meditation on the thought of God, the Being of God, forgetting absolutely one's limited self. And the realization is this, that then whatever voice comes to one is God's voice, every guidance is God's guidance, every impulse is divine impulse, every action is done by God. It is in this way that the soul is made free, and in the freedom of the soul lies the purpose of life.

THE IDEAL LIFE

WHEN SPEAKING on the subject of ideal life, the words of the Prophet of Islam may be quoted, where he says, 'Every soul has its own religion'; which means that every soul has a certain direction which it has chosen, a goal to attain to during life. This goal is a certain ideal which depends on the soul's evolution.

For instance a young man in a family understands that he has the responsibility for his mother and father, who are old. It is a duty, and not only a duty but a virtue on his part, that he should devote all that he earns, and give every service that he can render them in their old age. His idea of virtue is that if he can be helpful to his aged parents with money or with service, he will devote both to them, and he considers that to be a virtue. That is the ideal thing for him to do, so he does it. Perhaps he does not perceive anything beyond it, but what he does perceive is virtue in his eyes. And that is why he wishes to do it, and in it lies his satisfaction.

Another person is in business, as the agent of a firm. He thinks, 'I am paid by my firm, and the head of my firm is so kind that it is my first duty to prove myself faithful to my firm'. He labours with enthusiasm and great zeal from morning to evening, seeing a great virtue in serving well, although he does not pretend to religion or spirituality. But he considers his service as his virtue, and as long as he considers that he is doing his duty, he is following his religion.

Religion in the East is not made into a thing apart from one's life, as in the West where business, profession, and other things on the one side of life, and going to church one day in the week on the other side, together constitute religion, with a prayer before going to rest. But strictly speaking, life is religion. When one has that ideal before one with whatever occupation one is concerned, business. industry, domestic life, or whatever it is, one carries it out, trying to be worthy of it, that is religion.

In the Hindu language, the same word *Dharma* means both duty and religion; both are expressed by one word. 'This is your Dharma' means: 'This is your faith'. How beautiful the thought is! Whatever kind of duty it is, so long as you have an ideal before you and are performing that duty, you are walking in the path of religion.

We, with our narrowness of faith or belief, accuse others of belonging to another religion, another chapel or church. We say, 'This temple is better, that faith is better'. The whole world has kept on fighting and devastating itself just because it can not understand that each form of religion is peculiar to itself. Therefore the ideal life is in following one's own ideal; it is not in checking other people's ideals. If a certain thing is one's ideal, that does not mean that another person will agree that it is best to offer prayers ten times a day. He may be doing better by following his religion in his shop than by going to a mosque and offering up a prayer twenty times a day. Perhaps somebody with that ideal cannot see that the other person's way is an ideal also. Leave everyone to follow his own ideal.

Does the ideal remain the same all the time? No, the ideal grows and improves as man grows and improves with the years. Perhaps at some time in his life a man thinks that it would be ideal to have a beautiful house, a beautiful estate, good clothes, and all manner of comforts. From that moment this is the path he ought to pursue. But then he arrives at another ideal. He comes to think, 'My surroundings are not important if the people in the town are not happy nor in good surroundings'. From that time he cares less for his own house and his beautiful things, and goes into the town every day and seeks to improve the health and happiness of others. He thinks, 'The poor in the town should be looked after'. This is his new ideal. Before he evolved his new ideal he was only enjoying his beautiful home; he was living up to a lower ideal.

And then later on he may come to say, 'Never mind about my town; I think of my whole country'. The whole nation comes in for consideration: what is beneficial to it, and what are the things that should be improved. His fortune may not be very great; perhaps his town is not so beautiful as that of someone who is thinking only about his town; but he is thinking about the whole nation, and so his ideal is still greater. It does not matter to him in which town he lives, his life is in the whole country, in the whole nation. He becomes the spirit of the whole nation. That is his ideal.

Is man the same, whatever his appearance? We see now that it is all a matter of his ideal whether a man differs from his neighbour, whether he is heavenly or earthly, as high as the Devas, the heavenly beings, or as low as the demons. His ideal makes him as high as the one, or as low as the lowest demons. The greatness of man lies in the greatness of his ideal.

That which makes us esteem those whom we esteem is their ideal. That which raises man from earth to heaven is his ideal; and that which pulls man down from the heavens to the earth is also his ideal. When he does not live up to his ideal he falls to earth; and when he raises his ideal he goes from earth to heaven. He can rise to any height, according to the stature of his ideal.

One person thinks, 'O, it does not matter; if I have a good dinner, never mind what others have'; another thinks, 'It is no pleasure to me to have had a good dinner, since my family still starve; it gives me much more happiness if I have only a frugal dinner, as long as my family are well satisfied'. This raises him higher than the person who thinks only of his own happiness. A third person thinks, 'It does not matter how I live, so long as I have brought some happiness to the people of my town, or village; that would be worth while'. His ideal is greater still.

The trust that is sent by heaven is the ideal given to man. That is his charge in life, his responsibility in life. To take care of this and prove worthy of this responsibility and position that has been given to us, that is what should prove to be our ideal, our religion, our Dharma. In the Gospel the 'talent' represents the same ideal; at first it is small, but it expands as we go through life.

This explains the fact that the sin and virtue of two people cannot be the same. For instance there may be two students, and one is sent to a university and is studying for an examination. There are only two months left, but he happens to see an exciting play advertised. He thinks he would like to see this play, and yet there is so short a time for study. 'But then it is only one evening, and I can soon make that up; I will go just this once, and it will make no difference', he says. He disregards the importance of the ideal he had: that of passing his examination. He has changed his ideal by thinking that the examination does not matter. So he goes this once, but next day he sees another play advertised, and again gives in to his pleasure; and again and again. His fondness for the theatre grows, and the evenings go by, and the time comes when he is no longer ready for his examination. So he fails. Seeing the plays was a sin, not because it was a sinful action, but because he failed to keep to his ideal. He was meant to study to pass his examination.

Again, there is another student. He is trying to become a good playwright, or orator, or actor. He sees the same advertisement. He goes to the play and enjoys it very much. Every play he attends adds to his experience and increases his knowledge. The same action has become a virtue, for by going to the theatre and giving his thought to the plays he has helped to accomplish his ideal. Therefore it all depends on our ideal whether the same action be a sin or a virtue. We have to follow and prove ourselves worthy of that ideal, and the further we go the more our ideal develops. However small it was at the beginning, we are always progressing as long as we follow it and wish to prove ourselves worthy of it; but when we stray from our ideal we lose the track. And if there is anything wrong or evil in the world, it is this: leaving the track of the ideal that we have set before ourselves.

A person may say that a religious ideal is the true ideal, or a moral, spiritual, or a practical life. Many people say it is much better to be in the world, to live in the world; others say it is better to live away from the wicked world, to get away and live in the forests, the jungles, or the caves. They say, 'This is the only way to live'. Others say, 'Just make merry, eat, drink, and enjoy life'. But others again say, 'The good life is in the service of man; as much service as we can give, as much kindness, as much love, that is the ideal.'

If we ask a hundred people, we will hear of a hundred ideals. Everyone thinks that he who follows his ideal is the best person, and whoever follows another ideal is wicked. Sufis, mystics, ascetics, in spite of all their high ideals, have been killed, beheaded, and tortured by different religious authorities, because these religious authorities had a different ideal, and were convinced that their own ideal was right and the other wrong. They said, 'My Church is the only Church which exists, the only one which can teach you the real truth'. Is it not true that every Church or every faith in which there is a willingness for others to join, thinks that its ideal and its belief is the best to follow? That is man's foolishness. He wishes everyone to follow the same ideal as his. He does not know that the prophets whom the whole world may follow, often could not get their brother or their wife or their child to follow them!

If we read the history of Abraham, Moses, or Mohammad, we see what happened. It was difficult for their own people to follow them, however many other followers they may have had, because every soul has its own peculiar ideal, and it wants to go on towards it.

True preaching would be asking everyone to develop his own ideal, however wrong it might appear to the outsider at the moment. Let each one develop his faculty of doing right in his own judgment. One will see that in time he will develop the real thing, because in him is the light of God and it will never misguide him.

Once I was with a sage whom many people went to see. He pleased them all, and he was not fond of disputing or discussing, because to a sage there is nothing to discuss. Discussion is for those who say, 'What I say is right, and what you say is wrong'. A sage never says such a thing; hence there is no discussion. But the world is always fighting and discussing and disputing.

Many would come and try to dispute with him, but he did his best to avoid dispute. I was very fond of listening to his way of dealing with enquirers. My friends wanted to discuss what the ideal life is. He said, 'Whatever you think it is.' But my friends were not satisfied with this; they wanted a discussion. They answered, 'Do you think this worldly life, with so many responsibilities, with strife from morning to evening, can be the ideal life?' He said, 'Yes'. They asked, 'Do you not think that the life you lead, retirement and seclusion, is the ideal life?' He answered, 'Yes'. They said, 'But how can we give up our present life, our responsibilities to our children, our occupations, and all these things that take up so much time; how can we leave that life in order to follow your ideal life?' He said, 'Do not leave it'. They went on, 'But if we do not leave it, how can we get on in the spiritual life?' Then the sage asked, 'What do you mean by the spiritual life?', 'We mean by spiritual life a life like yours', they answered. He said, 'If you think my life is a spiritual life, be like me; if you think your life is a spiritual life, keep to it. It is not possible to say which life is best. If you think your worldly strife brings you happiness, just keep to it; if you think my life gives you happiness, give up your own. Whatever makes you happy and makes you think you are doing right, do it from that moment, and see what the result is. If it gives you more happiness, go on regardless of what others say. If it gives you happiness, if you are satisfied while doing it, while reaping its effect, then it is all right. Go on with it, and you will always be blessed.'

Therefore when the question of the ideal life arises, no one on earth can tell us that this or that particular way is the ideal. The one who presumes to know this says absurd things. He only tells us what he thinks the ideal; it is not necessarily the ideal for us. Whatever we think best, we should follow it; for then we are on the right path, in whatever direction it may lead, whether to heaven or to earth; both will lead to the same goal if pursued to the end.

THE JOURNEY TO THE GOAL

THE WORD journey may be applied to life. As life has two aspects, it may either be called a journey or a goal.

Why should life be called a journey? Because there is a change in nature and a change of experience. One goes from one experience to another, and that is also the meaning of the word journey: going from one place to another, passing from one experience to another. The whole of the external life is nothing but a succession of experiences, one after the other, night and day. That is why it is called a journey.

Yet there is a part of life from which this life of changes has sprung; the life which is everlasting, which is eternal, the life to which all things return; and that life is the goal. Therefore life is not only a journey, it is a goal. The goal is the stable part of life, the source of life; the manifested life called creation is the journey.

In this way we see there are really two journeys. There is the journey from the goal to the life in the world, and there is the journey from the life in the world to the goal. And both journeys are natural. As it is natural to go forth from the eternal goal, so it is necessary to go from the changing life to the life which is unchangeable.

Which is the most desirable thing in life, to seek for the goal or to dwell in this changing life? The answer is that every person's desire is according to his evolution. That for which he is ready is desirable for him. Milk is a desirable food for the infant, other foods for the grown-up person. Every stage in life has its own appropriate and desirable things. The desire to attain to a goal must be there before reaching it; when he does not feel the desire, it is not necessary for a man to seek it.

All things are worth while when we seek after them; then only do we appreciate their value; then only are we happy to have them. We do not need the things we do not know and do not desire. We need them when we know them and desire them.

The law of nature is that this external life develops gradually, stage by stage, through rocks, through vegetables, through animals, through man. Its depth is intelligence, which is named *'Ilm* by the mystic. The joy of the whole life is the fullness of intelligence, and intelligence comes to its fullness in the human kingdom. It is there that life and the primitive intelligence have their eyes opened to see and understand and think. 'God slept in the mineral kingdom, dreamed in the vegetable, woke in the animal, and became self-conscious in the human'. But in the human stage we find that not everyone has the same capability of thinking and understanding and knowing. It is his thinking quality that distinguishes man, that is why the real man is the thinker, he who is capable of thinking. The more thoughtful, the more awakened the mind, the more can be found in man the fullness of that attribute for which the whole world was created.

When he begins to think, the question arises why all this was created. And the answer is that all this gradual development is towards one single development, that of human life; and in human life towards the development of mind. Throughout the whole universe that which has really developed is the mind, which begins to know the use of all things and all forms, their secret and the way in which all things and all forms are controlled.

Another question comes to the thinking mind, after realizing the secret of all things and all forms, and after knowing the way in which all forms and all things are utilized, and that is, 'Is this enough? Is there not something else that man desires?' Then he the will find that there are four different desires: the desire to know, desire to love and be loved, the desire for joy, the desire for peace.

After the toil of the day there is a desire to rest and be away from people. Then there is the desire to get a certain amount of pleasure or joy in things one feels delighted in, such as going to museums and theatres. Another finds comfort and happiness in loving and being loved. The scholarly mind who wishes to know and understand things, has happiness and joy when he understands them. If any of these four desires is absent, one is unhappy.

The world is engaged in four different kinds of occupations. To one person some of them may be repellent and undesirable, while to another they seem desirable. Everyone has his own occupation in which he seems to be happy, but that of another seems to him useless, foolish or undesirable. In Sanskrit these occupations are called *Kama, Artha, Dharma,* and *Moksha.* The occupation of Kama is love, affection, attachment, or infatuation, to such an extent that nothing else matter in life neither money nor position, nothing. Kama is the thing he wants; it is his one occupation.

Artha is the occupation in which a person pursues money; he wishes to be rich, to have property, to make trade prosper. Love does not appeal to him. He calls the lover crazy, foolish, out of his mind. He believes that everybody will like him if he has money, and that it is crazy to pursue love!

Dharma is the occupation of pursuing duty. Such a person says, 'These things are not right. The right thing is to do one's duty.' Perhaps he is interested in his family, in family duty to mother, father, wife, or children, saying, 'This is my virtue'; or in the people, the nation, the poor, or the rich. Whatever he considers his duty he gives his life to. He may be a soldier, a teacher, or a merchant; but he feels justified according to the way he does his duty. The person who is after money thinks he is a fool. The lover thinks he is a fool too. For him the first thing is to convert people to his Church; to do something good for his nation, city, or village.

The fourth occupation, Moksha, is different again. This means to work for paradise, for heaven, for heavenly peace. What is the use of bothering about one's duty? The whole aim is heaven; that is the happiness to look for. All things will change, all will pass—wealth, earthly love—they are all changeable. But paradise, the happiness one can get in the hereafter after all the suffering here, that is the unchangeable. A man who thinks thus is pious. He suffers all his life; he goes through all kinds of pain; he is seeking for that paradise. The lover may say, 'How foolish; my paradise is on earth. My beloved is my love. What a foolish person to sacrifice all this, and who knows what will come hereafter?' But the other says, 'I can create my own paradise with my wealth'.

These four paths are diverse; and everyone considers his own the best and wisest. The Sufi looks on all with tolerance, and knows that there is a path for everyone. The path of the lover is for him, the path of the one seeking for wealth is for him, the seeker after paradise is following his path, it is all a journey. It is simply that there are four different routes by which the journey is made. The Sufi sees the same goal at the end of each; the lover has to meet the seeker after wealth, and both have to meet the one who has done his duty. Therefore at the end of their journey there is a place where they can meet. What does it matter if one does not go by a certain path? Let each choose the way that belongs to his own temperament and tendency. Therefore the Sufi does not worry. He gives no preference to one or to the other. He sees the journey of life being made along one or other of these roads. The saying of Buddah, 'Forgive all', comes true. Forgiveness does not come by learning, it comes by understanding that a person should be allowed to travel along that path which is suited to his temperament. As long as he is journeying with open eyes, let him journey.

The great thing is that one should journey with one single desire. There should be the single desire: whether to love a beloved, to collect wealth, or to do some good for the world of humanity, or to attain paradise; there should be the desire to journey to the goal. So many do not know which is the goal or what it is. One thinks wealth is the goal, another paradise, another the beloved. They do not see that there is a still further goal. They are naturally prompted by the desire to get to the goal, and yet are not conscious of the further goal.

As it is said in the Bible, 'Seek ye first the kingdom of God, and all things shall be added unto you'. The real desire is for that kingdom of perfection, the goal of everything, but how can a person desire that of which he does not realize the meaning? Desire comes by knowing the thing to be desired. If we do not know what the goal is like, how can we be attracted to it?

Rumi, the great Persian poet, speaking about this, says, 'Every soul is a captive on earth'. And this captivity is in the limited physical body, which man calls his individuality or personality; while the nature of the soul is peace and joy and freedom. In this captivity it lacks these things. That is why the soul begins to feel it, wants this or that: paradise, duty, a beloved, wealth. Reason may suggest, 'This is it', and the soul goes after it, but having acquired it, it begins to feel, 'No, this is not the thing that I wanted.'

All this shows that there is a constant desire of the soul to find its own nature; and until it finds it, it is always looking for something, though what it does not know. Is it not true of every individual in this world that, whatever may be his desire, as long as he has not attained it he is unhappy, and eager and anxious to achieve it? He is longing and suffering and doing all he can to attain it; but when he has succeeded, he does not feel happy. At once a new desire arises; if he has a thousand he wants a million; if he has done one duty there is another, and after that another. So it is with love affairs; so it is with paradise. He will never feel contented and satisfied, because fundamentally it is not the desire that he is really concerned with. Though he crosses the boundary wall of the desire he finds himself again with a new desire. And this itself proves the fact that there is only one fundamental desire underlying all others: the desire for spiritual perfection.

One is not capable of setting out on the journey to the eternal goal unless the four desires and occupations have been surmounted. In the first place the motive limits one to certain lines of accomplishment; and it does not allow one to accomplish anything beyond the scope of that particular motive. As long as a person has the desire to attain to something with a particular motive, he cannot go further. That is why the sages have said, 'Rise above the earthly motives. Accomplish all you wish to accomplish in life, whatever be the motive, and then that itself will lead you to a stage from which you can rise above them, and above the earthly desires of the body'. They have never said, 'Stop, and go into the jungle, and see life from our own point of view'. Everybody's path is for himself. Let everyone achieve the fulfilment of his own desires so as to be able to rise above them to the eternal goal.

There are four different paths recognized as leading to the attainment of that goal. The Yogis call them *Hatha Yoga, Raja Yoga, Mantra Yoga, Bhakti Yoga.*

Hatha Yoga is the path of abstinence. This is a form of self-control, achieved by practising different postures, sitting quietly and trying to slow down the circulation or follow a certain rhythm, or quieting the nerves by a certain kind of breathing. This is all a process of mastery of the body and mind. Sufis call this mastery *Vilayat.*

It is practice rather than study that helps in controlling the nerves of the body, the rhythm of the circulation, the mechanism of the body. The adepts are able to stop every pulsation of the body at will, for a few seconds at a time. There have been experiments made by doctors verifying this power. However surprising it may seem for the external pulse to be controlled in this way, what would it seem like if we could see still more deeply into the life of the adept! The control of mind is so much greater; words can never explain it; one must experience it oneself. The control of the self means the control of everything.

What does it mean when we see a person fail time after time, or another person succeed time after time? It is just a matter of holding the reins of our affairs in our hands. When there is no rein there is failure. Failure means that there has been lack of self-control, whether it is a failure in affairs or in health. Illness always comes when a person has lost the control of self. It is because this is the main theme of metaphysics that Hatha Yoga has been considered of the greatest value. All the miracles and all the wonders that have ever been known in this world have been done by those who have been able to control themselves by abstinence, and therefore to control life. However much were said upon this subject, it would still not express it. To begin with a person is puzzled by it, and he wonders whether he should believe it or not. That is why in the East the adepts never speak of their experiences in the spiritual life. They only tell their disciples to lead it and practise for years. 'That will make it clear to you', they say.

The other path on the spiritual journey is that of Raja Yoga. This is the path of life, going through all life's experiences and accepting its responsibilities. On this path there are four stages.

Brahmacharya-shrama is that path where a person works with the intellect. He wishes to know about things, reason about them, and understand them. It is the intellectual attainment of knowledge.

Gruhastha-shrama is the attainment of knowledge through the experience of the responsibilities of life, of home, children, servants, neighbours, friends, and enemies; the experience of living among them, doing one's duty to them, loving them, being kind to them, and taking upon one's shoulders every kind of responsibility; the experiences of welcoming the neighbour, the friend, with a smile even when in distress and despair, or in any difficulty. This itself becomes a lesson.

Wanaprastha-shrama is the service of the world, of humanity. This means considering not only one's own family as one's responsibility, but also one's townsfolk, one's race, the world at large.

Sannyasa-shrama is retirement, love of solitude, silence, contemplation, and resignation in regard to all the things of this world.

By these four stages of development perfection is gradually attained.

Mantra Yoga, strictly speaking a system of Yoga based on the repetition of and meditation on sacred words, aims at the attainment of perfection by means of wisdom, understanding life, and seeing through it. The best word to use for such a person is 'seer'. He sees into life, into the depth of life, through a person, through an affair, through a thing. He sees not only the outside, the surface, but by means of concentration he sees through things as with a torch that illuminates whatever is seen. This seeing is called *Jnana*. The journey through life is made by that means.

In Mantra Yoga a person comes in touch with the mysticism of sound when he begins to see and understand; he begins to see that he gains power by sound, that in every vowel, word, composition, a certain effect or element is hidden, because life and the whole of manifestation is the outcome of what may be called vibrations. The scientist today says that life is motion, but the mystic has said so for thousands of years. At the same time he has worked with what the Hindus call *Nada Brahma*: sound-God or vibration-God. He has worked with life according to the law of vibrations, and has seen what great power vibration has. The whole of Mantra Yoga is based on this law of sound or vibrations. But this is a very big subject.

Bhakti Yoga is the most important yoga, especially for those who have the quality of love and kindness, because all the beauty that there is in life is after all what we call love. From it all the virtues spring. The whole beauty of life is in it, and it is as the English song says, 'The light of a whole life dies, when love is done'. Life's light is love; and when the heart is empty of love, a man is living and yet not living; from a spiritual point of view he is dead. When the heart is asleep, he is as though dead in this life, for one can only love through the heart. But love does not mean give and take. That is only a trade; it is selfishness. To give sixpence and receive a shilling is not love. Love is when one loves for the sake of love, when one cannot help but love, cannot do anything but love. Then one is not forced to love; there is no virtue in that. One does not love because another does. It is simply there; it cannot be helped. It is the only thing that makes a person alive. If a person loves one and hates another, what can he know of love? Can you love one person fully if at the same time you cannot bestow a kind glance on some other person? Can you say you love one person fully when you cannot bear him to be loved by someone else as well? Can you hate a person when love is sprinkled like water in your heart? Love is like the water of the Ganges; it is itself a purification. As the Bible says, 'God is love'. When love is awakened in the heart, God is awakened there. When a man has journeyed, he reaches the goal as soon as his heart has reached love.

The Sufi says, 'The Ka'ba, the divine place, paradise, is the heart of the human being'. That is why he has respect for every heart. Every heart is his Ka'ba, his shrine. The human heart is the place toward which he bows, for in this heart is God.

THE PRESENCE OF GOD

SPEAKING about the presence of God, I begin by saying that everything present seems to us real, and that which is absent seems to us less than real; and therefore the conditions in life which are facing us at the moment seem to be real, and have their fullest effect on us. Whether they are joyful or sorrowful, whether they bring us happiness or unhappiness they are the ones that are real at that moment; when they are not present they are only like a tale that is told.

During the night while a person is dreaming, whether it is a dream of horror and fear, or one of joy, it is real to him for that moment. When the morning breaks and his eyes are open, then he calls it a dream. The experience has vanished. It was only during the presence of the experience that he took it to be real. Once it has passed, he calls it a dream.

When we think of our disappointments, our sorrows, and our pleasures and happiness and joy at different times in the past, are they nothing to us now? At the moment of experiencing intense pain it seems as if we cannot live a moment longer; but when it is past and the pain gone, and we look back on it later, it is only like a tale that was told. Today it is only a dream, a story. True, there is some impression left; but that which is past is past. What counts with us is the present; what is here just now is the only thing that counts.

People have different ideas about God. To some He is the Creator. This means He was present when the world was created, but now He is absent. To some He is the Judge; He belongs to the Day of Judgment. Therefore He must be absent just now, since they perceive there is no justice in the world. To such persons there is a hope that some day they will be placed before the Judge of the world and then perhaps they will know that God is really there; at present He is not. Then there is another who may think, 'God was present when He created me, but He is not before me now. He is not present where I am, for He is in heaven and I am on the earth. Therefore I am not in the presence of God.'

Thus it is clear that not only unbelievers in God, but even the believers, who look upon Him as a heavenly Being who dwells in heaven, are both absent from God to the same extent.

Then, coming to the philosophy of Presence, we find that what we see and hear and experience with our senses around us is what we call 'present'. That which our senses cannot perceive seems to be absent. But in reality there is something else present besides all that we perceive; and in spite of the presence of all that brings comfort or pleasure or happiness, man is generally unhappy because of an unconscious longing for it. One can be in great agony living in a palace, surrounded by pleasures, and in spite of the wealth and attentions one receives one may yet be unhappy. And it is possible for a person to be very happy even in the absence of all the means of pleasure, happiness, luxury, and comfort.

What is the meaning of this? It is that in reality the world outside is more distant from us than the world within, and that there is a world within which is immediate to our being and the first we are conscious of. Because we are in the presence of the outer world, we do not recognize that world within, yet its effect is just the same. This means that a person who lives in happy surroundings with luxuries and sources of pleasure and comfort, may be envied and imagined to be a very happy and lucky man. In reality, however, he may be very unhappy. The external world has given him all he wished, but the inner world, the inner being, is unhappy. There is something absent, and he wants it to be present; there is something missing inwardly. This shows that the inner presence is required; the external presence is not the only comfort.

But we may ask, the inner presence of what? Many will say, 'We know we are unhappy sometimes in spite of wealth, comfort, happiness, friends, or beloved'. But perhaps they will not believe that it is another lack, the lack of a divine ideal, that makes them unhappy. Others consider that life requires scope for progress, and that it is the lack of scope that causes the greatest unhappiness. Such persons think that they cannot prosper in the work that they are doing, that they cannot be any better off than the others. Such a thought is worse than death. Life is unlimited, and it wants scope to expand and rise. Without that scope life is unhappy. One finds this not only among human beings, but also in nature. Look at the constant progress of sun and moon, rising and reaching the summit, the zenith, and then setting. See the rising of the crescent, and how it progresses till it becomes a full moon. That means there is scope between the crescent and the full moon. This progress is the only thing that gives happiness or pleasure or joy in life; its absence means nothing but death.

However disappointed a person may be at not being in a particular profession or in a particular calling or rank in life, he develops enthusiasm and energy as soon as he sees some scope for progress. His disappointment is only there when he sees no more scope. Even if he were in the depths of the earth, it would not matter as long as he could think that he would some day rise to some height.

Another wonderful thing we see, which supports this philosophy, is the tendency of everything in nature to rise. The tendency of earth is to rise as mountains and hills. When we see the mountains and hills, and how high they are, our heart also seems uplifted; when we climb them then our heart becomes uplifted; as we look up to them from below, it seems as if the earth itself is desiring to rise and go upward.

Then when we look upon the perfection of water, of the ocean, we see that it also rises as waves; and every wave, as it rises up, seems to be stretching its hands upward as if saying, 'Take me up, take me up, higher and higher'. It is the same desire that is behind all nature, making it strive to rise upward and to reach something higher.

So it is with fire. They called the ancient people of Persia sun-worshippers, or fire-worshippers. In reality this is only a symbol to show how in its blaze the fire wants to ascend. It shares the desire of all things to go upward.

So it is in our own life. A person who seeks wealth desires to be richer and richer, to do better and better; the person who is in a high position desires to rise higher and higher. Whatever the goal, every heart's desire is to reach higher. But these are all external desires. The external surroundings cannot fulfil the purpose of man, because there is a higher world. We may call someone wicked because he always delights in doing evil, in causing another person harm, and in being unkind; but if we were to study his nature we should find that he too has a dislike for evil and wickedness; it is only that his sense of justice has not yet awakened. If evil is done to him he feels it; it is only the evil he does to another that he does not feel. He is intoxicated by doing evil, and therefore does not feel it. That he does not like it when another does it to him shows that he too really seeks goodness.

There is a desire for goodness in every heart. When a person thinks of goodness, loves goodness, admires goodness, and looks for goodness in everyone in the world, that person so to speak collects good. When we recognize the goodness in any person it is like collecting the seeds of goodness and sowing them in our hearts. But when a person looks for evil, then he can see nothing but evil in every person. In this way he grows so accustomed to it that his world becomes full of evil. He has contemplated it and looked for it and created it. We will always find a complaining person complaining about this one or that one having done wrong. We will find perhaps he has a record of a thousand people having done wrong. The world is a record in his heart, a record of all those who have done wrong or evil. But if we study him we will see that he has as much evil as he has recorded, perhaps even more; because if a man has evil in him, he collects a thousand evils; he becomes a storekeeper of evil, although he is really discontented with evil.

When someone tells another about some evil, he thinks that he himself is so good, so free from all evil. This side of human nature we see even in children. One child will come and tell how naughty the other is, thinking, 'I must be called good'. Such a tendency grows and develops; life gathers the wickedness in people; the heart becomes impressed; in time the evil is stored up. That which is the store becomes the treasure, the world within. He who stores evil cannot see good; because there is no good in this world that has not a little spark of evil in it; there is no evil in this world that has not a little spark of good. If a person only tried to find the spark of good, he could find it; but if a person seeks to find a little spark of evil in every good, he can do that also. Someone may say of another, 'He is very good', but the neighbour says,

'Yes, he is good, but you do not know this about him: I will just tell you what he does'! Is there anyone who will never contradict when somebody praises another? There has never been anyone in history about whom somebody has not spoken evil.

What is really good? The answer is, there is no such thing as good or evil; there is beauty. That which is beautiful, we call good. That which is ugly compared with the beautiful, we call evil, whether it is manner, custom, idea, thought or action. This shows that this whole phenomenon of the universe is the phenomenon of beauty. Every soul has an inclination to admire beauty, to seek for beauty, to love beauty, and to develop beauty; even God loves beauty.

In all ages the various religions have given different standards of good and evil, calling them virtue and sin. The virtue of one nation has been the sin of another; the virtue of the latter the sin of the former. Travel as we may through the world, or read the histories and traditions of nations as we may, we shall still find that what one calls evil, another calls good. That is why no one can succeed in making a universal standard for good and evil. The discrimination between good and evil is in man's soul. Every man can judge that for himself, because in every man is the sense of admiration of beauty. But he is not satisfied with what he does himself; he feels a discomfort, a disgust with his own efforts. There are many people who continue some weakness or some mistake, or who are intoxicated by some action which the world calls evil or which they themselves call evil, yet go on doing it; but a day comes when they also are disgusted. Then they wish for suicide. There is no more happiness for them. Happiness only lies in thinking or doing that which one considers beautiful. Such an act becomes a virtue, goodness; that goodness is beauty.

What is beauty? One sees beauty of form, and beauty without form; beauty of thought, beauty of feeling, beauty of ideal. Not only does one see beauty in flowers and fruit and trees, but one sees still greater beauty in imaginations and thoughts. One feels one could give all one's wealth or life for a beautiful thought or a beautiful dream.

A great many rewards were given in ancient times to the poets, the writers, the thinkers, expressing their beauty in poetry and writing. Yet one comes to the realization that sufficient reward can never be given for beauty of thought or beauty of imagination. But there is a still greater beauty: the feeling of kindness, of self-sacrifice, of devotion, of love. The beauty which has been so impressed upon the world that it never dies, the beauty which is seen in the life of Christ, the forgiveness, the love for humanity, the gentleness, the humility, nothing can be compared with it, it is so great. Therefore it cannot be limited to name or form or to the external world.

There is beauty of thought, and great beauty of feeling, of sentiment, of kindness, of self-sacrifice, of selflessness. And yet there is a still greater progress that a soul can make: the seeking of the source of beauty. It is said, 'The gift is nothing without the giver'. There is no doubt a beauty in listening to the composition of a great musician, but there is at the same time a desire in the heart to meet that composer and thank him personally. What a satisfaction, when we have not only heard the music but seen the composer! We can say how delighted we are, and how much his music has pleased us. Or there is a very good picture which we have admired; but it would be a still greater delight to be able to tell the painter how much we have enjoyed it. So it is with the love of goodness: that constant gathering of goodness, the constant comfort of looking for goodness in everybody, the constant consciousness of doing good to another, the constant delight in one's own goodness. There is no limit to such progress. One may say, 'This goodness belonged to my father, to my mother, to my beloved, to my friend, to my acquaintance, to a stranger'. But when it is all summed up, to whom does it belong? Is there nobody whom one can thank for it?

A person may see different places and palaces, beautiful gardens and museums, and meet people of all kinds; but would that be his final desire? No, it would be to meet the king! 'If only I could greet him, since all that I have seen and admired makes me wish to see the sovereign!'

One may have corresponded for a long time with someone at a great distance. In every letter one reads delightful things and admires his thoughts. Will not one's greatest pleasure be to see him, and be face to face with him? So in the end it is the desire of every soul to be face to face with the Owner of beauty, to whom all beauty and goodness belong.

Whether we look at this subject religiously, philosophically, or scientifically, from whichever point there is no difference. There is only one conclusion: that the whole of life, with all its manifestations and variety, is simply the manifestation of one life. The believer and the unbeliever will both agree that there is one life behind it all, one source of all manifestation; one constant life which is a stimulus, a food, a source and goal for the whole of manifestation. No one who sees this with sentiment, thought, feeling, and admiration, could deny that it would be the greatest happiness to discover that source of all beauty and goodness which one has admired and sought for all one's life in one's progress along the path.

No doubt there may be some who are so absorbed in their daily wants and pursuits as not to feel inclined to search after this source; yet an unconscious yearning to get to that source is always present. If it is not to be face to face with the Lord, it will be an ideal: if one is fond of music, to see the composer; if fond of painting, to see the artist; if interested in reform, to see the leader of reform; if admiring great people, to see the greatest man there is. Whatever attracts a man, he will always be very glad to see the person whom he can identify with what he admires.

But how can one be face to face with the Deity, the Formless, the Nameless, whom one can never picture, never dream of? This is a question, and unless it is solved, a person who claims to be face to face with his Lord is a pretender. But one can only answer this question after having found out whether the Deity is a separate being, or is formless, nameless, above all limitations.

No doubt it is the desire for the presence of God that accounts for man's tendency to make idols and worship them. It was the desire to see the Deity and worship Him that made man stand before the sun and worship it, to stand before a tree and worship it. But this could not satisfy, because it was worshipping a limited thing. In reality the first lesson about the presence of God is, as a philosopher says, 'If you have no god, make one for yourself.' How true it is that before one comes to the real conception of God, the first thing is to build Him in one's heart. The word God has the same origin as the word good, but its original in the old Hebrew means 'ideal'.

What is ideal? Ideal is something we make. When we believe a person is very good we think of that goodness; it surrounds that person, and our artistic and idealistic tendencies help to paint his goodness as beautifully, as well as we can. We can crown it by our artistic faculty; that is called an ideal. When a man wishes somebody to be wicked, he paints his wickedness and all the badness that is there; he makes him an ideal of wickedness. When he thinks of his mother or friend he paints till he makes the ideal of goodness. No one can paint it for you as well as you can for yourself.

There is a saying of Majnun, the great lover of Persia. 'Oh, Majnun', they said, 'your girl is not as beautiful as you think. You are sacrificing your life; you grieve for ages and ages for that girl; but she is not so beautiful.' Majnun answered, 'You should see my Leila with my eyes; it is the eyes of my heart you need. My heart has made my Leila.' That is called an ideal; and the ideal of perfection makes it beauty.

The ideal of perfection is the ideal of God, and we will turn to it in our troubles or worries or fears. If we are afraid of death, yet have that ideal by our side; we feel protected. If we are disappointed in anything, still there is that ideal by our side, to reassure us; we say, 'I do not mind, I am not really disappointed; for Thou art present in my heart; I feel Thy presence; Thou hast become my ideal'. In trouble, in pain, in poverty, in difficulty, or friendless, in all these things which no one in the world can escape, there He is beside us. The older we grow, the more we feel, 'As long as I can be of use to the world, so long will the world want me. As soon as I can be of no service, of no use, then the world will get tired of me, it will not want me. The world wants that which is not myself. If I am wealthy, the world is after my wealth, not me; if I am in a high position, the world is after me because of my position, not because of me. The world goes after false things. The world is false. The only protection from it is to have that ideal of God alive and constantly present. With that ideal I can be satisfied, and have rest and peace; not only on earth but even in the hereafter I shall be in the arms of the Divine!'

No one can ever be so dear, so close, neither children, husband, wife, nor friend as that perfect Ideal. That Ideal will never fail. He will always be with us here and hereafter. We belong to Him. From Him we came; to Him we return. By feeling the presence of that Ideal always in our hearts, we feel the springing up of every kind of beauty, of every impulse, thought and imagination, of everything that comes out of ourselves or that we see all round us. We identify it all with God in the end. To the person who creates the presence of God the whole life around becomes one single vision of the Immanence of God.

THE SPIRITUAL HIERARCHY

IN THE Qur'an we read that God is the Light of the heavens and of the earth. This explains to us that if the Creator is the light of the heavens and of the earth, if the Creator Himself is light, then the whole creation is His light also. Therefore if we wish to know the secret of the nature of the heavens or of the earth, we can learn it by studying the nature of light. There is nothing more attractive to our eyes than light, nothing more elevating. Every heart feels full of delight in the light of the sun.

The nature of light is to throw out its rays. The nature of the Light of God is the same. If we study the rays minutely we shall see that from whatever angle we view them there is one central ray shooting forth with more intensity and with much more light than all the others. That means there is a central ray. Actually the emblem of the cross, which is most ancient, is derived from the study of light. The first glance shows the one central ray; the second glance develops that ray into a horizontal line, and the two lines then form a cross.

But light is everywhere. Whether electricity, or gas, or candle, it is all the same; though light in its perfection, as in the sun, can be observed better than the smaller forms of light. Science has come to understand that the light of the sun is in all things, but all religions have understood this from the beginning. The Hindus and Egyptians taught it. All over the East the worship of the sun was the first to come into existence. Only later were the sun-worshippers considered infidels, or heathens, or pagans. But as sun-worship is the natural religion, it is true that every religion can be traced to it. The external light was the first thing that impressed the heart of man with the idea of God. No doubt the inner light helped, but that too is light. Therefore both the external and the inner light reveal the mystery of the source and secret of all religions.

We can see the same thing in different aspects of life. For instance the falls and springs of water, the different channels, all show one big central current of water, which scatters as it falls. It touches different rocks, spreads into many streams, and yet ultimately unites again. In vegetable life we see the same. A tree with fruit and flowers and so many leaves and branches has yet one central part of its being: its stem. The life of the stem is the life of the whole tree. It is not so much that the fruits and other forms appear upon the tree as that the stem itself is repeated over and over again. Every branch is a stem to smaller branches. This again shows how the light which we call life takes a main channel for its expression, and spreads through all the different organs, the small channels or boughs.

We see it in man's form. There is the spine which is the stem. The breath runs through the centre of man's body, although the hands and legs and face and various organs have different directions. This central life is more important than any other part of man.

Then we see it in the life of people. Perhaps in every house there is someone whose sorrow means sorrow to the whole family, whose pleasure or happiness means some pleasure or happiness to all the others. Perhaps a whole town acts through the strength, energy, enthusiasm, and initiative of one person. A whole nation may move through the man of the day. However many wise people there are, however intelligent and capable they may be, there is still one person like the stem, through whom the whole activity is kept going. It has never been otherwise, whether the age was aristocratic or democratic. Even if the age was one of democracy, a democrat has nevertheless represented that stem, just as in the age of aristocracy an aristocrat held that place. No nation, no town, no city, no family exists without that one soul on whom the happiness, unhappiness, degeneration, or evolution of the whole depends.

Once, on being asked whether one person's influence or understanding could be better than that of five people, it was evident to me that the questioner thought that in these days one individual is no better than another. But the answer is, 'Five people? That is very few. There are some persons who know and understand more than five thousand!' In all ages we find musicians, poets, and others of the greatest repute, who were seen by thousands of people who yet did not understand them. Millions of people may have adored them after they were gone. Poets, reformers, scientists have been considered crazy for thinking out something impossible. Yet they have been the greatest men in the world. Is not such a man equal to fifty thousand people? Surely.

Even today we can see in everyday life how people argue and dispute without coming to a conclusion. Then perhaps another comes and sets the whole thing right. The discord of thousands of people could be resolved, and thousands of people could be united into one harmony by the presence of one who unites them all.

Whether the democrat accepts it readily or not, it does not matter. Even in a democratic land like Russia there is the influence of a leader just the same. Whatever nation one goes to there will be one person who equals thousands.

This natural condition is the basis of ancient civilization. We see it in the reverence and honour which was given to age: the old person has experience. However intelligent someone may be, it is the older person's experience of life, the life he has seen, that tells.

Honour has been paid to learning. The learned person was respected because he understood more. Honour was paid to goodness. If a person showed goodness to his family, proved to be honest, virtuous, and good to his neighbour, they had respect for him also and made him a leader of the village or town. The social life was based on the appreciation of virtue, intelligence, and experience. Thence came the idea of the king, raja, chief, pasha, or sultan; whatever name he received, he received it by virtue of his goodness, kindness, education, experience, or bearing. He became the leader of those who wished to become like him.

Those who believed in religion had faith in their Church; they believed in their tradition. They had a regard for it. Others had faith in their king. In the story of the dervish and the procession of the king* we see how easy it is, under the delusion of democracy, to go against all tradition, education, authority, experience, and age. But if we avoid that delusion then we find the real democracy, that which comes from showing an ideal to others and honouring and respecting that ideal ourselves. It is a crude spirit which says; 'I do not care about your education, your experience, your age,

* See page 172.

I do not care if you are thousands of years old'. That is the false democratic spirit. The true democratic spirit feels within itself that there is nothing one cannot be, and at the same time appreciates, respects, and understands all that it sees in age, experience, goodness, righteousness, piety, or virtue. To follow such a spirit means evolution; not to follow it means degeneration.

So we come to the idea of the religious hierarchy. It is natural for those who admire art to admire those who have painted beautiful pictures. Those who have a taste for music naturally admire the composers of the past, who dedicated their lives to the study and contemplation of music, and have benefited us by that deep pursuit of music, and enabled us to start from the point at which we begin today. This inclination is inherent: to admire, respect, and feel grateful to the masters of the past. We feel the desire to be near them, to get still closer.

It is the same in all directions of life. There is always the desire to get near to those lives which have helped humanity in music, science, reform, philosophy, or religion. Whatever we know today is the result of thousands of years of experience. No country or nation can say, 'We were the only discoverers of this, or that'. No, the discovery of the very least thing is the discovery of the whole of humanity. How could we understand language, if we were not taught? Books, reading, civilization, seeing life, all have helped so much that no one can say that something is only due to a particular person or nation. The whole of humanity has shared in everything that we think new today.

In the case of the spiritual cults, we find that all the mystical and occult schools gratefully recognize the masters of the past who have given their experience, sometimes by dedicating their efforts, sometimes by surrendering their happiness, sometimes leading a very hard and restricted life, sometimes renouncing all the happiness and wealth and possessions of this world, rejecting all the temptations of life by going to live in mountain caves or forests.

Every cult of mystics has used certain names. There are certain names in the cult of the Hindus, under which they recognize certain masters. We find them also in the Semitic races, mentioned in the Bible, the Kabala, and the Qur'an. Naturally, the human mind has its limitations. If we had no limitations we should be perfect. So it has always been that man has recognized as masters only those who are found in his own tradition. He only recognizes the spirituality or greatness or blessedness of those whose names he finds in his own tradition. In the Hebrew tradition there are the names of Abraham and Moses; in the Christian tradition there is the name of Jesus Christ, and after him those of the saints; in the tradition of Islam there are other names again, Mohammad and many Muslim saints; and in India there are, for instance, Rama, Shiva, Vishnu, and Krishna. And as there was little means of communication in ancient times, it was only natural that the tradition of one country should not be known to the others, and that it should become corrupted as it passed to another. The names used in one nation thus came to be different from those in another. Brahma, Abraham, Bahram in Persia, are all related names. If we tell some people that one name is really the same as another, they will not accept it, because they do not wish to think another tradition is the same as their own. Those of their own tradition are the only ones!

There is no blame in this, seeing the tendency in man to revere, appreciate, be grateful, and to link himself with their piety, virtue, goodness, spirituality, or power. It does not matter as long as the greater thing is recognized. If he does not recognize it now, he will perhaps do so later. In just the same way no particular school or group of scientists has been the only help. When we look deeply into life we see that every person in this world has been helped in his evolution, and all have helped each other. We see how one person is illuminated by another, how one learns from another. Whatever the name of the teacher, there is still the one stem of life and light. As long as the tree of this manifestation exists, the stem will exist. The names are all names of one current of life and light that runs through the tree. The one Spirit of life is given different names, the sacred names; and we more easily recognize the current by the particular name to which we are accustomed. So far we are right, but the mistake we make, and it is to our loss, is to ignore or deny the same truth because it is given to us in another form and under another name. We limit it. We say the truth existed only in that period when certain teachers came to the world, and that after that it stopped. But the spirit of illumination can never stop as long as life goes on. Illumination has continued from the beginning, and will always continue until the manifestation ends; so long will the spirit of illumination continue to spread out its rays.

We accept some forms and ignore others. It is the natural tendency of mankind. It is this that accounts for so many religions. Even if a person cannot see things in this light, he can at least be tolerant of other people's religions. He can respect the religion because he sees others respect it, even if he himself has no respect for its teacher. After all, spirituality means respect, advancement. Man shows his evolution according to his respect, his consideration, his thoughtfulness. If we could only develop that faculty in our mind, it would not matter not believing or recognizing the Spirit of Guidance shown in different human forms. If we held our own teacher or master in the greatest esteem it would do a great deal of spiritual good. The disharmony of the world is usually caused by religious differences, as were the wars of ancient times, and the differences are caused by men failing to understand that religion is one, truth is one, God is one. How can there be two religions?

It is natural to regard highly the teachers who have passed away, for when a person has passed he is unapproachable, and the goodness of his spirit can be recognized. When the spirit is in physical form, it is more difficult to recognize spirituality in him and give him the same esteem as one who has passed. Sages and teachers in all ages have usually been recognized after they have died; in their lifetime they were neglected and even met with opposition.

The mystic understands that illuminated souls, guiding souls, are on earth today too. They were not only in the past; they are here now also. Were there none on the earth now, how could illumination be continued? It is the present that is the best, not the past. What is present today will be the past tomorrow, so the mystic does not lose the opportunity of recognizing the spirit in the present as well as in the past. The Sufis use such terms as *Wali, Nabi, Ghauth, Rasul, Qutb*. But names do not matter, though the grades are necessary. The influence of one soul may be felt in a village, of another in a county, of another in the whole country.

What is the sign of such souls? In the East it is believed that some people bring good luck, some child in the house, a guest, or a friend. The good luck may be brought to one person, or it may be brought to ten or fifty. This shows that there is some influence, and we can recognize it as something which is beneficial, good, harmonious, to five, ten, a hundred or even more. The soul is as great as the circle of its influence.

Human beings are all in limited form; they are so tall or so short, but the soul is much wider. One person's influence may hold a thousand people. There is a saying in Gujerati, 'It is possible that the world may be saved by the virtue of one; it is possible that a whole ship may sink by the sin of one'.

We see this also in practical life. An incapable foreman in a factory will bring nothing but disappointment; an inefficient manager in an office or shop will bring nothing but bad luck. One person's influence, capability, knowledge, enthusiasm, initiative, strength of mind, will-power, are perhaps far greater than those of a thousand people. When we look at it from a spiritual point of view one person's soul is emitting a blessing and goodness to thousands.

There are two forms of this. Firstly there may be a soul in a very humble guise, so that nobody would think that soul could possibly be very spiritual, or pious, or good; it may be a soul working as a servant, one who scrubs the floor; yet there is such a great influence of goodness and light and blessing in that soul, that unconsciously wherever it goes it brings some blessing, some goodness, light, harmony, joy, and peace.

In the East this has always been believed and still is. Therefore a child is taught to be careful not to offend anybody, however humble or weak he seems. We do not know what is hidden in his humbleness or weakness. He may be uneducated, or possess no money, position, or sign of high birth, or anything noticeable to the eyes of the world; and yet a beautiful soul may be hidden there like a precious gem lying for thousands of years under a rock, until someone finds it and puts it in a crown to be worn by a king, where everybody can see it.

A person who welcomes everybody, who sees virtue in everybody, who is faithful and considerate to everybody, his soul develops so that in time others perceive his light. Wherever the light is, it can be perceived.

But it is not necessary for the jewel to be so hidden. Sometimes it is not. It is not hidden where there is a special task in life that a soul has to do. There may be a task to give a divine message, or to uphold a country or nation that is becoming degenerate. Such a soul may have to guide it through its difficulties and preserve its harmony and peace.

As in the days of Noah, there may be need of a warning. That soul comes to give it. The light that is usually hidden now comes forward to bring something to view that was buried in the depths of life. At one time such a soul was called a prophet, or teacher, or godhead, or incarnation. Others claimed to be prophets, healers, or warners. But in the time of man's maturity, of the whole world's maturity, such things are no longer called by these names, and yet the work is needed. The personality has been the sign, the evidence; the message has been the sign, the evidence of its truth or falseness. There was a time when the world was not capable of seeing. Humanity did not have enough realization to recognize the message, that is why the claim of prophecy had to be made. But now the world can recognize, sooner or later, what is right and what is wrong. The warner, the master, the messenger of today will not claim; he will only work. He will leave his work to prove for itself whether it is true or false.

Those who view life mystically consider that they are not only at one with the teachers of this or that tradition of the past, but that in every soul there is a spark of that teacher. No soul is without the light of that spiritual teacher. Therefore they have regard and respect not only for the spiritual hierarchy, but also for the spark of that light which has made every soul a part of the spiritual hierarchy. So they regard with respect and reverence every human being in the world.

The whole vision of life, the whole of manifestation becomes one single evidence of the sublimity of God.

SUBLIME KNOWLEDGE

THE RESULT of spiritual attainment is so vast and great that words can never explain it, for the very reason that all that words can explain is limited, is learnt and taught, or bought and sold; but something that is higher than that cannot be put into words. With spiritual attainment, however, the first thing one begins to see in oneself is that thoughts such as 'I cannot' or 'it is impossible' or 'I am helpless' or 'it cannot be done', cease to exist. A soul naturally becomes positive and will say, 'If it is difficult today, tomorrow it will be easy; if it cannot be done just now, it can be done later.' This optimism is not only in the imagination, but it springs from the spirit; its root is in the spirit, and it strengthens man immensely in accomplishing things. The fear of death that everyone has, more or less, disappears, and when fear of death disappears there is nothing else that really frightens a man, for that is what frightens him most. Many say that they are not frightened of death, but they will not continue to say that when death is before them.

A story is told in India of a woodcutter who, when he was overcome with self-pity after having worked all day long, used to say, 'O, what a life! What a terrible life, having to work all day long in the hot sun cutting wood; I wish I were dead.' And sometimes he used to say, 'O death, why do you not come? I would rather die than live such a life!' And one day Death took pity on him and appeared before him. But the moment he looked at Death, he was so frightened that he began to beg him to leave him in this world a little longer; he said he would never invoke his name again, that he would very much like to live a few more days on earth. So it is with everyone. They call death when death is not present, but when death comes, then they are frightened.

It is the spiritual soul who as a result of spiritual attainment begins to rise above all fear. As Ali has said, 'Fear no longer remains in the heart of the spiritual ones.' For fear is like the darkness, and the illumination is light. When illumination comes obscurity disappears.

When a person has arrived at spiritual attainment, his doubts cease to exist. But without spiritual attainment, however intelligent a man may be, he still has doubts; and very often the more clever a person, the more doubts he has. And there are many among the most intelligent ones who cannot make a decision: they cannot make up their minds, for they doubt; and doubt is the decay which destroys every action. There is only one thing that raises a man above doubt, and that is not belief, but conviction; and conviction comes by spiritual attainment.

We will very often hear a learned man who has studied many books and who is most intelligent say, 'I suppose it is so,' or, 'It can be so', or, 'It may be so'. The mystic never says that. The mystic says, 'It is so', or, 'it is not so'. There is conviction. It is spiritual attainment that gives conviction to a person.

Have the prophets and sages said, 'There may be a hereafter, there may be a soul', or, 'Perhaps there is a Judgment Day', or, 'Maybe there is a God'? No, they have said, 'It is so'. They knew. Besides the soul which begins to see a way to immortality does not doubt or fear. It looks with open heart to what is coming.

Spiritual attainment also makes the sight penetrating. In other words, before the eyes of the spiritual person objects and people unfold themselves; they reveal their nature and character and secret. It is just like a master chemist; whatever drug there is, he knows how to utilize it, how to make medicine out of it. In the same way everyone stands before the spiritual soul with the record of his nature and character, together with his past and present and future. Every person is like a written letter, although a letter is not really a good comparison; for a letter is dead, and here is something living, something communicating and most revealing. A letter can reveal very little, but a person reveals a thousand-fold more. All that words can never express is confided to the spiritual soul in the twinkling of an eye.

Very often people are deluded by the great compassion, by the graciousness, fineness, saintliness of spiritual souls. They perhaps see in their negativeness a lack of power; but it is not really so. On the contrary, behind the refinement, behind that saintliness and that sympathetic and compassionate attitude, a great power is hidden, a power of resistance, a power of accomplishment.

Only, they do not make the most of their powers. The greater, the more spiritual they are, the less they use their powers. It is like a child-soul and a ripened soul: if you give money into the hand of a child-soul, that person will go to the shops and market places and will buy things that attract him; he will waste that money and in a short time he will have nothing left; but a ripened soul who has got the same amount will use it more slowly, more thoughtfully, and make the best of it, giving happiness to himself and to others with it.

And so the spiritual person does not make use of his inspiration or of his power for small, worldly things. He uses it more economically than the same power or one-hundredth of that power would be used in the hands of an unrefined soul. For instance, if an ordinary person knew all about his surroundings he would abuse that insight if he were still inquisitive and so small as to speak to everybody about what he saw. And this is what most people do. Man is most inquisitive if it concerns another person, but he cares very little to know about himself. Therefore the smallness of his nature must first be shaken off. When one rises morally above the tendency to devote one's time and thought to other people's affairs which do not concern one in any way, speaking about them, forming opinions about people, when all this is given up, then a person becomes entitled to spiritual attainment. And a person who is childish enough to use his powers, if he has any, in performing miracles or in accomplishing things of an everyday worldly nature, abuses spiritual power too.

Once a scientist asked me if there was any way of raising a pen, which was lying on the table, by spiritual magnetism. I said, 'Nothing is impossible to a mystic. But why spend time in raising a pen, when there are so many human beings waiting to be raised higher? This would bring about a much better result than raising a pen!'

What people want to do today is to get spiritual insight and power and use it for their material advantage. They think that if they can make things more profitable in their worldly life, it is worth doing. This is like spending pearls to buy pebbles. They would do better to pay for pebbles with pennies than to spend spiritual pearls on pebbles.

Business and industry and all other concerns require effort, perseverance, qualifications, intelligent work. If one does it that way one is successful. But the belief that spiritual attainment should only be used for worldly success would make of it a very small aim to be accomplished. Spiritual attainment is success itself; all things come to the spiritual person. If he is a business man, he will be more successful; but he should not try to attain spiritually in order to succeed in business. The accent must be on spiritual attainment and all things will follow as a matter of course. As Christ has said, 'Seek ye first the kingdom of Heaven and all these things shall be added unto you.' Therefore whatever a man's profession, be he a writer, a poet, a politician, or an inventor, whatever the profession, spiritual attainment will always help, in every direction.

There is no greater success than spiritual attainment, because it is the finer success, a success which is reflected in everything one does and which brings about fruitful results. That is why people of old have called it the philosopher's stone, for whatever the philosopher's stone touches, whether it is iron or copper or brass, it turns it into gold. In other words, whatever the heart of the spiritual person touches, it turns it into life.

A person who has spiritual attainment need not cultivate sympathy morally, for sympathy comes as a matter of course without his cultivating it. A spiritual person cannot be otherwise than sympathetic. It is a continual outflowing of love that manifests by spiritual realization. It goes out both to the wise and foolish, to the good and to the wicked, just as Christ's forgiveness was always ready for the wicked, his affection for the good.

It is love manifesting in different aspects as compassion, forgiveness, kindness, graciousness, as affection, as sympathy; it is one and the same. And in the end a spiritual person does not see in another person a separate entity. His realization makes him feel, 'It is myself', and once he begins to see the other person as himself he cannot wrong him any more. No one in the world seems to him to be different and distinct from himself, but he sees in everyone the various aspects of his own being. It is in this way that the spiritual soul expands and attains to perfection.

INTELLECT AND WISDOM

OFTEN people confuse the two terms intellect and wisdom; sometimes they use the word intellect for wisdom, sometimes wisdom for intellect. In point of fact these are two different qualities altogether. The knowledge which is learned by knowing names and forms in the outside world belongs to the intellect; but there is another source of knowledge, and that source of knowledge is within oneself.

The words 'within oneself' might confuse some people. They might think 'within oneself' means inside one's body; but that is because man is ignorant of himself. Man has a very poor idea of himself, and this keeps him in ignorance of his real self. If man only knew how large, how wide, how deep, how high is his being, he would think, act, and feel differently; but with all his width, depth, and height, if man is not conscious of them he is as small as he thinks himself to be.

The essence of milk is butter, the essence of the flower is honey, the essence of grapes is wine, and the essence of life is wisdom. Wisdom is not necessarily a knowledge of names and forms; wisdom is the sum total of that knowledge which one gains both from within and without. An intellectual person will argue, will dispute, but very often about a subject which he himself does not know fully; and frequently one finds that he does so for the very reason that he does not know the subject fully. Superficially the argument of such people makes one believe that they know it, but for the very reason that they argue it is evident that they do not. The one who knows does not need to argue; he knows; and he is so satisfied with this knowledge that he does not have that hunger which is felt by the person who argues.

In nature a trace of wisdom can be found by studying instinct: among birds, the art of making a nest, among fishes the art of swimming, and the science that exists among animals and birds, which know their medicine when they are ill. In the ancient traditions of the East there exists a belief that medicine was first learned by the bear. The reason was that the bear knew, when it was ill, where to go and what herb or remedy to find and to take, in order to bring about a cure.

What we call intellectual study is a collection of knowledge which has been given to man as something to learn, and he thinks of it as something to depend upon; but that is not all knowledge; it is only a limited part of knowledge. There is another aspect which can be drawn from the essence of life. That which is called instinct in the animals and birds, in the lower creation, that same instinct when developed in man becomes intuition. It is not true as some psychologists say that all that a child knows it has learned, whether it be a favourable or an unfavourable attitude, whether a good manner or an ill manner. If two children of different parents or different races were brought up without special training, one would find that each would exhibit different manner and tendencies. If one were to consider how much one learns from the outside world and how much one learns from within, it would not be an exaggeration to say that one learns ninety-nine per cent from within and one per cent from without —if that. It is not the outer learning which causes a man to become a really great person or personality in the world; it is the inward learning that helps him to become that. This does not at all mean that outer learning is not required, outer learning as the means of expressing in a better form that learning which one gets from within; yet, if anyone has ever learned anything, it is from within that he has learned it.

Intellect, in every phase of its development, is a step towards the knowledge of truth, and therefore intellectual activity should not be condemned as an unworthy means of reaching the truth. All the same, it is presumptuous on the part of man to try to estimate the truth by means of the intellect. Intellect is the mould which is formed by all that we have learnt and experienced, and through this mould intelligence works; intelligence is the knowing quality.

Intellectual knowledge has much to do with the brain, while wisdom comes from within the heart. In wisdom both head and heart work. One may call the brain the seat of the intellect, and the heart the throne of wisdom; but they are not actually located in the brain or in the heart. Wisdom may be called spiritual knowledge but the best definition of wisdom would be perfect knowledge, the knowledge of life within and without.

How does one pursue the wisdom which is within? By first realizing that intuition exists within oneself. It is perhaps not every person who even believes in intuition; and among those who do, not all trust their intuition. No doubt they have a reason for not trusting it, for an intuition often seems to be futile knowledge; but for what reason does intuition prove to be wrong? It is because it was not an intuition; they only thought that it was. Not every person is able to catch his first impulse, for the activity of the mind always goes from one thing to another. As soon as a thought comes from within, the activity of the mind makes it go to another thought, and thus the mind believes it has thought of one idea while in reality it has gone on to another idea.

In this way one begins to distrust intuition; and when one distrusts one's own intuition one has no confidence in oneself; and the meaning of faith is self-confidence. Whatever be the faith or belief of one who has no confidence in himself, it will not be substantial. If a person came to a wise man and said, 'I believe in you, I trust you, but I cannot trust in myself', he would say, 'I appreciate very much your trust and belief, but I cannot depend upon you'. If, however, another person comes and tells him, 'I trust myself, but do not yet know if I can trust you', he will say 'There is hope for that man', for he will know that that person has already taken his first step; he has now to take the next step. The man who cannot trust his own intuition is perplexed, he does not know what he wants. He will always depend upon outer things which give him reasons; but the things of the outer life which are subject to continual change, to death and destruction, are not dependable. These things are called by the Hindus *Maya* or illusion. A person who calls himself a positivist because he depends upon outer reason, is depending on something changeable and subject to death.

It is not easy to recognize an intuition. The thought-waves are just like voice-waves. It is quite possible for the thought of another person to float into that field of which one is conscious, and one may hear it and think it is one's intuition. Very often a person feels depressed or hilarious without any particular reason. This may be a kind of floating thought or feeling from another person which passes through his mind and being, and he, for that moment, begins to feel happy or unhappy without any reason. And it happens frequently to everyone during the day that there come thoughts and feelings and imaginings which he has never had himself or which he had no reason to have. It would not be right to call these intuition. Water which is found in a shallow pool is not the same as the water which is in the depth of the earth. Therefore the thoughts which come and go, floating on the surface, are not to be depended upon; real intuition is to be found in the depth of one's being.

There is also a difference between intuition and impulse. Impulse is just like a straw floating upon the surface of the water; and this straw becomes an impulse itself when it is pushed by the wave coming from behind. That is why a man gets credit for a right impulse and is accused for a wrong impulse. If one saw what is behind an impulse, one would be slow to express one's opinion on the subject.

Impulse when it is pure is intuition, but it is seldom pure because it is spoiled by reason.

The first thing one must learn is to believe in the existence of such a thing as intuition. The next is to be able to follow one's intuition, even at the cost of something valuable. Even if one is deceived for some time, one will not continually be deceived. Therefore in the end one will find oneself on the right path. But the third thing is to make one's mind one-pointed by the help of concentration, which will permit one to perceive intuition properly. Just as for hearing the ears are so made that the voice waves resound in them and become clear, so the mind should be made a kind of capacity, or mould, in which the intuition may become clear. The difficulty is that outwardly the work of the ears is different from the work of the eyes; but the mind does both seeing and hearing at the same time.

The mind is perceptive as well as creative, but it cannot at the same time perceive and create; for creating is expressing, and perceiving comes by receptivity. There are two temperaments among men, called in Sufi terms the Jelal temperament and the Jemal temperament. The Jelal temperament is expressive and the

Jemal is receptive. That is why there are some people who like to listen and others who like to speak; there are many who like to be active, while others like to see others act. The one who works is glad to work; the one who remains seated prefers to sit; Both enjoy what is akin to their temperament. The one is creative, the other receptive. But one can master one's life by taking these two different faculties in hand, and by trying at times to be creative and at other times to be receptive. The one who is creative needs, no doubt, action and a knowledge of action; but the one who is receptive needs concentration and the attitude of mind which is receptive. There is a third temperament which is at the same time receptive and creative; this temperament, called Kemal, does not give results.

The mind can become a receptacle for the knowledge which comes from within. If we look at people, we shall find that among a hundred there are ninety-nine who are creative by nature, but only one who is receptive enough to receive through his intuitive faculties. The difficulty with the mind is that when one wishes to receive, the mind wishes to create; when one wishes to create, then the mind wishes to receive. The Hindus liken the mind to a restive horse. A horse, unless one has put reins on it, will not be controlled and will not go in the direction which one wants it to take. Therefore that wisdom which is like the essence of life and which is to be found within oneself can only be attained by first making the mind obedient; and this can be done by concentration. People will easily understand if one tells them about voice production, how necessary it is in order to sing well to train the voice; also they can easily understand why it is necessary to learn physical culture in order to make the muscles strong; but when it comes to training the mind a person asks, in the first place, 'Is there a mind? I thought that there was only a brain', and even if he happens to believe in the mind, he does not know what can be done with it. Anything else he will find more valuable than the training of the mind. He may even think that it is an occupation for lazy people, who have all sorts of luxuries to give their time to. The greatest mistake that a man can make is to keep away from a child that culture which is most necessary as a training.

One may ask if a child does not learn concentration when he

goes to school; but on the contrary, he mostly loses his concentration in school. When a little child begins by learning mathematics, he loses his concentration. The child never has an opportunity to sit quiet for a moment; he has no opportunity to think of only one thing at a time. Then what happens? Children become nervous; today one finds that nervousness everywhere.

Besides after being educated one has to make use of that education. If a person's mind is not under control, how can he use it? It is one thing to learn, and another thing to make use of the learning. It does not suffice to learn a song; that does not make a person into a singer; he must learn to produce his voice also. And so it is with intuitive knowledge. When a man has become qualified by studying for a long time, and yet cannot use his knowledge, what was the good? There is a sufficient number of learned people; what we want today is people with master minds, those who do not only see the outer life, but also the life within, who do not only draw inspiration from outer life, but also from the life within. Then they become the expression of that perfect Being which is hidden, hidden behind the life of variety.

It is not meant by this that everyone should become a kind of super-being. It is not meant at all that people should be able to perform wonders or miracles; it is only intended that they should live a fuller life and become real human beings, in order to bring about better conditions in the world. What do we want? We want human beings. It is not necessary that everyone should become religious, or exceedingly pious, or too good to live. We want wise men in business, in politics, in education, in all walks of life; those who do not live only on the surface and those who do not believe only in matter, but who see life both within and without. It is such souls who will produce beauty; it is such souls who will harmonize the world, who will bring about the conditions we need today. We do not only need the knowledge of matter or spirit, we need living in all walks of life, so that in one's business, in one's industry, in every art or science one may practise, one can use that wisdom which is perfect in oneself. When the individual and the multitude find beneath their feet a solid foundation on which they can stand, from that day we may hope for better conditions in the world.

SIMPLICITY AND COMPLEXITY

WE READ in the Vadan, 'Simplicity is the living beauty.' Man today has made life so complex that whatever he seeks after, he wants to find in complexity. All things in life which have importance, beauty, and value are simple; and simplest of all things is the divine truth. The one who cares little for it thinks it is too deep water to go into, and the one who cares much for it thinks that it is so difficult that it would be very hard to find it. In this way both the lover of truth and the one who does not care look for complexity. Knowing his nature, the wise have guided man gradually to the truth. Nevertheless, Jesus Christ, the Prophet Mohammad, Moses, all the different prophets who in their time have given the message of God and truth, have given it in perfect simplicity. Today man with all his knowledge complicates that truth and gives it a form which is not understood. The general tendency is that when a man does not understand something, he believes by the very fact of his not understanding it, that there must be something in it.

Can there be any truth which the human soul has not known? If the soul had not known it, it could not be truth; for truth is not a knowledge, it is the very self of man. The truth is not a newly invented theory, not a dogma, not an idea; it is reality itself. At the back of it is the self of man; therefore it is simple. But it is not simplicity that man seeks; he is longing for complexity. Anything which will confuse he is glad to take interest in. If it is simple, he says, 'I know it already.'

Spirit is generally considered to mean the source and goal of all things and the essence of life, that spirit from which the whole of manifestation comes and the same to which the whole of manifestation is drawn. We also use this word in the case of a person who has passed from this earth. This is another meaning of the word spirit. From a metaphysical point of view it is the mind and the soul and their activity which is spirit, but there is still another meaning of the word spirit that we use in everyday language:

influence, power, radiance, enthusiasm; those also are called spirit.

This chapter deals with the spirit which we call manifestation or life. Many ask what was the reason at the back of this manifestation, of this creation. The reason is beyond all reasoning. There is no reason. It is nature itself; love cannot but manifest. It is its nature. When poetically expressed, the great ones have said that God was lonely and in order to realize his predisposition which is love, in order to experience it, He manifested. It is poetic and it is true. But the process of manifestation can be understood by knowing the nature of manifestation: that the spirit is likened to the sun and what we call souls are the rays of the spirit. If the spirit is eternal, then the souls are eternal. If the sun is eternal, the rays are eternal because the sun and the rays are not two things; rays are the unfoldment of the sun and souls are the unfolding of the spirit.

In manifesting, the souls enter into three spheres. No sooner does a soul come forth as a ray, than it enters what may be called the angelic sphere. In order to make this intelligible, the wise of ancient times have pictured angels in human form. Nevertheless, it was in order to make man that the whole of creation was made; it was not only the angels, but the rocks and shells, fruits and flowers, birds and beasts, all show in their form a preparatory stage of the human being. As we read in the scriptures, man was made in the image of God. The whole of creation was a process to make that image which was the image of man. Man was the finished image. For this reason God was recognized in the image of man.

The nature of the beings of this sphere is such that it can be said that they are happy, innocent, musical, lyrical, poetical, pure, and full of worship. When we see that nature in a human being we say, 'Here is an angelic soul'. Perhaps one person may show this more distinctly than another person. It is not necessary in order to be wise, that one should not be innocent. It is not necessary for an innocent person to be an ignorant one; it is the foolish person who is ignorant. The most wise are innocent because they hear all things and do not hear; the foolish are innocent because life does not speak to them; their heart is closed.

The soul on its further journey pierces another sphere, the

sphere of the jinns. The qualities of this sphere are represented by the soul in intellectuality, in poetic gifts, in musical talent, in art, in science, in all those attributes which belong to the mind. It is for this reason that we call such a person a genius.

After this sphere, the soul manifests in the physical sphere where it adorns the physical garb which is the human frame. Every soul that has been projected as a ray from the spirit, must pass through all these three spheres. Sometimes it remains in one sphere longer than in another. It remains or it goes further, just as some of us in art, in science, in learning, in the pursuit of knowledge, go so far and no further. So it is with souls; those which are satisfied in one sphere remain there; they may behave like any creature of the lower creation would—eat, drink, and make merry and be quite happy. There are others who feel uncomfortable until they have penetrated into another sphere where they are more contented; some are not satisfied in that sphere either and look for another sphere. We human beings here have this tendency and it is also the tendency of the soul. Wherever it finds interest, joy, and pleasure, it remains, it settles there. But again, every soul is bound to its goal, it *must* reach there, and in order to reach the goal it must return. The condition of that return is that it must give up the garb of the particular sphere it has dwelt in, in order to enter another sphere. It is not allowed to enter into the inner sphere with the outer garb. These three spheres: angelic, jinn, and physical, have each a particular garb. This garb may be called the body of that sphere which the soul has to adorn. And when returning, it must give back that garb to the same sphere from which it borrowed it. And this giving back of the garb to the sphere from which it was borrowed, we recognize as death. Since man does not know his soul and is only acquainted with the garb, when the garb is given back man says that it is the end of life. But in reality it is only the beginning—just another act of the play which is the further journey it must make.

There are, however, three different ways of returning, or one should really say going forward. One is the way of the drunken man; another of the man who is asleep; and the third is the way of the man whose eyes are open. The way of the drunken man is the general way. What is life? Life is drunkenness. Whether a man is in business or amuses himself, whether he is in a profession or has any other interest in life, what is it all? It is a wine. He is drunk. Afterwards he knows nothing except that particular intoxication. He is intoxicated by the life he has lived. That is his world: ambition, aspiration. He is taken back against his wish like a drunken man. This is the general way that a soul goes towards the goal.

Then there is the way of the man who is asleep. He knows not what death and life and birth mean. He does not know why he came here, why he is going away. He is happy because he is asleep. He is taken wherever he is taken.

Thirdly there is the way of the man who journeys with open eyes. The one with open eyes will see all the beauty on the way. He is the one who will enjoy the journey, who will appreciate the beauty of travelling. For him every step forward provides a new experience, a greater joy, a particular blessing. He experiences the dance of the soul, and what the dance of the soul is may be understood by watching the water in a tank and the running water of a stream. In the tank it is stagnant, dead; in the same way a person can be dull, heavy, depressed. The water of the running stream is dancing at every step, and the dancing soul attracts everything towards itself like the stream of water, and will bring pleasure and satisfaction to all who can see.

This process by which every soul comes forth and returns is the very process that the mystics of all ages have realized here on the earth; and the true meaning of mysticism or spiritual attainment is to know fully, here on the earth, about the way that the soul has manifested and is bound to return. The question is: how do the mystics know this explanation of the journey we have made? To understand this it is necessary to make intelligible to our minds that this journey is only an idea. In reality the soul has never been away. If one thinks of the soul as a line, one end is attached to the goal, and the other end is manifested; but when we look at the centre of the line, it is one line. Neither is God man, nor is man God; and yet man is God and God is man. The difference is in how we look at it. If the soul of man is attached to the goal, then it has not departed from any sphere it has once penetrated. It is still there. But man is unconscious of those spheres that he has gone through, because he is so open to this visible sphere that his soul has closed its eyes to the sphere within. Heaven is not a place where the virtuous are sent. Heaven and hell are both within man. All the higher spheres of which man talks are within, but he never realizes nor imagines that he can find the higher spheres within himself.

The analysis of the spirit is simple: spirit is fine matter and matter is the dense spirit. It is only a difference of words, and most difficulties that arise come from a difference of words. Words are to cover truth, not to explain it. Truth cannot be explained in words. The spirit is likened to water; matter is likened to snow. Water and snow are the same, it is only the condition of water that makes it snow; thus it is a condition of spirit that makes it matter. It is in this process that man must realize and come to understand the great fullness of the purpose of life and of all that he seeks after through life.

It is related among Hindus that the Lord Indra, the God of the heavens, had fairies at his court, Upsaras whose work was to dance. Once one of them went to the earth and saw a mortal being, and she fell so deeply in love with him that she lifted him up and brought him to the spheres of Indra. And when it was known that the mortal man had been brought there, Indra commanded that he should be dropped back to the earth to live the mortal life, and that the fairy should be sent to the other end of the world to overcome her Karma.

This story conveys that every soul is born to dance before the throne of Indra, God. In reality every action of beauty, of harmony, every action of love, of kindness, of compassion is the dance of the soul. But when the soul becomes conscious of this dance, then the presence of Indra becomes clear to that soul. To be in the presence of Indra is to be in the presence of God. It is the greatest joy and happiness which nothing on the earth can give. As Rumi has written in the Masnavi, where the soul is likened to a reed flute: 'Why does the music of the flute appeal to you? Because it laments, it cries; it longs for that spirit, for that being which was its stem. This reed was cut away from its stem and holes were made in its heart. That made it cry. It cries with longing to rejoin the stem.'

So it is with every soul. The restlessness, the uncomfortable feeling of every soul, is always for one and the same reason, though each one gives a different reason. The one would like to possess earthly wealth; another suffers from the contempt of friends; another cannot approach his beloved; another has troubles at home; another has a case in court. But in reality there is only one trouble and that trouble is the sorrow of the spirit. As it is the inclination of every river to go and meet the sea, so it is the inclination of every soul to go and meet the spirit.

At this time, when materialism prevails everywhere, there seems to be a great hunger after truth. It is natural that people should hunger after truth. The very fact that there is so much materialism shows that every soul feels uncomfortable and begins to long for spiritual attainment. But how do they pursue spiritual attainment? Generally there are two kinds of seekers. There is one kind who is curious, who wonders if there is anything or not; if it is really true that there is a soul and a hereafter. They look for some phenomenon in order to try and prove it. They use psychometry, palmistry, clairvoyance, and all such different means. There may be hundreds and thousands wandering about in delusion looking for phenomena. And there may be another one who is perhaps more intellectual, who reads books on occult science, often because he has seen them recommended in the newspapers, and in the end he will surely become more and more confused.

Is this the way of learning? Is it not enough that from childhood one has to learn in school? And after having read all those books, all that there is to be read, at what does one arrive? At confusion. One does not know which is false and which is true.

Learning is one thing and unlearning is another, and unlearning means rising above what we call worldly learning. Very often what we call knowledge keeps our soul away from the knowledge of itself, a knowledge which is most essential because the knowledge acquired by learning is very complex. People think that if it is simple it cannot be truth, they value what is complex. But in this way by one's own tendency one covers over the truth in oneself which is one's own being.

DEPENDENCE

THERE are three different ways in which a person depends upon another. One way is that of a child which has been given into the care of its parents. The child has not sought it, it has not asked for it, it does not know even that it depends upon them; and yet it is put in a situation where it depends upon the parents.

And there is another aspect of dependence, where one depends upon someone to whom one has given one's confidence, one's trust. This way of depending is different; it is one's own choice. In order to depend in that way one must have some reason also. One says, 'Because my friend is sincere', 'because I trust him', 'because this is my relative', or, 'because this is someone whom I know I can depend upon'. It is just like depending upon a ship to carry one over the sea. There is every reason for one to depend upon the ship. One knows that this ship has sailed perhaps a hundred times from this port to the other port and has always come back safely; everyone knows it. Therefore this is a dependence acquired by reasoning. This dependence is the one we generally see in life.

Then there is a third kind of dependence, known better by the ancient peoples. In this world, in this age of materialism and commercialism, this dependence seems to have disappeared. It is dependence upon the unknown. When one reads in the Bible that even the lilies are clothed by nature, and when one reads in the Masnavi that even the smallest insect is taken care of by Providence, one should believe that if we did not do anything today, we should still be taken care of just the same; but then a person thinks, 'Bread is going up in price; what will become of me tomorrow?' and that person cannot believe in dependence upon the unknown. Today people think, 'If the lilies are clothed, I should be clothed according to the latest fashion!'

All this shows that we have become too artificial, and that is why, far from following this principle, we cannot even believe in it. There is a great deal of pessimism in all parts of the world, and the more civilized the country, the greater the pessimism and the greater the strife. It is not that the support of the Unknown has been taken away from man, but life is so difficult today that, far from his depending upon the unknown, it is difficult for even the idea of the unknown to reach him.

When we think of the hundreds and thousands of men at this time not knowing from one day to the next what they should do, anxious about how they can get on in life, we see that there is no progress. A progress that can make a person worried and anxious so that he cannot depend upon life, how can we call it progress? Progress means ease, relief, peace, happiness, less strife, less struggle; that is progress. Progress does not mean greater struggle, greater uneasiness, greater anxiety, and greater worry. A good example of this was the case of a man whose father had enormous wealth, so that he and his family could live for many generations quite comfortably; and this man was anxiously looking for some work. He came to ask me about it, and I said, 'I am very surprised that you are looking for work, and want to do something. What are you looking for?' He said, 'Some business, some industry, something to produce. That is the only real field of activity: where you can produce money.' I said, 'Is there no other field where you can produce something better than money? You have enough to live on.' 'But what will people say? I must do something', said the man, 'and I can only think of doing that, and nothing else!'

There is much in the world that can be done for the poor, the needy, the ignorant, and for those who are not yet awake but are still asleep; for the conflicts which exist between nations, for the prejudice between races. There is no end of work one can give one's thought to instead of thinking, 'No, I must produce some money'. Yet that is the only activity which is accepted by the world. If a person does not do that, people think that there is something wrong with him! And what has it done? It has wrecked the nervous system of the present generation. After a hundred years we shall see that the race will begin to suffer tremendously from it. Working beyond the limit, from morning till night, what do people gain? Some of them perhaps may make money, but many have only a loaf of bread in the evening. After a whole day's toil that is all they can get.

For mankind there is no other ideal left except money; and wherever there is a lack of it people feel it strongly because they do not believe in anything else. If you go to the capitalist, his God is the same; if you go to the socialist, his ideal is the same: money. All the different morals and arguments and theories and discussions aim at civilizing the world; but how can one civilize the world as long as money remains the ideal of the people? There is a very large number of people who do not wish to make a home and do not have a family for the one reason that they are waiting for money. Imagine, hundreds and thousands and millions of examples of this, waiting for the time when there will be enough money to live in a society as artificially as is done today!

The ideal of a home in ancient times was quite different. The home of each man was a palace for him. It might have been a home of straw, reeds, bamboo, brick, earth, or marble, but everyone's home was a palace. If they had simple bread and water, they were thankful to have it. They did not think that because another person had a home of marble they should not marry unless they had a home of marble too; that they should wait all their lives until they had a marble home. And this attitude is destroying the happiness of the world. It is spreading discontent; and lack of money, without any real reason, is felt more keenly. What must come as a result of this is the desire to snatch the money from the hands of others. All the different ways of improving the economic conditions of the world will not prove satisfactory as long as man does not look at the spiritual ideal as something greater and more worth while, forgetting for a moment the things of the earth.

A pessimistic person will object and say, 'Suppose I went and sat before the City Bank and raised my hands in prayer and said, "Million francs, million francs, million francs, I depend upon you, million francs!" will it come?' To such a person the Prophet Mohammad gave a very good answer. When the man said, 'I depend upon God', the Prophet said, 'Yes, but first tie your camel to the tree. Do not let your camel walk loose, and then depend upon God.' This was a practical hint the Prophet gave, but at the same time when we come to think about dependence upon the unknown, we go into a much deeper subject, a subject of the greatest value in our everyday life. It is true to say, 'Tie your camel to a tree', but do we not see that very often with all his strife and struggle and worry and anxiety a person gets nothing in the end? And very often we see that to a person who does not strive and struggle the hand of Providence comes naturally and shows him, 'Here you are. Here is what you want'. In the East there is a saying, 'When God gives, He pours it through the roof, so that it comes into the house'; and this is true also. We cannot see it because we do not want to see it, because we do not open our eyes; but it happens in everyday life.

Do you think that strife brings money, or struggle the things that you want in life? Do you think that anxiety produces what you wish for? Never; it is quite the contrary. Very often a person tosses about in his bed for months on end and says, 'Million dollars, million dollars', and he does not get it; or a person may go out and work from morning till evening to gain a million dollars, and he does not get it; yet there is another one who gets it very easily. America is the best example of this philosophy; people with nothing at all have gone there and worked, and have got everything. This shows that when it comes, it comes amply; when it does not come, it does not come. Does that not show that somewhere there is a key to it, a treasure-house from which one can draw? It shows that there is a hand of wisdom working behind all things. And the one who does not look for it, does not depend upon it, does not recognize it, makes a great error, for all through life he lives with the treasure and yet he does not know of it.

But if one looks at it from a metaphysical point of view, one will find that some action is necessary; not only depending, but also some development in one's own self. Even among the spiritual people of today, those who are engaged in so-called occult sciences or psychic practices, many have intellectual ideas, but when it comes to dependence, that is an idea they do not know of.

In order to depend upon anyone, we should have faith in that person; and our dependence upon him is a mechanism which gives him a responsibility. When we look at nature's phenomena we find most beautiful examples of this. When the little sparrows do not yet know how to fly and depend upon their parents, not only the mother but also the father brings grain in its beak and gives it to them. It is a most wonderful phenomenon to look at from this point of view of dependence. The young cannot fly, they depend upon the parents, and the day they begin to fly and collect grain themselves, then neither the mother nor the father has any inclination to share their grain with the little ones. From that day they leave them alone. This shows that if we look for the grain while saying, 'My mother and father must look for me also', it cannot be and it will not be. The day we have awakened to the realization that we are looking for our own grain the mother and father have lost their responsibility.

Our relation with the unknown is exactly the same. As soon as we begin to depend upon the known source and on our own faculties to get all we wish, the unknown becomes still more unknown. Just as the parents of the sparrows withdraw and do not appear any more to the young ones, so God Himself disappears more and more. The more we look after ourselves, the more the known source disappears. It is not that it is disappointed or angry; it is an automatic process. Naturally a mother, whose heart is always focused upon her little ones, is watchful at every move her child makes, in case it might tumble. But for how long? As long as the child has not gained control of itself. The moment the child has control of itself and looks where it is going, then the mother puts her mind to something else. It does not mean that her love has lessened; it only means that the moment the child is able to move about without depending upon the mother, then that much responsibility is removed from the heart of the mother. It is exactly the same thing with the Heavenly Father.

When a man is poor, but can just live with the means he has, one may wonder whether it would be right for him to give away all his belongings and in that way make himself dependent upon others. But what is good? This is very difficult to decide, for good is peculiar to every person. There is a story of the great Indian composer Sayn Aliyas. He was an ascetic, and for his daily food a loaf of bread was enough. It happened that people gave him more; but he would never keep anything for tomorrow; he would always give away what he had not eaten that day. And if one asked him why he made himself dependent upon other people, he would answer, 'We are all interdependent. As long as I do not force myself upon others, it all comes from God and it all goes to God's creatures'. So it all depends on the point of view, on how one looks at it.

Sufis are the best examples in the world of dependence upon God. One will find numberless examples in the history of the Sufis of how they have practised that dependence upon God as something spiritual. How have they practised it? Not only for their food, but for everything in life they have developed dependence in their nature. While everybody has looked for independence they have practised quite the opposite, dependence, and the wonderful results that they have achieved by practising this are worth studying: dependence on life with food and without food; dependence on health while considering it and without attending to it. And in this way they have not only made themselves independent of the world, but they have made the unknown known to them. It is in this way that they have found the nameless, the formless, the unseen, the unknown God. In the terms of the Sufi this is called *Tawakul,* which means dependence upon God.

FRIENDSHIP (1)

FRIENDSHIP is a word which we all use in our everyday language, and yet it could take one's whole life only to realize its meaning. However learned a person may be, however pious, spiritual, or experienced, if he has not learned the nature and character of friendship he has not learned anything. This is the first and the last thing we have to learn. We so often use this word lightly, calling every acquaintance a friend, or professing to be somebody's friend; but the more we realize the meaning of it, the less we are able to claim friendship. For everything in life we are tested, examined, and tried, but to pass this examination of friendship is the most difficult thing in the world.

What is the reason for this? Why is it so difficult to be a friend? One would think that it was the easiest thing there is! The reason is that there is something in ourselves which is always against our being friendly. It is the self, the ego, which the Sufi calls *Nafs*. As long as this ego is standing and lives, a man cannot claim to be anybody's friend. And when he is not somebody else's friend he is not even his own friend, for one learns friendship by being a friend to another. A selfish man may seem to be a friend to himself, but it is on the surface, not in reality. He has not yet learned how to be a friend to another, so he cannot be a friend to himself. In our pursuit of truth we want to learn a great many things: the nature of life, the secret of life, the character of life; and to understand the meaning of friendship seems so easy and simple that we never trouble to think about it, nor about the responsibility of being a friend. The great error we make in our lives is that we begin to claim friendship before we have learned the meaning of friendship. In this world of illusion, where at the end of the examination we find everything to be of little importance, of little worth, if there is a sign of reality, of something that one can depend upon, and in which one can recognize a sign of eternity, it is in the constancy of friendship.

Man, absorbed in the active life of this world, has a desire for friendship, though he never practises it. Yet this tendency to friendship can be found even among the animals. There is a story of a hunter who was shooting birds one day in the forest, and saw two birds sitting on a branch of a tree. He shot one bird and it dropped to the ground. As this man was at a distance it took him some time to arrive at the spot, and while he was walking towards it he saw that the other bird had come down to look at its mate. It touched it with its beak and found that it was dead, and by the time the man arrived he found both birds dead. 'From that day,' he said, 'I gave up shooting, for I had seen a friendship among birds which one cannot find among mankind.'

It is a simple lesson, and it is a lesson that we have to learn; today when nations are against nations and races against races, when communities are against communities, and one religion against another, it is now that friendship is so much needed. Besides, friendship is the first lesson of spirituality that one can learn. One may think that friendship, a personal friendship, means nothing; that one does not become spiritual through a personal friendship. But one does. A person begins his spiritual accomplishment by learning how to be a friend. For one who is really treading the path of friendship need not go anywhere to learn morals. Friendship itself teaches him sincerity, gratitude, sympathy, tenderness, appreciation; all these things that we must learn in this world, friendship teaches us. And once a man begins to learn these things through friendship with one person, he will naturally show to others the same virtues which he has acquired by going along this path; just as someone who has learned how to sing beautifully will naturally sing every song that is given to him beautifully. The one who has cultivated his heart through friendship will naturally be inclined to be friends with others.

It is not belief in God which leads us to the goal, nor is it the analysis and the knowledge of God that bring us there. It is the friendship of God. For someone who learns the lesson of friendship in this world, this lesson develops in the end into friendship with God. But when a person exacts in return from his friend all that he does for him, then it is not friendship, it is business. It only means: I give you a shilling and you give me twelve pence. When a person judges his friend, then the spirit of friendship is not awakened in his heart, for a friend never judges. When a person talks to another about his friend, when he blames him, when he criticizes him, he does not know what friendship is. The meaning of friendship is too sacred to realize. All other relationships and connections in this life are empty if friendship is not at the back of them to strengthen them. The relationship between mother and daughter, father and son, brother and sister, husband and wife, teacher and pupil, all these connections need a spirit behind them; and this spirit is the spirit of friendship. When a daughter says, 'I am friends with my mother', there is something beautiful about it. It makes the connection between a mother and a daughter a different thing, it makes it living. In every relationship it is the same. When there is friendship to bind the relationship it makes it secure, it gives it life. Love is life, and life is symbolized by water. When one wants to bring water up out of the ground one has to dig for it, and the first thing which one finds is mud. And if one is disappointed by that, one has fooled oneself, for beneath the earth is water; it can be found but one must have patience to dig for it, to dig deep enough to find the water.

If one has made a friend it is not something that one has made to order, that must just fit in according to one's expectations and wishes. Every individual has his own characteristics, and as long as the spirit of forgiveness is not developed, friendship cannot last. It is a continual forgiveness that helps friendship to endure. Much can be learned by study, but not unselfishness. Unselfishness can be learned by one thing only and that is by treading the path of friendship. And it brings beauty into one's life; a friendly person, whether in business or in a profession, in whatever capacity he stands, gives one a feeling of warmth; in other words an atmosphere of life. One is always glad to meet a friendly person in a shop, in a factory, in an office. When this spirit is awakened one can feel in his words, in his voice, in his expression, in his atmosphere, that he is a friendly person, that there is something that goes out to meet others, a continual tendency to harmonize with others.

Once this spirit is developed the ever-complaining tendency vanishes. If it is not developed then this world is full of thorns that prick. Then one will have no peace, no happiness, whatever one's position in life. If a person wants to make his life easy, if he wishes to create happiness in his life, he must try to crush that ego, that Nafs, that thought of self which keeps one continually absorbed in one's own thoughts and in one's own affairs. By rising above it he will learn the spirit of friendship. And then for him the same path which was full of thorns will become full of roses. For some souls that same world which can be hell to many others, is heaven. For friendship changes man's point of view. An unfriendly man, as soon as he sees another person, sees him from his own critical point of view. He has his preconceived ideas, and therefore he is not allowed by Providence to see the good side of the other. But the one in whom the friendly spirit is awakened always overlooks little errors, faults, mistakes; his sympathy and his love naturally help him to rise above the faults of man. That is the story of Jesus Christ, the friend of humanity, before whom the greatest sinners were brought; but the attitude of the Master was always forgiving. Those who brought them were unfriendly; the Master was friendly.

Life is as we look at it. If we wish to find faults we can find faults in the best person in the world, and if we wish to find good points we can find good points in the worst person in the world. It is as we see life. Someone went to Jami, the great seer of Persia, and asked him if he would accept him as his disciple on the spiritual path. Jami asked him, 'Have you loved, have you learned the manner of friendship?' He said, 'No, not yet.' Jami said, 'Go into the world again, and learn it.' The first lesson on the spiritual path that one has to learn is the manner of friendship. Once that is learned then all other parts of the spiritual journey will become easy. Where do all the disturbances, such as wars, revolutions, disagreeable experiences among nations, fights among parties, come from? They all come from lack of friendship. And the most extraordinary thing is that one party may perhaps have been fighting another party for years, but if we investigate their particular ideas we find that they are not even friends among themselves, for fighting against the other party produces and develops this unfriendly spirit in them. It is a kind of intoxication.

In education, in religion, or in anything else, the best thing one can do is to introduce the spirit of friendliness. And how can we introduce it? This is something which cannot arise only by reading some books about it. There exist innumerable societies and institutions of brotherhood everywhere, but they prove to be anything but brotherhood. Therefore that is not the way. The way is for an individual to be brought to understand fully that the essence of morals and of religion and of education is one, and that one essence is the manner of friendship. Sufis of all ages have named it *Suluk*, which means divine manner, beneficence. That is why the best education is beneficence: how to bring pleasure and happiness to another; and one can begin to learn this by understanding fully what friendliness is and by practising it at the same time.

FRIENDSHIP (2)

RELATIONSHIP is nourished by contact, kingship is maintained by reciprocity, but friendship is developed with love. There is no relationship that can be compared with friendship, for it is in learning the law of friendship that one understands ethics and morals, and also the relation between man and God.

There are three principal things to be understood in connection with friendship. The first is understanding without words. If there is no understanding between two persons, words are of no use. They may talk and talk, and discuss and discuss, and it will only go from bad to worse, for argument will never end. As it is said in the Vadan, 'Why? is an animal with a thousand tails. At every bite you give it, it drops one of its curved tails and raises another'. Can argument bring about understanding? Never. Argument only increases argument, and so one can go on till two persons turn their back upon one another. Understanding is a gift of God, understanding is a soul's unfoldment, and understanding is the greatest fortune one can have in life. It is with understanding that the foundation of friendship is established, and it is in understanding that friendship is secure. Without understanding there is no friendship.

And the next thing is a disinterested attitude. When a person thinks that by friendship he can get some benefit from the friend, or that the other may benefit by him, that is just burning the roots of friendship. In these material days so few of us understand what friendship means. Whenever there is a question of friendship the first thought is: what shall I gain by this friendship, can his influence be of some use to me? That is not friendship. Whenever a thought of self-interest creeps in, that means the ruin of friendship. Every little thought of profiting by it means destruction; it can never develop into a real friendship, it will only develop into a business relationship. It will last as long as the business relationship lasts, it will prosper as long as the business relationship prospers, and then it will vanish. Such a relationship can never be called friendship.

In this world every individual is helpless in some way or another, and every individual is of use in some way or another. It can happen that a person depends unconsciously upon his friend for his own interest, and even then it will turn out to be a wrong attitude. It cannot bring about fruitful results, for friendship must be built upon a solid foundation, a foundation where there is always a desire to give, to be helpful and serviceable to the friend: no thought of taking, always a thought of giving and keeping back nothing. A real friend holds his life cheap for his friend. The one who considers anything more important, more precious than friendship, has not yet learnt the first lesson of friendship. There is no sacrifice too great, if it is made for a friend. If a sacrifice is not made for a friend, then for whom should one make it? A person would never learn how to make any sacrifice if it were not for a friend.

In our daily life we take the word friendship too lightly, and we confuse the words 'friend' and 'acquaintance'. An acquaintance is someone whom we have met, and he has seen us, and we recognize one another. We may have been introduced at a dinner party. We use the word 'friend' so freely in everyday language that we have forgotten the meaning of it. Generally we call anyone whom we have seen at a reception or party a friend; or anyone that belongs to our club. But even to have one friend in one's life is the greatest good fortune.

And the third important thing in friendship is overlooking. No man in the world is faultless, no soul in the world is perfect. If on our part there is no desire to overlook our friends' shortcomings, there can be no more friendship. Friendship is maintained by recognizing that a human being is imperfect, that he has his faults and shortcomings. There is always something in him to overlook, and if we go on doing so, there is always the possibility that he may develop those very qualities which are lacking, for we may add to our friend qualities that are wanting in him. Sometimes people meet once, and they feel they are friends. Sometimes people know each other for months and years, and so they grow to be friends; their knowing one another and coming together in the end brings about the fulfilment of friendship. In such cases it develops as a result of their knowing one another.

Another odd thing sometimes happens, and that is when two persons are at daggers drawn for many months or years, and then suddenly throw their daggers away and become friends for ever; but this is unusual. I myself have seen people who have been enemies working against one another for years, and from the day they became friends they have been the closest friends. Those who say, 'I was his friend and he was my friend but now we are not friends any more', should realize that they have never been friends. It was a presumption on their part, a false impression. Can friendship be such a false thing, can gold be gold at one time and not at another? Gold is gold, it never changes, it remains the same. Constancy in friendship is the soul of friendship. And that custom whereby a friend writes to another 'Yours as always' is wrong. If a plant remains as it has always been, it does not grow, and that which does not grow is not living, and that which is not living is dead.

When a person thinks, 'I am too good or too kind to you, I have been too devoted to you', that person forgets that kindness, goodness and devotion are larger than the horizon. No one can be too good, no one can be too kind, and no one can be too devoted. And when there is a discussion between friends, and one says, 'I have done so much for you, I have suffered so much for you, I have had so much pain on your account, I have had such a difficult life for your sake,' then he is entering into business. He wants to keep a diary of what he has given in the form of love and kindness and goodness and sacrifice. A true friend makes every sacrifice he can and never thinks about it; he does not even allow his mind to ponder upon the subject. Real friendship means regard, a deep regard for the pleasure and displeasure of the friend. Is there anything in life which is more delicate than friendship—taking care that no words should hurt the friend, that no action should harm him, that not the slightest shade of coldness may fall on his heart? It is most difficult. If a person has learnt the manner of friendship he need not learn anything more; he knows everything. He has learnt the greatest religion, for it is in this same way that one will make a way to God. The one who has never learnt the manner of friendship will never know the way to God. He may be God's worshipper, but he cannot be the friend of God.

There is an attitude which one often sees in friends, and that attitude reveals a divine secret. It is the tendency to cover up any fault that one's friend has committed from another person; and not only to cover it from the sight of others, but even from one's own sight. Never thinking about it, never looking at it, interpreting it differently, such a man turns the wrong of his friend into right. And every little good point of his friend, even though it may only weigh an ounce, he makes into a pound. He appreciates and admires it so much, he raises it so high, he considers it so great, that another person cannot imagine how this insignificant idea, this slight merit, can be valued so highly.

In the beginning of my spiritual pursuit, when I went to my murshid there was no end to my enthusiasm, there was no end to my devotion, there was no end to my excitement about it. I told everybody I met how I felt about the personality of my murshid. Once, in answer to my deep feeling, my murshid said, 'Friendship in the path of God, friendship in the path of truth is greater than any friendship in life.' And at that time I met a very learned man in Hyderabad, with whom I spoke about the deeper things of life. He was interested to hear such deep thoughts from a young man, and said that he would like to see more of me. And in my great enthusiasm I said, 'If you saw my teacher you would realize that there is no one in the whole world who can be compared with him, so great is he, so wonderful is his personality, so blessed is his presence, so inspiring his glance, so peaceful his atmosphere.' He said, 'I would like very much to see him. Where does he live?' I told him, and then he exclaimed, 'There? I have lived there for twenty years; it is just next door to my house! What is his name?' I told him, and he said, 'I have known him all these years, but I never thought he was so great!' In twenty years he had not seen what I had seen in a few months. It is friendship that enlightens one; and it is distance that keeps one's eyes covered.

If we are friends, and if we cannot understand one another, then we are not yet friends, we only think we are friends. But if we understand, then all the beautiful points in us both are made a thousand times more clear because of that friendship. In friendship there is no limitation.

Lastly we come to that most mysterious expression, and yet an expression which is known to all on the religious path: the Grace of God. What is it? It is the friendship of God. It is the friendly emotion of God. It is not the judging quality of God. When God's grace comes, it does not come by saying, 'Are you worthy, are you unworthy, do you deserve it, do you not deserve it?' It comes as emotion, love, devotion, admiration comes from friend to friend. There are no limits to it. It is all right for someone to say that because in the past incarnation he has done so much evil, in this life he has a bad time with much suffering; or that in the past incarnation he has done so much good, that this time he has become rich. And it is all right for others to say that when they go to hell for their sins they will be whipped and thrashed and put into the fire. But when you look at the grace of God, you forget all these things; no rules, no laws, no deserving or undeserving can be distinguished any more. There is only one thing, and that is love; love that stands above law.

God's grace does not come specially to the pious, it does not come necessarily to the people who are very good, nor does it come readily to the people who are very occult or mystical. It comes as love comes from friend to friend. When love comes it comes without a conception of right and wrong. It is an emotion, it is the rising of the wave, it is a divine feeling that comes. It rises as a stream, and it falls upon the person in the form of a thousand gifts. It may be as inspiration, it may be as comfort, it may be as health, it may be as peace, it may be as rest, it may show itself in a thousand different forms.

The knowledge of what will please your friend, if it comes to you at all, will only come if you really know what friendship is. Otherwise you may presume you are a friend, and all your life you may try to please your friend, but you will never really be able to do so.

It is the same with God. You may do all possible good actions and offer a thousand prayers, and yet if you do not know what pleases God, you cannot please Him. But it does not come from knowledge; it only comes from friendship. Friendship is an automatic action, it is an innocent devotion, an unconscious outgoing, a pure feeling with depth, with life. Automatically that feeling brings about grace. Therefore no one can say why a person is another's friend. We cannot be the judge of it; we cannot understand it. And so no one can say why God is pleased with this person or that person. Sometimes we see that people who do not deserve it have great wealth; and then here are others who, if they had money, would really make the best use of it. Some do not seem to deserve the position or rank they hold; others perhaps in our eyes deserve more; and yet in the eyes of God it is different. It is because they deserve it, though we do not see why and how. And it is the same with friendship. When someone said to Majnun, 'Majnun, Leila is not beautiful, why are you so devoted to Leila?' Majnun said, 'To see Leila you must borrow my eyes.'

When we judge people do we see with the eyes of God, do we see what feeling God has towards them? And when we cannot see in this way we have no right to question why others are in this or that position in life, why some people are rich, why they are in a big position; it is all a kind of battle with God. And those who learn this one principle: that with a friend one should do one's very best to the end, in order to prove worthy of his friendship; and those who try to do their utmost to regard the pleasure and displeasure of God without any thought of reward or of any answer from Him, it is those who really know the meaning of friendship.

THE FOUR PATHS WHICH LEAD TO THE GOAL

THERE is one path which may be called the way of the intellectual. When an intellectual person has risen above his intellectuality it is then that he may be called an intelligent person. For there is a difference between the intellectual and the intelligent. An intellectual person is he who has gathered knowledge by impressions, by studies; and he is the king of the domain of his intellect. What he has learned, what he has studied, what he has experienced, he has kept in the book of his mind; and that is his world. But it makes him captive to a limited horizon of knowledge, and it is the rising above that knowledge which may be called intelligence. Yet it is the intellectual person who is capable of being intelligent; intellect is a cover over intelligence, and when this cover is taken off then a person becomes intelligent. The intelligent one is he who perceives for himself, who learns for himself, who understands for himself, who recognizes things by himself, who is a pupil and who is a teacher within himself at the same time.

Once a person has risen above the boundaries of his limited knowledge, then the higher knowledge begins to come to him by itself. He begins to learn more in one moment than an intellectual person would learn after having read all the books in the library during many years. When once an intelligent person has got an insight into the hidden laws of nature, he begins to see a way opening to the higher knowledge. His reasoning changes its nature; it becomes the essence of reason. He does not see things through the reason he has learned from the world, but he begins to see the reason of all reasons, the reason which is covered by ordinary reasoning.

Man is born intelligent; it is afterwards that he covers his intelligence and that he is glad to call it intellect. Then he is recognized as being learned, and he thinks that he has acquired some knowledge, but it is at this point that he makes his intelligence limited. And as long as his intelligence is limited, he cannot see further than he sees.

There is a time in a person's life when he is learning, and there comes a time when he himself is knowledge. It is at the time when the soul becomes knowledge itself that it begins to have glimpses into the hidden laws of nature; and this illumination may develop so that a person sees the whole of manifestation clearly and fully in the light of intelligence. The Qur'an says, 'God is the Light of the heavens and of the earth'; and if there is any spark of God that can be found in man, it is his intelligence. Naturally, therefore, when this divine light which is hidden in man is once brought to a blaze and has risen as a flame, it illuminates his path towards perfection.

The second path to perfection is the path of righteousness, of duty, of good actions. A person may not be intelligent, but conscientious in what he does and what he should do, always using his goodwill to do a righteous action; and by doing so he is fulfilling that law of harmony which automatically raises his soul to perfection. Very often one wonders about friends or relations who one thinks are goodness itself, their actions being righteous actions, and yet they never seem to show any tendency towards religion or meditation; and then one often thinks what a pity it would be if they did not arrive at spiritual perfection. But it is quite possible that they will arrive at that perfection before the seeker who makes too much fuss about it and does little; before a person who talks too much about spiritual things and knows little; before the one who is clinging to the outer signs of religion and spirituality. Merely by his righteous actions, by his good deeds, such a person will attain the goal. He may not know it, but it will work automatically, because he is taking the path of righteousness which will surely lead him to perfection.

The third path is the path of discipline, and it is in this path that concentration, meditation, contemplation, and all different forms of discipline are necessary, in order to bring about that realization which is the ultimate goal. The path of meditation enables man to experience different planes of life, not always classified as people do when speaking about this plane and that plane, this grade and that grade. The real experience of inner life cannot very well be classified. For instance, if one asks a meditative person, 'Are there seven planes of existence?, he will say, 'Yes it is so.' But when another person says, 'I have read in a book on Greek philosophy that there are nine planes of existence; can it be true?' he will answer, 'Certainly'. Then another one comes and says, 'I think that there are only three planes', and again he will agree. He does not say this to please; he is able to see these planes as five, seven, nine, in as many forms as he likes, because he actually sees them so. Go to a beginner in music and ask how many notes there are. He will answer, seven; and perhaps he will mention the semitones besides. But if you asked of an experienced musician who has given all his life to music and has come to understand the essence of sound, 'Is it not true, as the Chinese say, that there are twenty notes in the octave?' he will say, 'Yes, it can be true, but when the Indians say that there are twenty-four notes in the octave, that is true too; it is how you look at it.'

All that man learns intellectually about metaphysics keeps him limited to book-learning. He derives no benefit but a passing interest; it is a surprise to him to know that there are so many different planes of our being. He does not go further, and if he wanted to see them and know what they are, he could not. But by meditation he can realize them, and by this realization he can give the interpretation of any philosophy, whether Buddhist, or ancient Greek, or Vedanta philosophy, any philosophy you put before him, for he knows what he has experienced through meditation.

No doubt the way of self-discipline is a very difficult way. It is the way of mastery, of power; but it is a hard and difficult path. Practising discipline by sitting in a certain pose or posture is very difficult to keep up for a long time. If one makes a vow to refrain from eating fruit, sweet or sour things, a vow of silence, of fasting, of standing so many hours, or walking, or staying up for part of the night or the whole night, it is not always easy to keep to it. Self-discipline is learned by going against one's own inclinations. Why should one go against them? Are inclinations not natural? One cannot say what is one's own inclination; all inclinations are borrowed here, and what one calls natural is what one has become accustomed to. The word 'natural' is a word that one can study for years and years, and one will find at the end of the study that there is no such thing as natural. There are natural inclinations to pleasure and comfort which clash with the still greater and deeper inclinations we have for more power and strength, for more light and for more life. So the inclinations can be divided into two aspects: the innermost inclinations, and the inclinations which one feels in everyday life. There is always a conflict between them; and the innermost inclinations are sometimes undermined by the outer inclinations. By learning self-discipline one learns to suppress the outer inclinations in order to make way for the inner inclinations to rise and to flourish, which finally culminates in what we call mastery.

The fourth path of perfection may be called the path of devotion, a path that cannot be compared in value or in depth with any other path. The reason is that devotion touches the Spirit of God. Not everyone is capable of this method, for in some people the heart is closed by the head quality, by intellect, but in others the heart quality is foremost. The first step on the path of devotion teaches selflessness; it makes one unselfish. Devotion is the tuning of the heart to its natural pitch; in other words, the healthiest condition possible in man is that in which devotion has blossomed. It is devotion alone that buries man's false self, be it devotion to a human being or to God. If truth is ever to be seen it is in devotion; for the world of heart is a different world from the world in which we all live; its law is different, the weather there is different, its sky is different, its sun and moon are different. The nature of that world is different; it is a world in itself. By devotion, heaven is brought to earth. And yet how very often a person says, 'But is it not a simple devotion?' It is in simplicity that the greatest subtlety is to be found; for it is the heart of the devotee which is liquid compared to the one which has become crystallized. It is awakened to sympathy, it is open to appreciate all beauty.

Women are more attracted to devotion than men, for generally the nature of women is to be more respectful towards human beings. This is natural, for if it were not for the love of the mother the world would not go on. This is the principle of devotion; it is in the quality of devotion which exists in women that the secret of the whole creation resides.

Krishna has said, 'I am with my devotees'. And therefore if one says, 'Where is God? Is He in the sixth heaven or in the seventh, or in a certain paradise or palace in which people imagine Him to be?' the answer is that the paradise or the palace or the dwelling-place of God is in the heart of His devotee. No doubt it is not easy for man to rise to devotion to God. It is on this account that the Sufis in all ages have practised devotion gradually, by their sympathy for their teacher, by the devotion to their Lord, and by the culmination of that devotion in God. It is devotion which raises the object of its devotion, or its ideal, to the highest heaven. It is by devotion that the rocks have been turned into gods. Someone asked a Hindu, 'By worshipping a God made of rock, what do you gain? Do you really believe that you have made a God?' 'Yes,' said the Hindu, 'my hands have made this God of stone, and my devotion has given life to it. If you believe in a formless God and have no devotion, you have not yet reached him. He is far away from you. My God is before me; your God is far away from you.' As the Bible says, God is love. If God is to be found anywhere, he is to be found in the heart of man. And when is He to be found? When the heart is awakened to sympathy, to love, to devotion.

HUMAN EVOLUTION

IT IS NOT only the human race that has evolved as time has passed, age after age, but an individual also evolves in his lifetime. In other words, humanity evolves gradually during a world's lifetime, while an individual, if he evolves at all, does so during his life. It is possible that the human race may take an opposite course; instead of evolving it may go back, and so it is with individuals too. But a person who is really evolving will not go back. If he did go back some steps he would feel uneasy and discontented, and he would go forward again. Perhaps he will go back a hundred times, but then a hundred times he will go forward again, for a person who has once experienced the joy and happiness of evolution will not be content with going back; feeling the discomfort of it he will go on.

No doubt the rhythm of every person's evolution is different. One can read in the Vadan that one soul creeps, another soul walks, another soul runs, and another soul flies; and yet they live on the same earth, under the same sun, and they are all called human beings. How strange it is that at the present time a new spirit has awakened in humanity, and one does not recognize the evolution of personality any longer! What one does distinguish is the nationality; whatever country one enters, the first thing they ask for is one's passport. It does not matter what evolution one has, and it does not matter what one's soul is experiencing; as long as one has a passport which distinguishes one as the subject of this or that country, that is the important thing. And very often people make a great virtue of saying, 'I am as good as you'. But imagine the insolence of it! The better one is the less one considers oneself to be. The one who is really better could not say, 'I am as good as you'. This means that the consciousness of the present-day man is inferior; he says, 'I am as good as you', because unconsciously he feels inferior in his mind.

Whose fault is it? One might say it is the fault of nations, of races, of education, and one might give many other excuses. But it is the times, it is the spirit of the times. It is no one's fault; yet at the same time it is not necessary to go through a condition in a kind of intoxication; it is better to awaken to the knowledge of that condition. It is better to become acquainted with the real condition of humanity today. When we study human nature from a metaphysical point of view, we shall see that the origin of human nature is the same as the origin of all other things; and the central theme of that origin is intolerance. Without reason, man's first feeling is that another must not exist. Later that feeling becomes modified, and man becomes more sympathetic, more harmonious and considerate; but the first feeling he has is that another should not exist.

Where does this feeling come from? In reality there is one life and there is one being; this world of variety is made of one being; it is the manifestation of the One. But at the same time in this world of variety, in this manifestation, the one Being loses that consciousness of being one, and there arises the consciousness of being many; in that way one being comes to stand against another being. Friendship, sympathy, harmony, attachment, devotion, all these come afterwards as man evolves, but they are not his first tendencies. The first tendency is a kind of jarring influence. For instance, how happy one feels when one is sitting in the train alone; but as soon as another person enters, one thinks that this is a great crime! One would rather he had gone to the other compartment and left one alone. It is a natural feeling when in a restaurant one is eating at a table alone, and a stranger comes to sit at the same table; he may be an angelic person, but as soon as he comes, one thinks, 'Why? Have they not got any more tables?' And this feeling comes even to harmonious people; I am not speaking of the inharmonious ones.

Is there then anything to be surprised at if in the history of the world there have been so many wars and battles? And for what? For nothing. Man is more fond of war than of peace. He likes peace after a war, but if he had loved peace before the war there would never have been a war.

What is the soul? If there is any explanation that can be given of the soul, it is the feeling of 'I am'. The feeling of one's existence, this is the soul; that part of one's being which feels that one exists. And what is the ego? Ego is what is gathered around the soul, and that is the knowledge of oneself. When a person says or feels, 'I exist', that is the feeling of the soul. But he goes further and says, 'I exist as what? I exist as a physical body, as hands, as feet, as head, as a tall person, as a short person, as a thin person, as a stout person'. It is that feeling of being a tangible and visible being, it is that knowledge surrounding the soul, which makes the ego, the Nafs. There are many friends in this world and there are many enemies; but the best friend and at the same time the worst enemy is our own ego. It is our best friend when it becomes a friend; but first of all it is the worst enemy. Every time a person takes offence at something, every insult that a person feels, every impulse to do something, it all comes from the Nafs.

The ego is like the rose and also like the thorns which surround the rose. It takes the place of the thorns when it is not cultivated, and it becomes a rose when it is refined. And the way to make it refined is to humble oneself and to crush one's desires. It is by the process of crucifixion that a person refines the ego. It is a hard grain, and it must be ground till it becomes a fine powder, out of which a paste is made.

When the ego remains in the condition of a thorn, more thorns come; and more and more, till it increases its thorns to such an extent that everyone who touches that person is dissatisfied. We all have friends to whom we should be most grateful if they would keep away from us. We love them, we like them, but we would be very glad if they would keep away. What is it? It is the thorns that hurt.

In what way do these thorns manifest? They manifest in the form of words, of actions, of desires, in the form of manner. Why does one feel annoyed with certain people in life, even before they have uttered one word? Because the thorn is pricking. Perhaps that person will say, 'But I have not said anything, I have not done anything,' but he does not know that he has thorns; there are perhaps so many that even before he utters one word, before he moves, his presence pricks us. It is a natural outcome of the ego. Either the ego develops thorns, or it develops into a rose; and when it develops into a rose, then everyone is attracted to it because of its beautiful petals, its delicacy, its fragrance, its colour, its softness, its structure. Everything about it is attractive, appealing, and healing.

For every soul there are four stages to pass through in order to come to the culmination of the ego, which means to reach the stage of the rose. The first stage is that a person is rough, thoughtless, and inconsiderate. He is interested in what he wants and in what he likes; as such he is naturally blind to the needs and wants of others. In the second stage a man is decent and good as long as his interests are concerned. As long as he can get his wish fulfilled he is pleasant and kind and good and harmonious; but if he cannot get his wish and cannot have his way, then he becomes rough and crude and changes completely. And there is a third stage, when someone is more concerned with another person's wish and desire, and less with himself; when his whole heart is seeking for what he can do for another. In his thought the other person comes first and he comes afterwards. That is the beginning of turning into the rose. It is only a rosebud, but then in the fourth stage this rosebud blooms in the person who entirely forgets himself in doing kind deeds for others.

In Sufi terms the crushing of the ego is called *Nafs Kushi*. And how do we grind it? We grind it by sometimes taking ourselves to task. When the self says, 'O no, I must not be treated like this', then we say, 'What does it matter?' When the self says, 'He ought to have done this, she ought to have said that,' we say, 'What does it matter, either this way or that way? Every person is what he is; you cannot change him, but you can change yourself'. That is the grinding.

When a thorn shows itself and you grind it as soon as you notice it, that same thorn by being crushed will turn into a rose, for the thorn also belongs to the rose bush. And when a person says, 'I will not occupy this position, I will not eat this, I hate it, I despise it, I cannot bear it, I cannot look at it, I cannot endure it, I cannot stand it,' these are all little thorns. A person may not know it, but they are thorns, and when they are crushed, then the rose comes out of it. How easy it is for people to say they want to know about mysticism and occultism. If there were an even bigger name, they would like to take an interest in that, and they believe that by reading books one can understand it, by learning lessons one can learn it, or by doing certain practices one can know it. But it is the everyday life that teaches us from morning till night.

Every moment of the day and night we are up against something that our Nafs rebels against; and if we took that opportunity to crush it, to put it down, in some years' time our personality would become a rose.

Is it then always wrong to be what is called an egoist? There are many kinds of egoists. There are good points and there are bad points in an egoistic person. The egoist is selfish, and selfish men can produce cruelty and dishonesty. But there is another side to it, and that is pride and independence and indifference, which give him contentment; besides when the real egoist, whose ego stands before him like a statue of rock, watches that ego, then after some time that ego becomes a living being. It comes to life and becomes the very being that one is seeking. Therefore the right egoist is right and the wrong egoist is wrong.

For whom shall we build a throne of soft cushions? For our own vanity's sake, thinking that we are better than others? No, for the pleasure of others, and not for our vanity. As soon as the question arises, 'Am I not better than others, am I not more spiritual or wiser than others?' then there is 'I'. That is wrong. What does it matter what we are as long as we are able to give pleasure to others, to make life easy for others? For this is the world of woes; there is no end to the troubles; from the king to the pauper, from the richest to the poorest, there are endless troubles hanging over the head of every individual. And if we can be of some little use to anybody, we can more easily learn what mysticism is; for the only real mysticism is when a person realizes that he pleases God by pleasing mankind.

It is only in this way that we can crush our ego. Every time that we notice its pinprick, every time that its thorns appear before our eyes, we should crush it and say, 'What are you? Are you not thorns, are you not the cause of unhappiness for others and myself as well? I do not want to see my own being in such a form, in the form of thorns! I want my being to be turned into a rose, that I may bring happiness, pleasure, and comfort to others.' If there is anything needed in spiritual teaching, in seeking truth, in self-realization, it is the refinement of the ego. For the same ego which begins by being our worst enemy, will in the end, if developed and cultivated and refined, become our best friend.

APPENDIX I

THE AIMS OF THE SUFI MOVEMENT

The Movement is based upon the Sufi Message brought to the Western world by Hazrat Inayat Khan in 1910.

In his studies as an initiate in one of the ancient Sufi orders, Inayat Khan recognised the basic love and wisdom through which humanity may realize the purpose of life. He saw these two principles as enshrined in the ideals of all religions. He held that by honouring all, and respecting their differences, a basis for mutual understanding could be reached which would not be possible by seeking to convert one to the views of another.

In pursuance of his vision he came to the West, and taught in Europe and America until 1926 when, shortly before his passing, he returned to India. He called his teaching the Sufi Message and to propagate it he founded a body called the International Sufi Movement. In the constitution are enshrined the following Sufi Thoughts:

1. There is one God, the Eternal, the Only Being; none else exists save He.
2. There is one Master, the Guiding Spirit of all souls, who constantly leads his followers towards the light.
3. There is one Holy Book, the sacred manuscript of nature, the only scripture which can enlighten the reader.
4. There is one Religion, the unswerving progress in the right direction towards the ideal, which fulfils the life's purpose of every soul.
5. There is one Law, the Law of Reciprocity, which can be observed by a selfless conscience together with a sense of awakened justice.
6. There is one Brotherhood, the human brotherhood, which unites the children of earth indiscriminately in the fatherhood of God.
7. There is one Moral Principle, the love which springs forth from self-denial, and blooms in deeds of beneficence.
8. There is one Object of Praise, the beauty which uplifts the heart of its worshipper through all aspects from the seen to the unseen.
9. There is one Truth, the true knowledge of our being within and without which is the essence of all wisdom.

10. There is one Path, the annihilation of the false ego in the real, which raises the mortal to immortality and in which resides all perfection.

The Movement has the following Objects:

1. To realize and spread the knowledge of unity, the religion of love and wisdom, so that the bias of faiths and beliefs may of itself fall away, the human heart may overflow with love, and all hatred caused by distinctions and differences may be rooted out.
2. To discover the light and power latent in man, the secret of all religion, the power of mysticism, and the essence of philosophy, without interfering with customs or belief.
3. To help to bring the world's two opposite poles, East and West, closer together by the interchange of thought and ideals, that the Universal Brotherhood may form of itself, and man may meet with man beyond the narrow national and racial boundaries.

Regarding the aims of the Movement, we quote as follows from the words of Inayat Khan:

"The purpose of the Sufi Movement is to work towards unity. Its main object is to bring humanity, divided as it is into so many different sections, closer together in the deeper understanding of life. It is a preparation for a world service, chiefly in three ways. One way is the philosophical understanding of life; another is bringing about brotherhood among races, nations, and creeds; and the third way is the meeting of the world's greatest need, which is the religion of the day. Its work is to bring to the world that natural religion which has always been the religion of humanity: to respect one another's belief, scripture, and teacher. The Sufi message is the echo of the same divine message which has always come and will always come to enlighten humanity. It is not a new religion; it is the same message which is being given to humanity. It is the continuation of the same ancient religion which has always existed and will always exist, a religion which belongs to all teachers and all the scriptures.

"Sufism in itself is not a religion nor even a cult with a distinct or definite doctrine. No better explanation of Sufism can be given than by saying that any person who has a knowledge of both outer and inner life is a Sufi. Thus there has never at any period of the world's history been a founder of Sufism, yet Sufism has existed at all times.

"The present-day Sufi Movement is a movement of members of different nations and races united together in the ideal of wisdom; they believe that wisdom does not belong to any particular religion or race, but to the human race as a whole. It is a divine property which mankind has inherited; and it is in this realization that the Sufis, in spite of belonging to different nationalities, races, beliefs, and faiths, still unite and work for humanity in the ideal of wisdom.

"The Sufi message warns humanity to get to know life better and to achieve freedom in life; it warns man to accomplish what he considers good, just, and desirable; it warns him before every action to note its consequences by studying the situation, his own attitude, and the method he should adopt.

"Sufism not only guides those who are religious, mystical, or visionary, but the Sufi message gives to the world the religion of the day: and that is to make one's life a religion, to turn one's occupation or profession into a religion, to make one's ideal a religious ideal. The object of Sufism is the uniting of life and religion, which so far seem to have been kept apart. When a man goes to church once a week, and devotes all the other days of the week to his business, how can he benefit by religion? Therefore, the teaching of Sufism is to transform everyday life into a religion, so that every action may bear some spiritual fruit.

"The method of world reform which various institutions have adopted today is not the method of the Sufi Movement. Sufis believe that if evil is contagious, goodness must be even more so. The depth of every soul is good; every soul is searching for good, and by the effort of individuals who wish to do good in the world much can be done, even more than a materialistic institution can achieve. No doubt for the general good there are political and commercial problems to be solved; but that must not debar individuals from progress, for it is the individual progress through the spiritual path which alone can bring about the desired condition in the world.

"The Sufi message is not for a particular race, nation, or church. It is a call to unite in wisdom. The Sufi Movement is a group of people belonging to different religions, who have not left their religions but who have learned to understand them better, and their love is the love for God and humanity instead of for a particular section of it. The principal work that the Sufi Movement has to accomplish is to bring about a better understanding between East and West, and between the nations and races of his world. And the note that the sufi message is striking at the present time is the note which sounds the divinity of the human soul. If there is any moral principle that the Sufi Movement brings, it is this: that the whole of humanity is like one body, and any organ of that body which is hurt or troubled can indirectly cause damage to the whole body. And as the health of the whole body depends upon the health of each part, so the health of the whole of humanity depends upon the health of every nation. Besides, to those who are awakening and feel that now is the moment to learn more of the deeper side of life, of truth, the Sufi Movement extends a helping hand without asking to what religion, sect, or dogma they belong. The knowledge of the Sufi is helpful to every person, not only in living his life rightly but in regard to his own religion. The Sufi Movement does not call a man away from his belief or chruch: it calls him to live it. In short, it is a movement intended by God to unite humanity in brotherhood and in wisdom."

From *The Sufi Message of Hazrat Inayat Khan,* Volume IX

APPENDIX II

HAZRAT INAYAT KHAN MEMORIAL TRUST

The Hazrat Inayat Khan Memorial Trust, located in New Delhi, has been created for religious and charitable purposes. It is founded on the Sufi Message of love, harmony and beauty, as brought by Hazrat Inayat Khan (1882-1927).

Its goal is twofold: It wants to unite all people longing for love, harmony and beauty; and it wants to create not only a physical opportunity for this to happen, but also to create the appropriate atmosphere.

Its original and first activity was—and remains to be—to take care of the Dargah (memorial tomb) of this Sufi saint and master, who has been working for human brotherhood, religious tolerance, mysticism in daily life, the unity of religious ideals and a practical life philosophy. Apart from his being an active and famous musician in the first decade of this century in India, he has been working mainly in the West, bringing about a greater understanding for the values, the philosophy and the music of India, thus preparing ground for later positive developments.

The Trust further undertakes, within the limits set by the donations by Sufis and others, to render financial, material and spiritual help to the needy and destitute, particularly around the Dargah. This help is given to improve the physical health, to leniate immediate suffering, to provide for better living conditions through education, and by providing food to children and other needy persons. The Trust also looks after housing problems in some cases.

During the last fifteen years the Trust has succeeded to make the Dargah into a dignified place and to start making it suitable for the Sufi work. It is becoming a place of peace and happiness, for silence and meditation, a home for everybody looking for these experiences within or without, its atmosphere charging every open-hearted visitor with upliftment and new energy. It is intended to become an ecumenical meeting ground in the real sense of the word for Hindus, Buddhists, Parsis, Sikhs, Jains, Jews, Christians, Muslims, and all others with sympathy in their hearts. At the same time it must be a place for help to our fellow-men. Here everyone can feel at home and free, and can meet people from other circles on 'neutral' yet warm and inspired ground. It is a centre for the spreading of the ecumenical Sufi Message of love, harmony and beauty: a Message of universal brotherhood and tolerance, a basis for inter-religious brotherhood, a platform for inter-communal understanding, a spiritual centre, and an 'akasha' for love, harmony and beauty.

Gradually, the land around the Dargah had become completely occupied by temporary dwellings, refugees and others. To enlarge the area for our direct use was a very difficult and expensive task, because the Trust wanted to help the tenants living on the spot in acquiring better accommodation, even with financial assistance to these tenants living in the very poor huts in this area. In other cases, the Trust has given some help to a tenant in starting a business.

In this way it became also possible to make some space available for the social, medical and educative programmes of the Hope Project Charitable Trust, another Sufi organisation working in the name of Hazrat Inayat Khan. The work of this Trust is to provide free social services to those living in the community around the Dargah. It includes the Hazrat Inayat Khan Health Centre, where medical treatment and referral services are provided; two dispensaries are being run, one homeopathic, the other allopathic, which help about 250 patients a day. In the Milk programme milk is distributed everyday to infants, pregnant mothers and the infirm. The Hazrat Inayat Khan Education Centre offers educational and vocational training for children and adults from the Basti; there is a school for women, girls and little boys for educational and vocational training, free of charge. The social work programme offers help to those who are in crisis situations, financial troubles, the disabled and anyone who is in need.

This is quite in the tradition of Sufi Dargahs in India: besides spiritual activities also the material requirements of those in need are provided for.

In 1988 the new Dargah building was inaugurated. It is constructed around the original mazaar (tomb) by ASEMA architects in close contact with the Trust. Its simple design in beautiful material and harmonious proportions may be a symbol for the scope each individual has for the design of his life and the development of his heart. With this new building new opportunities are opening up.

Even before that time the activities of the Trust have grown steadily, and have become more intense. During a greater part of the year there are daily prayers and meditations, weekly qawalli concerts, weekly classes of the Inner School; each month Universal Worship is held, where texts from the sacred scriptures of the major world religions are read; occasionally there are concerts of spiritual classical Indian music, music playing such an important role in Inayat Khan's Message; regularly lectures and courses on modern Sufism are being given. On special occasions there is langar, the free distribution of food to the local population. There is a small library in a preliminary form, on the fields of Sufism, philosophy, psychology, mysticism and (comparative) religion.

Further new activities are being envisaged. The first of these is realised by the publication of this series of volumes on the Sufi Message by Hazrat Inayat Khan. Brotherhood meetings will be organised amongst followers of different religions in order to increase mutual tolerance through understanding and realisation of the essentials we have in common. Courses will be developed on the Sufi Message on subjects such as: the unity of religious ideals, moral culture as the way to God, the development of personality; the tuning of mind, heart and spirit, etc. Further opportunities will be created to participate in meditation, silence, prayer, and spiritual music in order to develop the feeling of sympathy within so that it may radiate. Staging concerts of spiritual classical Indian music will be continued, following the tradition of the great musician, Hazrat Inayat Khan has been. The library may develop into a scholarly one. In close contact with the Hope Charitable Trust further facilities will be offered in the field of social and welfare programmes.

In 1987 the Circle of Friends of Hazrat Sufi Inayat Khan was inaugurated. It is open to all those sympathising with the Sufi Message of today, who feel stirred by the ideas and ideals of love, harmony and beauty, balance and tolerance, understanding and moral culture; those who look for spiritual development yet standing in the world; who want to strengthen the unity of religious ideals; to all those, therefore, who want to unite with other friends in order to share and to contribute to the development of these ideals within oneself, amongst one another, and around, on a foundation of ever growing sympathy. In the meantime meetings of the Circle of Friends are taking place regularly.

For further information on the work of the Trust or on its Circle of Friends apply to:

Hazrat Inayat Khan Memorial Trust
129, Basti Hazrat Nizamuddin Aulia
(opposite Lodhi Hotel)
New Delhi 110 013
Tel. 4625833

Appendix III

ABOUT THE SERIES

Volume I. *The Way of Illumination*
The traditional Sufic outlook on life's values and purpose is re-expressed by Hazrat Inayat Khan in universal and contemporary concepts.
Included are: *The Way of Illumination; The Inner Life; The Soul; Whence and Whither;* and *The Purpose of Life.*

Volume II. *The Mysticism of Music, Sound and Word*
Sufism traditionally used music as a means of transmitting the essence of mystical insight. Hazrat Inayat Khan integrates this concept of music with elements like sound and silence, vibration and the word, thoughts and inspiration, creating new dimensions for our lives, and thereby recomposing a musical concept extending beyond the tradition of time and culture.

Volume III. *The Art of Personality*
This volume contains the substances of Hazrat Inayat Khan's teaching on our Divine heritage and human relationships, including the science of life's forces. He suggests that the art of personality is the completion of nature and the culmination of heredity. Development of the personality is taken from before birth to the deepest aspects of consciousness.
Included are: *Education; Rasa Shastra; Character-Building and the Art of Personality; Moral Culture.*

Volume IV. *Mental Purification and Healing*
In this volume the Sufi principles are explained concerning the influence the mind may exert on the body, in relation to the spiritual power within us, and concerning the possibilities of spiritual healing in conjunction with modern science.
Included are: *Health; Mental Purification; The Mind World.*

Volume V. *Spiritual Liberty*
This volume contains a wealth of information about different aspects of Sufi mysticism.
Included are: *A Sufi Message of Spiritual Liberty: Aqibat: Life after Death; The Phenomenon of the Soul; Love, Human and Divine; Pearls from the Ocean Unseen.*

Volume VI. *The Alchemy of Happiness*
Hazrat Inayat Khan always insisted that spiritual or mystical aspirations are of no avail if one's life is not lived as it should be. Under this title, forty lectures are collected that deal with life in all its aspects.

Volume VII. *In an Eastern Rose Garden*
Talks given by Hazrat Inayat Khan on a variety of subjects. His ability to communicate the unity and relativity of his viewpoint on diverse subjects illustrates the essence of his mystical perception of life.

Volume VIII. *Sufi Teachings*
A collection of talks on various practical and esoteric aspects of traditional Sufi teachings developed by Hazrat Inayat Khan in a modern and universal context.

Volume IX. *The Unity of Religious Ideals*
A systematically arranged collection of Hazrat Inayat Khan's addresses on what is perhaps the most important part of his teaching: the underlying unity of all religious thought and experience.

Volume X. *Sufi Mysticism*
Hazrat Inayat Khan situates the traditional concepts of initiation, discipleship, spiritual teaching and other esoteric aspects of Sufism in today's world. Besides the main part consisting of: *Sufi Mysticism* and *The Path of Initiation and Discipleship*, these subjects are included: *Sufi Poetry; Art: Yesterday, Today and Tomorrow; The Problem of the Day.*

Volume XI. *Philosophy, Psychology and Mysticism*
These later talks by Hazrat Inayat Khan, given during the last two years before his death, contain a clear overview of these topics in terms of his Sufic vision. This series of lectures may be considered his *magnum opus*. The Aphorisms at the end are sayings noted down by his pupils which Hazrat Inayat Khan expressed at different times and places to soothe or clarify the seeker.

Volume XII. *The Divinity of the Human Soul*
The first part of this volume deals with the relationship of man and God. The second part is autobiographical. The third part contains four short plays written by Hazrat Inayat Khan for his pupils.
Included are: *The Vision of God and Man; Confessions; Four Plays.*

Volume XIII. *Sacred Readings: The Gatha's*
This volume contains the teachings derived from classes given by Hazrat Inayat Khan to his pupils at the earlier stages of their training.

Volume XIV. *Index to Volumes I-XIII*
The volume is published for the first time. It will be of great interest for the student of Sufism.

The Dance of the Soul
This collection of aphorisms is just a gem of wisdom and mysticism with a touch of humour. It helps you to discover your very being at the same time as hinting practical solutions for your daily life: feeling, thinking, speaking, acting.

Bowl of Saki (1994)
Wisdom for everyday. The book contains one saying for each day of the year. Space is left open to accommodate the signatures of your friends.

Those desiring particulars regarding the activities in all countries of the Sufi Movement founded by Hazrat Inayat Khan should apply to the International Headquarters of the Movement as follows:

(for activities in India)	(for activities outside India)
Sufi Movement India, Dargah Hzt. Inayat Khan 129, Basti Hzt. Nizamuddin New Delhi 110 013	General Secretariat, Sufi Movement, Anna Paulownastraat 78 2518 BJ The Hague Holland